VIETNAM

TOP SIGHTS, AUTHENTIC EXPERIENCES

Iain Stewart, Brett Atkinson, Austin Bush,
David Eimer, Phillip Tang

Contents

Plan Your Trip

Nanning

CHINA

MACAU

HONG KONG

Son

en

Hong Gai

hong

**HALONG BAY
p71**

h

Gulf of
Tonkin

Hainan
Island
(China)

inh

Dong Hoi

Dong Ha

**HUE
p107**

Danang

**HOI AN
p135**

Quang
Ngai

SOUTH CHINA SEA
(EAST SEA)

Kon Tum

Ba

Quy Nhon

Tuy Hoa

Buon Ma
Thuot

Nha
Trang

**DALAT
p171**

Phan
Rang

ay Ninh

Bien Hoa

Phan
Thiet

**MUI NE
p161**

A

g
ho

**HO CHI MINH CITY
p189**

ng
eu

**CON DAO
ISLANDS
p229**

N   0
            0   400 km
                          200 miles

Welcome to Vietnam

A land of staggering natural beauty and cultural complexities, of dynamic megacities and hill-tribe villages, stupendous beaches and towering mountains, Vietnam is Asia at its most exotic and compelling.

Self-confident and fast-developing, Vietnam is a country going places. Economic progress is booming in the country's metropolises, where the pace of change is intoxicating. Here ancient, labyrinthine trading quarters of still-thriving craft industries are juxtaposed with grand colonial mansions from the French era, all overseen from the sky bars of 21st-century glass-and-steel high-rises.

Away from the urban centres, you'll find unforgettable experiences everywhere. There's the sublime: gazing over a surreal seascape of limestone islands from the deck of a traditional junk in Halong Bay. The inspirational: exploring the world's most spectacular cave systems in Phong Nha-Ke Bang National Park. The comical: watching a moped loaded with honking pigs weave a wobbly route along a country lane. And the contemplative: witnessing a solitary grave in a cemetery of thousands of war victims.

Take time to savour Vietnam's incredibly subtle, flavoursome national cuisine on a street-food tour or attend a cooking class. Scoot around the rural back roads that fringe the historic old trading port of Hoi An or hike the evergreen hills of Sapa. And for horizontal 'me' time, you'll find outstanding spas – from marble temples of treatments, lotions and potions, to simple, inexpensive family-run massage salons.

...you'll find unforgettable experiences everywhere.

Sapa (p84)
EFIRED/SHUTTERSTOCK ©

MYANMAR
(BURMA)

Ou

Lao Cai

Cao Bang

VIETNAM

SAPA
p85

Yen Bai

Lang

Thai
Ngu

Mekong

LAOS

HANOI
p35

Ca

Hai

Nin
Bir

Thar
Hoa

Vinh

Ha

VIENTIANE

PHONG NHA-KE BANG
NATIONAL PARK
p97

THAILAND

Mekong

BANGKOK

Siem
Reap

CAMBOD

Andaman
Sea

*Gulf of
Thailand*

PHNOM
PENH

Mekong

Chau Doc

Long
Xuyen

Vir

Lo

PHU QUOC
p253

Can T

Rach Gia

Sc
Tra

MEKONG DELTA
p239

Bac L

Ca Mau

Hoi An (p134)
NOINA/SHUTTERSTOCK ©

Plan Your Trip
Vietnam's Top 12

MICHAL JASTRZEBSKI/SHUTTERSTOCK ©

Hoi An

Temple-rich trading port and culinary mecca

Vietnam's most civilised and cosmopolitan town, this beautiful
ancient port is bursting with gourmet restaurants, hip bars and
cafes, quirky boutiques and expert tailors. Immerse yourself in history in the warren-like lanes of the Old Town, and tour the temples
and pagodas. Dine like an emperor on a peasant's budget. Then
hit glorious An Bang Beach and bike the back roads. Yes, Hoi An
(p134) has it all.

Ho Chi Minh City

International, but unmistakably Vietnamese

HCMC's (p188) visceral energy will delight big-city devotees. This in-your-face city doesn't inspire neutrality: you'll either be drawn into its thrilling vortex or find it overwhelming. Dive in and be rewarded with a wealth of history, delicious food and a vibrant nightlife that sets the standard for Vietnam. The heat is always on; loosen your collar and enjoy.

Phong Nha-Ke Bang National Park

Cathedral-like caves and jagged limestone peaks

The mist-wrapped hills and rainforest of the Phong Nha-Ke Bang region (p96) form one of Vietnam's most spectacular national parks. Head underground for even more delights. A fortunate few can experience Hang Son Doong (pictured), the world's largest cave; more accessible is Hang En, and ziplining and kayaking Hang Toi.

3

4

Halong Bay

Two thousand limestone islands in an emerald sea

Halong Bay's (p70) stunning combination of karst limestone islands and sheltered, shimmering seas is one of Vietnam's top tourist draws. Definitely book an overnight cruise and make time for your own special moments on this World Heritage wonder – rise early for an ethereal dawn, or pilot a kayak into grottoes and lagoons. To escape the crowds, consider heading to neighbouring (but less touristy) Lan Ha Bay.

5

Hue

A majestic, fascinating former imperial capital

The capital of the nation for 150 years, Hue (p106) is perhaps the easiest large Vietnamese city to love and spend time in. Its situation on the banks of the Perfume River is sublime, its complex cuisine justifiably famous, and its streets are relatively traffic free. And that's without the majesty of the Hue Citadel to explore. On the city's fringes are some of Vietnam's most impressive pagodas and royal tombs, many in wonderful natural settings.

Hue Citadel (p110)

Hanoi

Captivating capital steeped in history and culture

Ancient but dynamic, the nation's capital hurtles towards modernity, cautiously embracing visitors. Sample Hanoi's (p34) heady mix of history and ambition by wandering the lanes of the Old Quarter, sipping drip-coffee or *bia hoi* (fresh draught beer). When you're done, check out the crumbling decadence of the French Quarter then zip up to cosmopolitan West Lake for finer dining and the low-down on Hanoi's burgeoning art scene.

6

Phu Quoc Island

Paradise island way down south

Lapped by azure waters and edged with the kind of white-sand beaches that make sunseekers sink to their weak knees, Phu Quoc (p252) is ideal for slipping into low gear, reaching for a seaside cocktail and toasting a blood-orange sun as it dips into the sea. And if you want to notch it up a tad, grab a motorbike and hit the red-dirt roads: the island's the size of Singapore. Dinh Cau Beach

Mui Ne

Adventure-sport epicentre and beach mecca

The relaxed, prosperous beach retreat of Mui Ne (p160) is a kitesurfing capital, with world-class wind and excellent schools for professional training. For those who prefer dry land, sandboarding and golf are popular alternatives. The resort has more than 20km of palm-fringed beachfront, stretching invitingly along the shores of the South China Sea. From guesthouses to boutique resorts, boho bars to fine-value spas, Mui Ne has a broad appeal and is readily accessible from HCMC. Kitesurfing (p165), Mui Ne Beach

ISTOCK/GETTY IMAGES ©

HEMIS/ALAMY STOCK PHOTO ©

ISTOCK/GETTY IMAGES ©

9

Cat Tien National Park

A rainforest refuge for primates

Accessible and impressive, Cat Tien National Park (p185) lies conveniently between HCMC and Dalat. Set on a bend in the Dong Nai River, there's something vaguely *Apocalypse Now* about arriving here. Popular activities include trekking, cycling and wildlife spotting: the Wild Gibbon Trek is a must. The park is also home to a primate centre, where gibbons and langurs are coaxed back into their natural environment. Left: bar-bellied pitta; Far left: Crocodile Lake (p186)

TAPPASAN PHURISAMRIT/SHUTTERSTOCK ©

TONKINPHOTOGRAPHY/SHUTTERSTOCK ©

CAO TRAN THO/SHUTTERSTOCK ©

Con Dao Islands

Divine beaches and a sombre history

These idyllic tropical islands make the perfect escape from urban Vietnam. Once hell-on-earth for a generation of political prisoners, Con Dao (p229) is now a heavenly destination of remote beaches and coral reefs. It's a wonderful place to explore by bike, in search of that dream bay, while the main settlement of Con Son is one of Vietnam's most charming towns.

10

LUKAKIKINA/SHUTTERSTOCK ©

Dalat

Atmospheric old French-colonial hill station

The queen of the southwest highlands, Dalat (p170) has been popular with international tourists since the French-colonial days. Grand Gallic villas are dotted around pine groves, and the centre of the town is a pretty lake, with numerous nearby waterfalls adding to its natural appeal. Adventure sports are also a huge draw with abseiling, canyoning, mountain biking, hiking, whitewater rafting and kayaking all possible in the temperate climate. Elephant Falls (p179)

BJORN PROFESSIONAL/SHUTTERSTOCK ©

Sapa

Hiking hot spot and colourful hill-tribe town

Undulating rice terraces cascade down to valleys inhabited by Hmong, Red Dzao and Giay villages. Up above, the sinuous ridges of the Hoang Lien Mountains touch the sky. Brushed with every shade of green in the palette, the countryside surrounding Sapa (p84) is a showcase of northern Vietnam's most superb rural vistas. This is prime territory for digging out your walking boots and hitting the trails.

Plan Your Trip
Need to Know

When to Go

Warm to hot summers, mild winters
Tropical climate, wet & dry seasons

Sapa
GO Mar–May & Sep–Nov

Hanoi
GO Mar–May & Sep–Nov

Danang
GO Mar–Sep

Ho Chi Minh City
GO Nov–Feb

High Season (Jul & Aug)

o Prices increase by up to 50% by the coast; book hotels well in advance.

o All Vietnam, except the far north, is hot and humid, with the summer monsoon bringing downpours.

Shoulder (Dec–Mar)

o During the Tet festival, the whole country is on the move and prices rise.

o North of Nha Trang can get cool weather. Expect chilly conditions in the north.

o In the far south, clear skies and sunshine are the norm.

Low Season (Apr–Jun, Sep–Nov)

o Perhaps the best time to tour the whole nation.

o Typhoons can lash the central and northern coastline until November.

Currency
Dong (d)

Language
Vietnamese

Visas

Some nationalities need a visa in advance for all visits, some don't. The standard length of stay for tourist visas is 30 days; for visa-exempt nationalities it is 15 days.

Money

ATMs are found throughout the country, even in small towns. Cash is king but debit and credit cards can be used in many hotels.

Mobile Phones

To avoid roaming charges, local SIM cards can be used in most European, Asian and Australian (and many North American) phones.

Time

Vietnam is seven hours ahead of GMT/UTC.

Daily Costs

Budget: Less than US$40

- Glass of *bia hoi* (draught beer): from US$0.30
- One hour on a local bus: US$1–1.50
- Cheap hotel: US$9–16, dorms less
- Simple noodle dish: US$1.50–2.50

Midrange: US$40-100

- Comfortable double room: US$25–50
- Meal in a restaurant: from US$8
- One-hour massage: US$7–20
- Ten-minute taxi ride: US$2.50–5

Top End: More than US$100

- Luxury hotel room: from US$80
- Gourmet dinner: from US$20
- Internal flight: US$30–100

Useful Websites

The Word (www.wordhcmc.com) This superb magazine has comprehensive coverage and excellent features.

Vietnam Coracle (http://vietnamcoracle.com) Excellent independent travel advice, including lots of backroads content.

Vietnam Online (www.vietnamonline.com) Good all-rounder.

Coast Vietnam (www.coastvietnam.com) Classy website concentrating on Vietnam's central coast.

Rusty Compass (www.rustycompass.com) Useful online travel guide with itineraries and videos.

Lonely Planet (www.lonelyplanet.com/vietnam) Destination information, hotel bookings, traveller forum and more.

Opening Hours

Hours vary very little throughout the year.

Banks 8am to 3pm weekdays, to 11.30am Saturday. Some take a lunch break.

Offices and museums 7am or 7.30am to 5pm or 6pm; museums generally close on Monday. Most take a lunch break (roughly 11am to 1.30pm).

Restaurants 11am to 9pm

Shops 8am to 6pm

Temples and pagodas 5am to 9pm

Arriving in Vietnam

Tan Son Nhat International Airport, Ho Chi Minh City

Taxi Taxis to central districts (around 190,000d) take about 30 minutes.

Bus The air-conditioned Route 152 bus (6000d, every 15 minutes, 6am to 6pm, around 40 minutes, see http://busmap.vn for route).

Noi Bai International Airport, Hanoi

Taxi Taxis to the centre cost 400,000d and take around 50 minutes.

Bus Jetstar shuttles (35,000d) and Vietnam Airlines minibuses (50,000d) run hourly. The Route 17 public bus to Long Bien bus station is 5000d.

Getting Around

Buses are the main transport mode for locals, but travellers tend to prefer planes, trains and automobiles.

Train Reasonably priced and comfortable enough in air-conditioned carriages (and sleepers), but there are no real express trains.

Plane Cheap if you book ahead and the network is comprehensive, but cancellations are not unknown.

Car Useful for travelling at your own pace or for visiting regions with minimal public transport. Cars always come with a driver.

Bus On the main highways services are frequent, although it's not a relaxing way to travel. In the sticks things deteriorate rapidly. Open-tour buses are very inexpensive and worth considering.

For more on **getting around**, see p299

Plan Your Trip
Hot Spots For...

Vietnamese Cuisine

Vietnamese cooking is a fascinating draw for travellers, the national cuisine combining Chinese and French influences.

Hoi An (p134)
Boasts an array of stupendous restaurants where you can try unique regional specialities.

Sea Shell
Innovative, contemporary Vietnamese cuisine (p157).

Hue (p106)
Ancient city famous for its complex, often highly refined imperial cuisine tradition and unique snacks.

Hanh Restaurant
Try Hue specialities at this famed restaurant (p126).

Hanoi (p34)
The capital is the place to get stuck into street food, which is diverse and delicious and everywhere.

Hanoi Street Food Tours
Take a gastronomic tour of Hanoi's street scene (p65).

National Parks

Vietnam has 31 national parks and over a hundred protected natural reserves. While wildlife can be elusive, there are stupendous landscapes and forests to enjoy.

Phong Nha-Ke Bang National Park (p96)
Hike through pristine mountain and valley trails, or take a river cruise, to some of the world's largest caves.

Paradise Cave
This cave is a highlight of the Phong Nha region (p103).

Cat Tien National Park (p184)
Has a range of excellent hiking trails and is home to a pioneering primate rehabilitation project.

Wild Gibbon Trek
Visiting the gibbons at dawn is utterly memorable (p185).

Con Dao Islands (p228)
These idyllic islands include Vietnam's best snorkelling and diving on healthy coral reefs.

Con Dao Dive Center
A recommended school for scuba action (p235).

Beaches

Vietnam is a beach lover's dream, its near-endless coastline dotted with surf-washed shorelines, tiny coves and hidden bays.

JIMMY TRAN/SHUTTERSTOCK ©

Phu Quoc (p252)
This tropical island has picture-perfect white-sand beaches and sheltered bays.

Sao Beach
A dazzling crescent of snow-white sand (p258).

Mui Ne (p160)
A broad, sandy shoreline, with towering sand dunes nearby and empty beaches up the coast.

Manta Sail Training Centre
One of Southeast Asia's best sailing schools (p164).

An Bang (p150)
Ride a bicycle from Hoi An to glorious An Bang's wonderful expanse of golden sand.

DeckHouse
Check out this eclectic shoreside eatery (p150).

Historic Sites

Fully loaded with historic interest, Vietnam has excellent war museums, Cham temples, grandiose private mansions, tombs and pagodas and fine French colonial architecture.

R.M. NUNES/SHUTTERSTOCK ©

Ho Chi Minh City (p188)
Boasts an excellent collection of museums, as well as Chinese temples.

War Remnants Museum
Poignant museum dedicated to the horrors of war (p196).

Dalat (p170)
This temperate highland city has a collection of curious, somewhat quirky, sites worth investigating.

Hang Nga Crazy House
Acid-trip architecture equals concrete anarchy (p178).

Perfume River (p118)
Hue's beautiful river is lined with monuments including an astonishing collection of emperors' tombs.

Tomb of Tu Duc
Mausoleum dedicated to a 19th-century ruler (p118).

Plan Your Trip
Local Life

Activities

Vietnam can be a culture shock for many travellers. Taking a tour can really help you understand the locals better. You'll find a terrific array of tour operators in Vietnam, offering everything from street-food tours to vintage scooter day trips and (of course) cruises of Halong Bay. There's superb hiking, particularly in the north of the country, where the weather is cooler. Adventure sports include kayaking, rock climbing, kitesurfing, diving and snorkelling, sailing and surfing. Always stick with reputable, well-established companies as regulations are not strict and accidents do occur.

Shopping

There's a great selection of handicrafts to choose from in all the main tourist centres, including great lacquerware, wood carving, mother-of-pearl inlay, ceramics and textiles. Head to Hoi An for made-to-measure clothes such as suits and dresses. There's also a great deal of fakery: sunglasses,

designer labels, football kits and even dodgy Lonely Planet guides. Communist propaganda art posters are wildly popular, and you'll find tempting art and photographic galleries. Avoid purchasing any animal products such as snake wine; many items have been sourced unethically or even illegally.

Entertainment

There's a small live-music scene in Ho Chi Minh City and Hanoi with rock, electronic and hip-hop artists. Cities have concert halls for classical and traditional performances, and cinemas. Elsewhere, look out for traditional dance performances, and do try to take in a water-puppet show, which is highly rewarding.

Eating

Showcasing fresh and vibrant flavours, excellent street food and elegant restaurants in restored colonial architecture, Vietnam is packed with superb opportunities for

HADYNYAH/GETTY IMAGES ©

eating out. Cookery classes, market visits and walking tours make it easy to discover the country's culinary heritage. Generally the more local the place is, the tastier the food; a place that bustles with Vietnamese is always a good sign. In towns popular with tourists, restaurants with English-language menus often tone down dishes for Western tastes. Seafood is nearly always live in Vietnam: just select what you want from the tanks. Beware that dog, cat and all manner of other 'delicacies' are eaten in Vietnam though they are virtually always consumed in specialist restaurants well off the tourist trail.

Drinking & Nightlife

Cafes serving Vietnamese-style coffee are found in towns and villages across the country. Bars are also wildly popular; look out for *bia hoi* joints, which are incredibly

★ **Best Cafes**

Sound of Silence (p151)

Café Duy Tri (p46)

Espresso Station (p158)

An Cafe (p183)

cheap. A craft beer scene is sweeping the nation, and you'll find brewpubs and interesting ales on tap in all the main cities. In clubs, most DJs mix pounding electronic beats and Vietnamese pop (which is not always easy on Western ears). As the government regulates nightlife carefully, most places open around 10pm and close early (usually 2am). Note that anywhere advertising karaoke is almost certainly a front for prostitution.

From left: Cruising Halong Bay (p74); Street-food vendor

Plan Your Trip
Month by Month

January

🎎 Dalat Flower Festival

Held early in the month, this is always a wonderful occasion, with huge elaborate displays. It's become an international event, with music and fashion shows and a wine festival.

February

🎎 Tet (Tet Nguyen Dan)

The Big One! Falling in late January or early February, Vietnamese Lunar New Year is like Christmas, New Year and birthdays all rolled into one. Travel is difficult at this time, as transport is booked up and many businesses close.

🎎 Quang Trung

Wrestling competitions, lion dances and human chess take place in Hanoi on the fifth day of the first lunar month at Dong Da Mound, site of the uprising against the Chi-nese led by Emperor Quang Trung (Nguyen Hué) in 1788.

March

🏃 Saigon Cyclo Challenge

On your marks...get pedalling! Ho Chi Minh City's fastest rickshaw drivers battle it out in their three-wheeled chariots to raise funds for charity. Takes place in mid-March every year.

April

🎎 Holiday of the Dead (Thanh Minh)

It's time to honour the ancestors with a visit to graves of deceased relatives to tidy up and sweep tombstones. Offerings of flowers, food and paper are presented. It's held on the first three days of the third moon.

🎎 Hue Festival (Biennial)

Vietnam's biggest cultural event (www.hue festival.com) is held every two years, with

THI/SHUTTERSTOCK ©

events next held in 2020. Most of the art, theatre, music, circus and dance performances are held inside Hue's Citadel.

🎆 Danang Firework Festival

Danang's riverside explodes with sound, light and colour during this spectacular event, which features competing pyrotechnic teams from the USA, China, Europe and Vietnam. Held in the last week of the month.

May

🎆 Buddha's Birth, Enlightenment and Death (Phong Sinh)

A big celebration at Buddhist temples with lively street processions and lanterns used to decorate pagodas. Complexes including HCMC's Jade Emperor Pagoda (p207) host lavish celebrations. Fifteenth day of the fourth lunar month.

★ **Best Festivals**

Tet, January–February

Hue Festival, April (biennial)

Danang Firework Festival, April

Buddha's Birth, Enlightenment and Death, May

Wandering Souls Day, August

June

🎆 Nha Trang Sea Festival

Falls at the end of May and the beginning of June and includes a street festival, photography exhibitions, embroidery displays and kite-flying competitions.

🎆 Summer Solstice Day (Tet Doan Ngo)

The Vietnamese keep epidemics at bay with offerings to the spirits, ghosts and

From left: Lunar New Year, Po Nagar; Danang Firework Festival the God of Death on the fifth day of the fifth moon. Sticky rice wine (ruou nep) is consumed in industrial quantities.

August

✥ Wandering Souls Day (Trung Nguyen)

Second in the pecking order to Tet is this ancient Vietnamese tradition. Huge spreads of food are left out for lost spirits who, it's believed, wander the earth on this day. Held on the 15th day of the seventh moon.

✥ Children's (or Mid-Autumn) Festival, Hoi An & Hanoi

This is a big event in Hoi An and Hanoi, when citizens celebrate the full moon, eat mooncakes and beat drums. The lion, unicorn and dragon dance processions are enacted, and children are fully involved in the celebrations.

September

✥ Vietnam National Day

Big parades and events are held across Vietnam on 2 September. Celebrated with a rally and fireworks at Ba Dinh Square, Hanoi (in front of Ho Chi Minh's Mausoleum) and there are also boat races on Hoan Kiem Lake.

✥ Hanoi Pride

Features parties, film screenings, talks and a colourful bicycle rally. It's held over a week between July and September; check the website www.facebook.com/vietpride. vn for details.

October

✕ Mid-Autumn Festival (Trung Thu)

A fine time for foodies, with mooncakes of sticky rice filled with lotus seeds, watermelon seeds, peanuts, the yolks of duck eggs, raisins and other treats. It's celebrated across the nation on the 15th day of the eighth moon and can fall in September or October.

✥ Cham New Year (Kate)

This is celebrated at Po Klong Garai Cham Towers in Thap Cham on the seventh month of the Cham calendar. The festival commemorates ancestors, Cham national heroes and deities, such as the farmers' goddess Po Ino Nagar.

✥ Khmer Oc Bom Boc Festival

The Mekong Delta's Khmer community celebrates on the 15th day of the 10th moon of the lunar calendar (late October or November) with colourful boat races at Ba Dong Beach in Tra Vinh province and on the Soc Trang River.

December

✥ Christmas Day (Giang Sinh)

Not a national holiday, but is celebrated throughout Vietnam, particularly by the sizeable Catholic population. It's a special time to be in places such as Phat Diem and HCMC, where thousands attend midnight Mass.

Plan Your Trip
Get Inspired

Read

The Quiet American (Graham Greene; 1955) Classic novel set in the 1950s as the French empire is collapsing.

The Sorrow of War (Bao Ninh; 1990) The North Vietnamese perspective, retold via flashbacks.

Vietnam: Rising Dragon (Bill Hayton; 2010) A candid, highly insightful assessment of the nation.

The Sympathizer (Viet Thanh Nguyen; 2015) Superbly written spy novel; Pulitzer Prize–winner.

The Sacred Willow: Four Generations in the Life of a Vietnamese Family (Duong Van Mai Elliot; 1999) Memoir of a middle-class family.

Watch

The Vietnam War (2017) Definitive documentary series, which examines the roots of the conflict, war itself, and consequences.

Apocalypse Now (1979) The American War depicted as an epic 'heart of darkness' adventure.

The Deer Hunter (1978) Examines the emotional breakdown suffered by small-town servicemen.

Cyclo (Xich Lo; 1995) Visually stunning masterpiece that cuts to the core of HCMC's underworld.

Vertical Ray of the Sun (2000) Exquisitely photographed family saga set in Hanoi.

Listen

Ohio (Crosby, Stills, Nash and Young; 1970). Anthem that captures the rage and anger of the anti-war movement.

Trinh Cong Son (Ngu Di Con; 1970s) A mother grieves for her son, a missing soldier.

Saigon Bride (Joan Baez; 1967) Protest song that deals with the horrors of war.

Vietnam (Jimmy Cliff; 1969) Jamaican reggae musician's very catchy protest song.

Doi (Suboi, 2016) Beat-driven, bass-heavy track from Vietnamese hip-hop queen.

19 (Paul Hardcastle; 1985) Electro classic referencing the average age of US soldiers.

Above: Hanoi (p34)

GRACETHANG2/SHUTTERSTOCK ©

Plan Your Trip
Five-Day Itineraries

Northern Adventure

Savour the delights of the capital and then cruise a Unesco World Heritage site by boat, taking in some of its 2000 or so islands.

FROM LEFT ALMUT ALBRECHT/500PX ©; MATT MUNRO/LONELY PLANET ©

Hanoi (p36) Experience the evocative Old Quarter, architecture and museums before a street food feast.
🚌 4 hrs to Halong City

Halong Bay (p70) Cruise this unique seascape, with more than 2000 limestone outcrops dotting the ocean.
⚓ 1 hr to Cat Ba Island

Cat Ba Island (p78) Enjoy the relaxed ambience of Cat Ba Town, dine on fresh seafood and visit beaches.

Southern Charm

This trip includes a taste of life in one of Asia's most exciting cities, the unforgettable spectacle of a floating market and a beach-blessed tropical island.

Phu Quoc (p252) Kick back and enjoy this island's turquoise seas, blinding white sands and surf-fresh seafood.

3

1 **Ho Chi Minh City** (p188) Revel in this cauldron of commerce by hitting the markets and indulging in the cuisine.
🚌 3 hrs to Can Tho

2

Can Tho (p246) Arise before dawn to experience the colour of a floating Mekong market at its magical best.
✈ 45min to Phu Quoc

1

3

Plan Your Trip
10-Day Itinerary

Caves Coastline & Culture

Central Vietnam contains some stupendous cave systems and two of the nation's most enjoyable small cities, both famed for their historic sites and regional specialities.

Phong Nha-Ke Bang National Park (p96) This truly remarkable national park is the world's greatest caving region.

Hue (p106) The old imperial capital of Hue has a unique walled citadel and a roster of impressive tombs and pagodas.
🚌🚗 5 hrs to Phong Nha-Ke Bang National Park

Hoi An (p134) Enjoy the town's unique ambience, tour temples, pagodas and museums, then hit the beach.
🚌🚗 3 hrs to Hue

Plan Your Trip
Two-Week Itinerary

North to South

Making the most of Vietnam's spectacular coastline, this route hugs the shore and is bookended by the country's two greatest cities. You'll have ample time to indulge at the beaches and hit the cultural sights.

Hanoi (p36)
Experience the Old Quarter's atmosphere and street life, and tuck into the terrific street food.
🚌🚗 4 hrs to Halong City

Halong Bay (p70)
Gaze over a horizon-filling expanse of seemingly innumerable jungle-topped islets.
✈ 1¼ hr to Hoi An

Hoi An (p134)
Search for souvenirs, hit An Bang beach, take in the My Son ruins and enjoy the cosmopolitan vibe.
🚌🚗 4 hrs to Mui Ne

Ho Chi Minh City (p188)
Eat some of the globe's best cuisine and take a day trip to the Cu Chi Tunnels.

Mui Ne (p160)
Rest up by the beach in this tropical idyll, or get stuck into some adrenaline sports.
🚌🚗 6 hrs to Ho Chi Minh City

Plan Your Trip
Family Travel

JANELLE LUGGE/SHUTTERSTOCK ©

Vietnam with Children

Children get to have a good time in Vietnam, mainly because of the overwhelming amount of attention they attract and the fact that almost everybody wants to play with them.

Big cities have plenty to keep kids interested, though in most smaller towns and rural areas boredom may set in from time to time. Vietnam has great beaches, but pay close attention: there are some riptides and lifeguards are not always present. Seas around Phu Quoc Island are usually more sheltered.

Eating & Drinking

Children generally enjoy local cuisine, which is rarely too spicy. Spring rolls, noodles and rice dishes usually go down very well. Comfort food from home (pizzas, pasta, burgers and ice cream) is an option too. The range of fruit is simply staggering, and it can be fun (and educational) to explore a market picking out exotica such as

dragon fruit and rambutans. Bottled water is available everywhere.

Getting Around

Travelling around Vietnam takes a lot of organisation, even more so for a family. Avoid long bus journeys along busy highways as they can get tedious. Internal flights are inexpensive. Definitely consider a train journey as children love the adventure of rail travel: four- and six-bed berths can be booked (so you're all in the same compartment). Many travel agencies can organise a minibus; reckon on US$100 to US$120 for a full day's travel.

In cities your biggest worry is likely to be walking across the road safely; traffic does not stop for pedestrians so you'll have to get used to negotiating your way through a flow of moving cars and motorbikes. Taxis are very affordable.

Discounts for kids are available for air and rail travel.

NADEZDA ZAVITAEVA/SHUTTERSTOCK ©

Packing

Pack plenty of high-factor sunscreen before you go as it's not that widely available. Antibacterial hand gel is a great idea.

Babies & Infants

Baby supplies are available in the major cities, but dry up quickly in the countryside. You'll find cots in most midrange and top-end hotels, but not elsewhere, and some restaurants can find a high chair. There are no safety seats in rented cars or taxis.

Breastfeeding in public is quite common in Vietnam, but there are few facilities for changing nappies (diapers).

★ Best for Kids

Jerry's Jungle Tours (p261)

Cat Tien National Park (p185)

Vintage Vespa tour (p215)

Water puppet shows (p63)

Cooking courses (p144)

The main worry throughout Vietnam is keeping an eye on what infants are putting into their mouths. Their natural curiosity can be a lot more costly in a country where dysentery, typhoid and hepatitis are commonplace.

From left: Dragon fruit; Golden Dragon Water Puppet Theatre (p217)

Ngoc Son Temple (p38)

HANOI

The Huc bridge (p38)

Hoan Kiem Lake (p38)

Map Locations

Old Quarter
This labyrinth of streets is Asia at its raw, pulsating best.

HO CHI MINH'S MAUSOLEUM

West of the Old Quarter
Visit Ho Chi Minh's expansive mausoleum complex, as well as the Temple of Literature and the Imperial Citadel of Thang Long.

OLD QUARTER

HOAN KIEM LAKE

Around Hoan Kiem Lake
Temples, gardens and a peaceful lake lie at the centre of this area close to the Old Quarter.

French Quarter
This elegant part of town is blessed with a collection of fine, though crumbling, colonial villas.

Hanoi (p58)
Old Quarter & Hoan Kiem Lake (p62)

Hanoi at a Glance...

Vietnam's graceful capital races to make up for time lost to the ravages of war. This is a city on the move: its streets surge with scooters while all around layers of history reveal periods of French and Chinese occupation.

The Old Quarter is where defiant real-deal farmers hawk their wares, while city folk breakfast on noodles and oldies practise t'ai chi at dawn on the shores of Hoan Kiem Lake. Dine on the wild and wonderful at every corner, investigate street markets, uncover an evolving arts scene and then toast the Hanoi night from the panoramic heights of a sky bar.

One Day in Hanoi
Rise early for a morning walk around misty **Hoan Kiem Lake** (p38). Visit the **Ho Chi Minh Mausoleum Complex** (p44) before taking a look at the **Fine Arts Museum of Vietnam** (p53). Lunch at **La Badiane** (p65) then drop by the **Temple of Literature** (p56). Immerse yourself in the chaos of the Old Quarter (p40) before eating at **Blue Butterfly** (p63).

Two Days in Hanoi
Head into the suburbs to the excellent **Vietnam Museum of Ethnology** (p52). Lunch at **Chim Sao** (p65) then take in the **Museum of Vietnamese Revolution** (p53) and adjacent **National Museum of Vietnamese History** (p39). After dinner at **Cha Ca Thang Long** (p63) or **Old Hanoi** (p64) it's drinks at **Tadioto** (p66).

Ho Chi Minh's Mausoleum (p44)

Arriving in Hanoi

Noi Bai International Airport (p68) About 35km north of the city, connected by airport shuttle buses; a taxi is US$20. The journey time is around 45 minutes.

Bus Hanoi has four main bus stations.

Taxis Readily available.

Train For southern destinations it's **Hanoi train station** (p68), northbound trains use **Tran Quy Cap Station** (p68).

Where to Stay

Most visitors to Hanoi find themselves staying in the Old Quarter, the most atmospheric, but chaotic and noisy, part of the city. Consider the quieter, nearby French Quarter for a more relaxing base. There are also luxury hotels in the northern suburbs, close to West Lake (Ho Tay). For more information on the best neighbourhoods, see p69.

The Huc bridge

BROSTOCK/SHUTTRESTOCK ©

Hoan Kiem Lake

This small tree-lined lake is the perfect place to begin exploring old Hanoi and get your bearings. It even has its own temple, accessed by a historic scarlet footbridge.

Great For...

☑ **Don't Miss**

Every morning at around 6am local residents practise traditional t'ai chi on the shore.

Hoan Kiem Lake

Legend claims in the mid-15th century Heaven sent Emperor Ly Thai To a magical sword, which he used to drive the Chinese from Vietnam. After the war a giant golden turtle grabbed the sword and disappeared into the depths of this **lake** (Map p62) to restore the sword to its divine owners, inspiring the name Ho Hoan Kiem (Lake of the Restored Sword).

Ngoc Son Temple

Meaning 'Temple of the Jade Mountain', Hanoi's most visited **temple** (Den Ngoc Son; Map p62; Hoan Kiem Lake; adult/student 30,000/15,000d; ☉8am-6pm) sits on a small island in the northern part of Hoan Kiem Lake, connected to the lake shore by The Huc bridge, an elegant red bridge, constructed in classical Vietnamese style.

St Joseph Cathedral

KWANGHAI.C/LONELY PLANET ©

ℹ Need to Know

The lakeside roads are pedestrianised on Sundays.

✕ Take a Break

For a bird's-eye view of the lake, and great coffee, head up to Cafe Pho Co (p46).

★ Top Tip

Don't miss the stuffed turtles inside the Ngoc Son Temple.

The temple is dedicated to General Tran Hung Dao (who defeated the Mongols in the 13th century), La To (patron saint of physicians) and the scholar Van Xuong.

St Joseph Cathedral

Hanoi's neo-Gothic **St Joseph Cathedral** (Nha To Lon Ha Noi; Map p62; P Nha Tho; ⊙8am-noon & 2-6pm) `FREE` was inaugurated in 1886, and boasts a soaring facade. Its most noteworthy features are its twin bell towers, elaborate altar and fine stained-glass windows. Entrance via the main gate is only permitted during Mass: times are listed on a sign on the gates to the left of the cathedral.

At other times, enter via the Diocese of Hanoi compound, a block away at 40 P Nha Chung.

National Museum of Vietnamese History

Built between 1925 and 1932, this architecturally impressive **museum** (Bao Tang Lich Su Quoc Gia; Map p58; ☎024-3825 2853; http://baotanglichsu.vn; 1 P Trang Tien; adult/student 40,000/10,000d; ⊙8am-noon & 1.30-5pm Tue-Sun) was formerly home to the École Française d'Extrême Orient. Exhibit highlights include bronzes from the Dong Son culture (3rd century BC to 3rd century AD), Hindu statuary from the Khmer and Champa kingdoms, jewellery from imperial Vietnam, and displays relating to the French occupation and the Communist Party.

Old Quarter

Hanoi's historic centre boasts over 1000 years of trade, commerce and activity. Exploring the maze of backstreets is fascinating, though the traffic and pollution are punishing.

Great For...

ⓘ Need to Know

It's very easy to get lost (day or night) – carry your hotel's business card.

★ **Top Tip**

Definitely try the street food: the Old Quarter has loads of good options.

You're likely to find negotiating the narrow streets of the Old Quarter an intimidating experience, at first. Waves of motorbikes compete with cars and pedestrians pushing their way through the maze of countless cheap hotels, shopfronts of knock-off wares and hawkers with their sizzling baskets, beneath an ever-present honking of horns and the heady aromas of exhaust fumes, street food and sweat.

Watch where you tread on the sticky pavements, employ a strategy and determination when crossing the street, and remember to look up when you can: glimpses of the old and the very old indeed peek out occasionally from behind garish, modern facades. You'll gain your confidence soon enough, and when you do, there's no better way to spend time here than to wander, soaking up the sights, sounds and smells.

Bach Ma Temple

In the heart of the Old Quarter, the small **Bach Ma Temple** (Den Bach Ma; Map p62; cnr P Hang Buom & P Hang Giay; ⊘8-11am & 2-5pm Tue-Sun) FREE is said to be the oldest temple in the city, though much of the current structure dates from the 18th century and a shrine to Confucius was added in 1839. It was originally built by Emperor Ly Thai To in the 11th century to honour a white horse that guided him to this site, where he chose to construct his city walls.

Pass through the wonderful old wooden doors of the pagoda to see a statue of the legendary white horse, as well as a beautiful red-lacquered funeral palanquin.

Dong Xuan Market

Heritage House

One of the Old Quarter's best-restored properties, this traditional **merchants' house** (Ngoi Nha Di San; Map p62; 87 P Ma May; 10,000d; ☺9am-noon & 1-6pm) is sparsely but beautifully decorated, with rooms set around two courtyards and filled with fine furniture. Note the high steps between rooms, a traditional design incorporated to stop the flow of bad energy around the property.

There are crafts and trinkets for sale here, including silver jewellery, basketwork and Vietnamese tea sets, and there's usually a calligrapher or other craftsperson at work too.

> ✖ **Take a Break**
> Head to the bustling New Day (p63) restaurant for authentic Vietnamese bites.

OUTCAST85/SHUTTERSTOCK ©

Long Bien Bridge

A symbol of the tenacity and resilience of the Hanoian people, the Long Bien Bridge (built between 1899 and 1902) was bombed on several occasions during the American War, and each time quickly repaired by the Vietnamese. Designed by Gustave Eiffel (of Eiffel Tower fame), the bridge, used by trains, mopeds and pedestrians, is undergoing reconstruction to restore its original appearance. It's colourfully illuminated at night.

Dong Xuan Market

The largest covered **market** (Cho Dong Xuan; Map p58; cnr P Hang Khoai & P Dong Xuan; ☺6am-7pm) in Hanoi was originally built by the French in 1889 and almost completely destroyed by fire in 1994. Almost everything you can think of from fresh (and live) produce to cheap clothing, souvenirs, consumer goods and traditional arts and crafts can be found inside.

Hanoi Ceramic Mosaic Mural

Spanning almost 4km along the Song Hong dyke, from its terminus at the Long Bien Bridge, this mural project holds the Guinness World Record for being the largest ceramic mosaic on the planet. The colourful mural lines busy roads, uses ceramics produced at nearby Bat Trang and depicts different periods in Vietnam's history. Both local and international artists commenced work on the project in 2007, completed in 2010 for Hanoi's 1000th-birthday celebrations.

> ☑ **Don't Miss**
> The quarter's tunnel (or tube) houses, so called because of their narrow frontages and long rooms.

Ho Chi Minh's Mausoleum

AQSHI VN/SHUTTERSTOCK ©

Ho Chi Minh in Hanoi

The father of the Vietnamese nation lived in Hanoi for extended periods, and it's possible to visit his modest home and grandiose mausoleum.

Great For...

☑ Don't Miss

The fascinating historic photographs inside the Ho Chi Minh Museum.

The Ho Chi Minh Mausoleum Complex is an important place of pilgrimage for many Vietnamese. A traffic-free area of botanical gardens, monuments, memorials and pagodas, it's usually crowded with groups of Vietnamese who come from far and wide to pay their respects to 'Uncle Ho'.

Ho Chi Minh's Mausoleum

In the tradition of Lenin, Stalin and Mao, **Ho Chi Minh's Mausoleum** (Lang Chu Tich Ho Chi Minh; Map p58; ☎024-3845 5128; www. bqllang.gov.vn; Ba Dinh Square; ⊙8-11am Tue-Thu, Sat & Sun Dec-Aug, last entry 10.15am) FREE is a monumental marble edifice. Contrary to his desire for a simple cremation, the mausoleum was constructed from materials gathered from all over Vietnam between 1973 and 1975. Set deep in the bowels of the building in a glass sarcophagus is the

Need to Know

(Map p58; ☑024-3845 5128; www.bqllang. gov.vn; entrance cnr P Ngoc Ha & P Doi Can)

Take a Break

Check out **Bar Betta** (Map p58; ☑0165 897 9073; 34 Cao Ba Quat; ⊗9am-midnight) for coffee (or a cocktail).

★ Top Tip

Plan to visit early in the day, as the mausoleum closes by mid-morning.

frail, pale body of Ho Chi Minh. The mausoleum is usually closed from 4 September to 4 November while his embalmed body goes to Russia for maintenance.

Dress modestly: wearing shorts, tank tops or hats is not permitted. Talking, putting your hand in your pocket and photography are strictly prohibited. The queue usually snakes for several hundred metres to the mausoleum entrance and inside, filing past Ho's body at a slow but steady pace. If you're lucky, you'll catch the changing of the guard outside – the pomp and ceremony displayed here rivals the British equivalent at Buckingham Palace.

Ho Chi Minh's Stilt House

This humble, traditional **stilt house** (Nha San Bac Ho & Phu Chu Tich Tai; Map p58; So 1 Ngo Bach Thao; 25,000d; ⊗8-11.30am daily & 2-4pm Tue-Thu, Sat & Sun) where Ho lived intermittently from 1958 to 1969 is set in a well-tended garden adjacent a carp-filled pond and has been preserved as Ho left it. From here, you look out onto Hanoi's most opulent building: the beautiful, beaux-arts **Presidential Palace** (2 Ð Hung Vuong), constructed in 1906 for the Governor General of Indochina. It's now used for official receptions and isn't open to the public. Visitors may wander the grounds if you stick to the paths.

Ho Chi Minh Museum

The huge concrete Soviet-style **Ho Chi Minh Museum** (Bao Tang Ho Chi Minh; Map p58; ☑024-3845 5435; www.baotanghochi minh.vn; 19 P Ngoc Ha; 40,000d; ⊗8am-noon daily & 2-4.30pm Tue-Thu, Sat & Sun) is a triumphalist monument dedicated to the life of the founder of modern Vietnam. The often-confusing exhibition is a mixed bag; highlights include mementoes of Ho's life, and some fascinating photos and dusty official documents relating to the overthrow of the French and the onward march of revolutionary socialism. Photography is forbidden.

TIPWAM/SHUTTERSTOCK ©

Coffee & the Cafe Scene

Cafe culture is deeply ingrained in the capital. With Vietnamese creations that make use of yoghurt, eggs and even fruit, ordering a coffee in Hanoi can be endlessly varied.

Great For...

☑ Don't Miss

In the heat and humidity of summer, an iced coconut coffee sure hits the spot.

Traditional Cafes

Western-style cafes are becoming increasingly common, but most pale in comparison to the traditional cafes dotted around central Hanoi.

Café Duy Tri

This caffeine-infused **labyrinth** (☎024-3829 1386; 43a P Yen Phu; ⊗8am-6pm) is a Hanoi classic. You'll feel like Gulliver as you negotiate the tiny ladders and stairways to reach the 3rd-floor balcony. Delicious *caphe sua chua* (iced coffee with yoghurt) may be your new favourite summertime drink.

Cafe Pho Co

One of Hanoi's most hidden cafes, this **place** (Map p62; 4th fl, 11 P Hang Gai; ⊗8am-11pm) has plum views over Hoan Kiem Lake. You'll need to order coffee and snacks

Caphe trung da

VINHDAV/GETTY IMAGES ©

before tackling the final winding staircase. Try sweet *caphe trung da,* coffee topped with silky-smooth beaten egg yolk.

Cafe Lam

A classic **cafe** (Map p62; ☏024-3824 5940; www.cafelam.com; 60 P Nguyen Huu Huan ⊙6am-10pm) that's been around for years – though these days it draws Converse-wearing and Vespa-riding bright young things refuelling on wickedly strong *caphe den* (black coffee).

Cong Caphe

Settle in to the eclectic beats and kitsch Communist memorabilia at this hip **cafe** (Map p58; http://congcaphe.com; 152 P Trieu Viet Vuong) with a *caphe sua da* (iced coffee with condensed milk).

Cool Cafes

It's not all about traditional cafes in Hanoi; there are also some unique and quirky places to imbibe your caffeine.

Loading T Cafe

Architecture lovers will especially love this **cafe** (Map p62; ☏0122 786 8686; 2nd fl, 8 Chan Cam; ⊙8am-6pm; ☜) converted from a room in a dilapidated French colonial house. Homemade cakes, fresh juices and coconut or yoghurt coffee are on the menu.

Hanoi House

A chic and bohemian **cafe** (Map p62; ☏024-2348 9789; 2nd fl, 47a P Ly Quoc Su; ⊙9am-11pm; ☜) with superb upstairs views of St Joseph Cathedral. Chill out on the impossibly slim balcony.

Old Quarter street cafe

Street Food & Bia Hoi

For atmosphere and authenticity, you can't beat mingling with Hanoians over street snacks and glasses of bia hoi *(draught beer). Squat down on a plastic stool and get stuck in.*

Great For...

ⓘ Need to Know

For something to chew with your brew, **Bia Hoi Ha Noi** (2 P Duong Thanh) does the best spare ribs in town.

★ **Top Tip**

The Viets like to start drinking early; *bia hoi* joints are busy from noon onwards.

Hanoi's Best Street Food

Deciphering Hanoi's street food scene can be bewildering but the city's best grub definitely comes from the scores of vendors crowding the city's pavements with smoking charcoal burners, tiny blue plastic stools and expectant queues of canny locals.

Bun Rieu Cua

Get to this incredibly popular **spot** (Map p62; 40 P Hang Tre; bun rieu 25,000d; ⏱7-9:30am) early, as its sole dish of *bun rieu cua* (noodle soup with beef in a spicy crab broth) is only served for a couple of hours from 7am. A Hanoi classic.

Bun Cha Nem Cua Be Dac Kim

Visiting Hanoi and not eating *bun cha* (barbecued pork with rice vermicelli) with a side of *nem cua be* (sea-crab spring rolls) should be classed as a capital offence. This is an excellent **place** (Map p62; 67 P Duong Thanh; bun cha 60,000d; ⏱11am-7pm) to try this street food classic.

Banh Mi Pho Hue

Banh mi (sandwich) vendors abound in Hanoi, although the phenomenon is less popular than in Ho Chi Minh City. **Banh Mi Pho Hue** (Map p58; 118 P Hue; banh mi 25,000-55,000d; ⏱8am-9pm) is usually packed with locals, which is always a good sign.

Pho Thin

Negotiate your way to the rear of this narrow, rustic **establishment** (Map p58; 13 P Lo Duc; pho 50,000d; ⏱6am-8.30pm) and sit down to some excellent *pho bo* (beef

Pork *banh mi*

noodle soup). A classic Hanoi experience that hasn't changed in decades.

Banh Cuon

Don't even bother ordering **here** (Map p62; 14 P Hang Ga; meals from 35,000d; ⊗8am-3pm); just squeeze in and a plate of gossamer-light *banh cuon* (steamed rice crêpes filled with minced pork, mushrooms and shrimp) will be placed in front of you.

Banh Goi

Nestled under a banyan tree near St Joseph Cathedral, this humble **stall** (Map p62; 52 P Ly Quoc Su; snacks 35,000d; ⊗10am-7pm)

> ✕ **Take a Break**
> On the southern bank of West Lake, Đ Thuy Khue features dozens of outdoor seafood restaurants.

AS FOOD STUDIO/SHUTTERSTOCK ©

turns out *banh goi*, moreish deep-fried pastries crammed with pork, vermicelli and mushrooms.

Bun Bo Nam Bo

Bun bo nam bo (dry noodles with beef) is a dish from southern Vietnam, but it's certainly travelled north well at this busy **venue** (Map p62; 67 P Hang Dieu; meals from 60,000d; ⊗7.30am-10.30pm). Mix in bean sprouts, garlic, lemongrass and green mango for a filling treat.

Bia Hoi Hot Spots

Hanoi is the *bia hoi* capital of Vietnam. This refreshing, light-bodied pilsener was first introduced to Vietnam by the Czechs. Brewed without preservatives, it is meant to be enjoyed immediately and costs as little as 5000d a glass.

A wildly popular place unofficially known as 'Bia Hoi junction' and 'Beer Corner' is at the corner of P Ta Hien and P Luong Ngoc Quyen, in the heart of the Old Quarter. It's now packed with backpackers though, and has lost most of its local charm.

An alternative *bia hoi* hot spot is where P Nha Hoa or P Bat Dan meets P Duong Thanh on the western edge of the Old Quarter. Good spots include **Bia Hoi Ha Noi** (Map p62; 2 P Duong Thanh), which also does great ribs; **Nha Hang Lan Chin** (Map p62; ☑024-3824 1138; cnr P Hang Tre & P Hang Thung; ⊗9.30am-10pm), famed for *vit quay* (roast duck); and **Quan Bia Minh** (Map p62; 7a P Dinh Liet; meals 90,000-130,000d; ⊗8am-late) for well-priced Vietnamese food and excellent service led by the eponymous Mrs Minh.

Speciality Food Streets

Pho Cam Chi, a narrow lane 500m northeast of Hanoi train station, is packed with local eateries turning out cheap, tasty food for a few dollars.

The northeast edge of **Truc Bach Lake** is famous for its *lau* (hotpot) restaurants.

Cho Am Thuc Ngoc Lam, on the east side of the Song Hong (Red River), is popular with locals and heavy on seafood.

Hoa Lo Prison Museum

XITA/SHUTTERSTOCK ©

Hanoi's Museums

Hanoi, as the capital, has a fine selection of museums dealing with everything from fine art to revolutionary history, tribal culture to Vietnamese women.

Great For

☑ Don't Miss

The flight suit of Senator John McCain (a Republican nominee for the US presidency) who was jailed in Hoa Lo Prison.

Vietnam Museum of Ethnology

A fabulous **collection** (☎024-3756 2193; www.vme.org.vn; Đ Nguyen Van Huyen; adult/ concession 40,000/15,000d, guide 100,000d; ⊙8.30am-5.30pm Tue-Sun) relating to Vietnam's ethnic minorities features well-presented tribal art, artefacts and everyday objects gathered from across the nation, and examples of traditional village houses. Displays are well labelled in Vietnamese, French and English. If you're into anthropology, it's well worth the approximately 200,000d each-way taxi fares to the Cau Giay district, about 7km from the city centre, where the museum is located.

Hoa Lo Prison Museum

This thought-provoking **site** (Map p58; ☎024-3934 2253; cnr P Hoa Lo & P Hai Ba Trung; adult/child 30,000d/free; ⊙8am-5pm) is all

Fine Arts
Museum of
Vietnam

Hanoi Station   Hoa Lo   Hoan
(Train Station A)   Prison   Kiem   Museum of
                       Museum   Lake   Vietnamese
                                              Revolution

Tran Quy Cap Station
(Train Station B)   Vietnamese
                       Women's Museum

ℹ️ Need to Know

Many museums close for a long lunch break.

✕ Take a Break

Head to the Maison de Tet Decor (p65) for healthy, mainly organic dining.

that are most poignant. There is a stunning collection of propaganda posters, as well as costumes, tribal basketware and fabric motifs from Vietnam's ethnic minority groups.

Fine Arts Museum of Vietnam

This excellent **Fine Arts Museum** (Bao Tang My Thuat Viet Nam; Map p58; ☑024-3733 2131; http://vnfam.vn; 66 P Nguyen Thai Hoc; adult/child 40,000/20,000d; ☺8.30am-5pm) is housed in two buildings that were once the French Ministry of Information. Treasures abound, including ancient Champa stone carvings and some astonishing effigies of Guan Yin, the thousand-eyed, thousand-armed goddess of compassion. Look out for the lacquered statues of Buddhist monks from the Tay Son dynasty and the big collection of contemporary art and folk-naive paintings.

that remains of the former Hoa Lo Prison, ironically nicknamed the 'Hanoi Hilton' by US POWs during the American War. Most exhibits relate to the prison's use up to the mid-1950s, focusing on the Vietnamese struggle for independence from France. A gruesome relic is the ominous French guillotine, used to behead Vietnamese revolutionaries. There are also displays focusing on the American pilots who were incarcerated at Hoa Lo during the American War.

Vietnamese Women's Museum

This excellent, modern **museum** (Map p58; ☑024-3825 9936; www.baotangphunu.org. vn; 36 P Ly Thuong Kiet; 30,000d; ☺8am-5pm) showcases women's role in Vietnamese society and culture. Labelled in English and French, it's the memories of the wartime contribution by individual heroic women

Museum of Vietnamese Revolution

Inaugurated in 1959 and housing over 40,000 exhibits, this **museum** (Bao Tang Cach Mang Viet Nam; Map p58; ☑024-3825 4151; 216 Đ Tran Quang Khai; adult/student 40,000/20,000d; ☺8am-noon & 1.30-5pm, closed 1st Mon of the month) enthusiastically presents the histories of conflict and revolution within Vietnam, from the liberation movements against the French occupation, to the establishment of the Communist Party and the Socialist Republic of Vietnam.

Local Life in the Old Quarter

This amble around the Old Quarter and the fringes of Hoan Kiem Lake is the ideal way to get to grips with inner city Hanoi. You'll encounter craftsmen carving, street vendors hawking and there's plenty to tempt your wallet en route.

Start Ngoc Son Temple

Distance 3km

Duration two hours

5 Continue via the city gateway to **Dong Xuan Market** (p43), which has hundreds of stalls.

P Ly Nam De
P Phung Hung
P Hang Cot
P Lo Ren
P Thuoc Bac
Hang Duong
P Cha Ca

6 Wind your way south via **P Thuoc Bac**, passing herb merchants, tin-box makers and silk shops.

P Hoang Dieu
P Nguyen Tri Phuong

OLD QUARTER

P Hang Thiec
P Hang Bo
P Hang Quat
P Hang Gai

P Duong Thanh

Take a Break... There's a cluster of good cafes around St Joseph Cathedral.

Đ Tran Phu

Cao Ba Quat

P Hang Ga
P Ly Quoc Su

FINISH
7

HOAN KIEM DISTRICT

DONG DA DISTRICT

Hanoi Station (Train Station A)

P Trang Thi

7 Graceful, neo-Gothic **St Joseph Cathedral** (p39) is one of Hanoi's most famous landmarks.

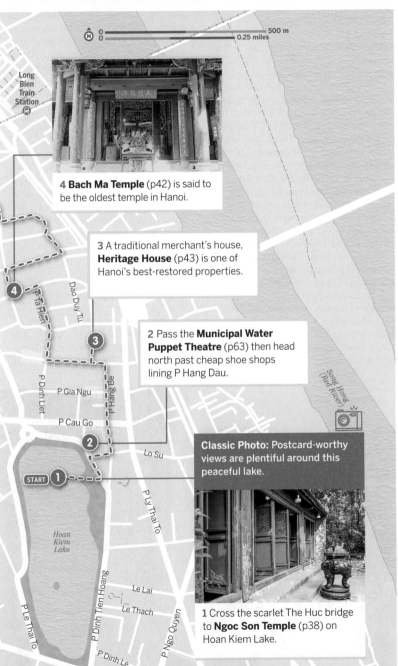

N 0   500 m
0   0.25 miles

Long Bien Train Station

4 Bach Ma Temple (p42) is said to be the oldest temple in Hanoi.

3 A traditional merchant's house, **Heritage House** (p43) is one of Hanoi's best-restored properties.

2 Pass the **Municipal Water Puppet Theatre** (p63) then head north past cheap shoe shops lining P Hang Dau.

Song Hong (Red River)

Classic Photo: Postcard-worthy views are plentiful around this peaceful lake.

P Ta Hien

Dao Duy Tu

P Gia Ngu

P Hang Be

P Dinh Liet

P Cau Go

Lo Su

START

P Ly Thai To

Hoan Kiem Lake

1 Cross the scarlet The Huc bridge to **Ngoc Son Temple** (p38) on Hoan Kiem Lake.

P Le Thai To

P Dinh Tien Hoang

Le Lai

Le Thach

P Ngo Quyen

P Dinh Le

⊙ SIGHTS

Temple of Literature   Confucian Temple

(Van Mieu Quoc Tu Giam; Map p58; ☑024-3845 2917; P Quoc Tu Giam; adult/student 30,000/15,000d; ⊗8am-6pm) A rare example of well-preserved traditional Vietnamese architecture, the Temple of Literature honours Vietnam's finest scholars. Founded in 1070 by Emperor Ly Thanh Tong, the attractive complex is dedicated to Confucius (Khong Tu) and was the site of Vietnam's first university (1076). The altars are popular with students praying for good grades, while the pagodas, ponds and gardens of the five courtyards make picturesque backdrops for student graduation photos. It is depicted on the 100,000d note.

University admission was originally exclusively for those born of noble families, but after 1442 became more egalitarian. Gifted students from all over the nation headed to Hanoi to study the principles of Confucianism, literature and poetry. In 1484 Emperor Ly Thanh Tong ordered that stelae be erected to record the names, places of birth and achievements of exceptional scholars: 82 of 116 stelae remain standing, mostly atop turtle statues. Paths lead from the imposing tiered gateway on P Quoc Tu Giam through formal gardens to the Khue Van pavilion, constructed in 1802.

Hai Ba Trung Temple   Buddhist Temple

(Map p58; P Tho Lao; ⊗6am-6pm Mon-Sat) Two kilometres south of Hoan Kiem Lake, this temple was founded in 1142. A statue shows the two Trung sisters (from the 1st century AD) kneeling with their arms raised in the air. Some say the statue shows the sisters, who had been proclaimed the queens of the Vietnamese, about to dive into a river. They are said to have drowned themselves rather than surrender in the wake of their defeat at the hands of the Chinese.

Hanoi Opera House   Historic Building

(Nha Hat Lon Ha Noi; Map p58; ☑024-3993 0113; http://hanoioperahouse.org.vn; 1 P Trang Tien) This glorious neoclassical centrepiece of Hanoi's French Quarter is unmissable with its Gothic pillars and domes. The French-colonial 900-seat venue was built

From left: Hai Ba Trung Temple; Temple of Literature; Tay Ho Pagoda; Imperial City of Thang Long

ROMAN BABAKIN/SHUTTERSTOCK ©

ROMAN BABAKIN/SHUTTERSTOCK ©

in 1911. On 16 August 1945 the Viet Minh–run Citizens' Committee announced that it had taken over the city from a balcony on this building. For some drama today, book ahead for a performance here, even if just to experience the grand interior. Most weekends you'll see Hanoi wedding couples getting photographed on the elegant front steps.

Lotte Observation Deck   Viewpoint

(☎024-3333 6016; www.lottecenter.com.vn; 54 P Lieu Giai, Ba Dinh; adult/student day 230,000/170,000d, night 130,000/110,000d; ☉9am-10pm) The city's best views can be found on the 65th floor of the landmark Lotte Center, opened in 2014, in the western corner of Hanoi's Ba Dinh district. From this uninterrupted vantage point, high above Hanoi's hustle and bustle, one can consider the size of the Old Quarter relative to the sheer scale of Hanoi's voracious growth. The tower also houses a hotel, all manner of restaurants, a rooftop bar and a department store on its lower floors.

Tay Ho Pagoda   Buddhist Temple

(Phu Tay Ho; Đ Thai Mai; ☉6am-7pm) Jutting into West Lake (Ho Tay), beautiful Tay Ho Pagoda is perhaps the most popular place of worship in Hanoi. Throngs of people come here on the first and 15th day of each lunar month in the hope of receiving good fortune from the Mother Goddess, to whom the temple is dedicated.

West Lake   Lake

(Ho Tay; Map p58) The city's largest lake, known as both Ho Tay and West Lake, is 15km in circumference and ringed by upmarket suburbs, including the predominantly expat Tay Ho district. On the south side, along Đ Thuy Khue, are seafood restaurants, and to the east, the Xuan Dieu strip is lined with restaurants, cafes, boutiques and luxury hotels. A pathway circles the lake, making for a great bicycle ride.

Imperial Citadel of Thang Long   Historic Site

(Hoang Thanh Thang Long; Map p58; www.hoangthanhthanglong.vn; 19c P Hoang Dieu; adult/child 30,000d/free; ☉8-11.30am daily & 2-4pm Tue-Thu, Sat & Sun) Added to Unesco's

Hanoi

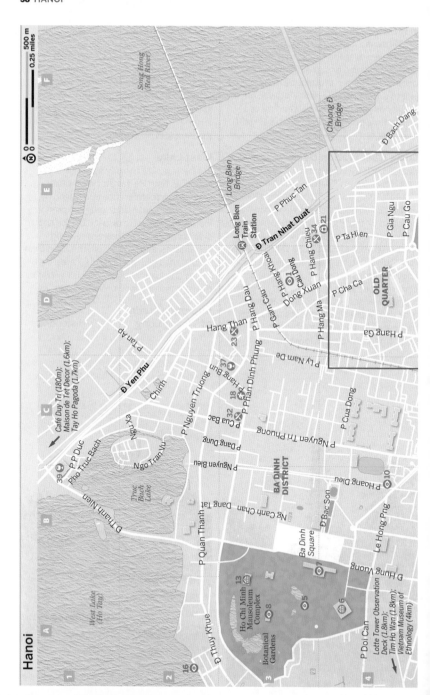

Song Hong
(Red River)

Long Bien
Bridge

Chuong D
Bridge

Đ Bach Dang

P Phuc Tan

Long Bien
Train
Station

Đ Tran Nhat Duat

34

21

P Ta Hien

P Gia Ngu

P Cau Go

OLD
QUARTER

P Cha Ca

P Hang Ma

P Hang Ga

P Gam Cau

Dong Xuan

1

P Hang Chieu

P Hang Ma

P Hang Khoai

P Hang Cau

P Hang Dau

Hang Than

23

37

18

32

P Ly Nam De

P Cua Dong

P Nguyen Tri Phuong

P Hang Bun

P Phan Dinh Phung

P Nguyen Truong

P Dang Dung

P Cua Bac

Đ Yen Phu

Chinh

Ngo Tran Vu

Ngu Xa

P P Duc

Pho Truc Bach

Đ Tan Ap

Café Duy Tri (180m);
Maison de Tet Decor (1.6km);
Tay Ho Pagoda (1.7km)

39

Đ Thanh Nien

Truc
Bach
Lake

P Nguyen Bieu

BA DINH
DISTRICT

P Quan Thanh

Ng Canh Chan

Đ Dang Tat

Ba Dinh
Square

Đ Bac Son

7

P Hoang Dieu

10

Le Hong Png

P Cua Dong

West Lake
(Ho Tay)

16

Đ Thuy Khue

Botanical
Gardens

Ho Chi Minh
Mausoleum
Complex

13

8

5

6

P Doi Can

Đ Hung Vuong

Lotte Tower Observation
Deck (1.8km);
Tim Ho Wan (1.8km);
Vietnam Museum of
Ethnology (4km)

500 m
0.25 miles

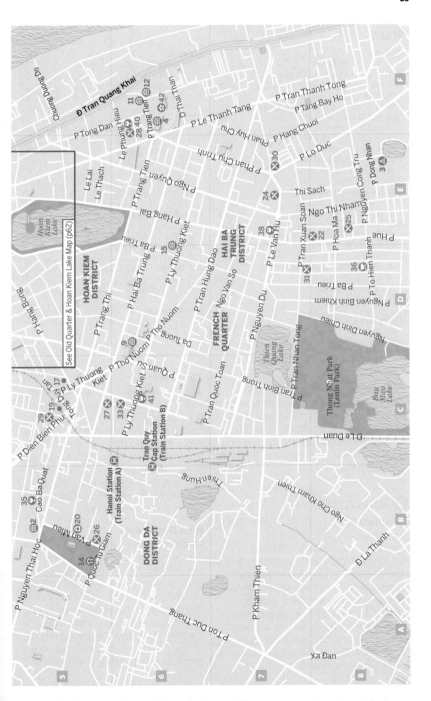

Chuong Duong Do

Đ Tran Quang Khai

P Tong Dan

Le Phung Hieu

P Trang Tien

P Trang Tien

11

28 40

4

12

42

D Thai Than

P Le Thanh Tang

P Tran Thanh Tong

P Tang Bay Ho

P Hang Chuoi

Phan Huy Chu

P Lo Duc

P Dong Nhan

30

P Nguyen Cong Tru

3

Le Lai

Le Thach

P Trang Tien

P Ngo Quyen

P Phan Chu Trinh

Thi Sach

Ngo Thi Nham

P Nguyen Binh Thanh

P Hang Bai

Hoan Kiem Lake

See Old Quarter & Hoan Kiem Lake Map (p62)

HOAN KIEM DISTRICT

P Trang Thi

P Hai Ba Trung

P Ba Trieu

P Ly Thuong Kiet

15

24

E

38

P Le Van Huu

Tran Xuan Soan

22

25

P Hoa Ma

36

31

P To Hien Thanh

P Ba Trieu

P Hue

D

P Hang Bong

P Trang Thi

HAI BA TRUNG DISTRICT

P Tran Hung Dao

Ngo Van So

P Nguyen Du

Nguyen Dinh Chieu

P Hang Da

Da Tuong

P Tho Nuom

P Tho Nuom

9

FRENCH QUARTER

P Tran Quoc Toan

Thien Quang Lake

P Tran Nhan Tong

P Tran Binh Trong

Thong Nhat Park (Lenin Park)

Bay Mau Lake

P Ly Thuong Kiet

P Quan Su

P Ly Thuong Kiet

41

P Duy Tan

17

19

29

P Dien Bien Phu

Tong Duy Tan

27

33

Tran Quy Cap Station (Train Station B)

D Le Duan

P Tran Binh Trong

Ngo Cho Kham Thien

P Nguyen Thai Hoc

Cao Ba Quat

35

2

P Van Mieu

20

26

14

P Quoc Tu Giam

Hanoi Station (Train Station A)

DONG DA DISTRICT

Thien Hung

P On Duc Thang

P Kham Thien

D La Thanh

Xa Dan

5

6

7

8

F

E

D

C

B

A

Hanoi

World Heritage List in 2010 and reopened in 2012, Hanoi's Imperial Citadel was the hub of Vietnamese military power for over 1000 years. Ongoing archaeological digs of ancient palaces, grandiose pavilions and imperial gates are complemented by fascinating military command bunkers from the American War.

❸ ACTIVITIES

Omamori Spa   Massage
(Map p58; ☑024-3773 9919; www.blindlink. org.vn; 52a P Hang Bun, Ba Đinh; 1hr massage from 190,000d) This not-for-profit organisation provides training and employment opportunities for the blind. Masseuses here are vision impaired and speak excellent English. The trained therapists give massages with a level of gentleness and body awareness that differs from traditional practitioners. Tips are not accepted; pricing and service are excellent.

Zo Project   Art
(Map p58; ☑0166 466 2433; http://zopaper. com; 27 Ngo 5A Tran Phu, railroad off 10 P Dien Bien Phu; workshops from 700,000d; ☺store 9am-7pm) If you love traditional Vietnamese paper, then this workshop–store is the place for handcrafted paintings, postcards or even artistic lampshades. Workshops here include calligraphy and watercolour painting. Profits help ethnic minority craftspeople in northern Vietnam.

Blue Butterfly
Cooking Class   Cooking
(Map p62; ☑024-3926 3845; http://blue butterflyrestaurant.com; 69 P Ma May; per person from 1,225,000d; ☺9am or 3.30pm) In this popular cooking class, you'll meet your chef/teacher in the restaurant kitchen, be accompanied on a shopping trip to the Dong Xuan Market, then return to the kitchen where you'll be instructed in the preparation and cooking of three dishes.

Once the class is over, enjoy the fruits of your labour in the restaurant.

🔒 SHOPPING

Tan My Design
Clothing

(Map p62; 📞024-3938 1154; www.tanmy design.com; 61 P Hang Gai; ⊘8am-8pm) Stylish clothing, jewellery and accessories, with the added bonus of a funky cafe when you need a break from shopping. The homewares and bed linen are definitely worth a look.

Indigenous
Arts & Crafts

(Map p62; 📞024-3938 1263; 36 P Au Trieu; ⊘9am-6pm) A top spot for quirky ethnic-style gifts and excellent fair-trade coffee. There's a great little cafe too, so you can choose your favourite Vietnamese java before you buy.

Three Trees
Fashion & Accessories

(Map p62; 📞024-3928 8725; http://threetrees. com.vn; 15 P Nha Tho; ⊘9am-7pm) Stunning, very unusual designer jewellery, including many delicate necklaces, which make special gifts.

Hanoi Moment
Arts & Crafts

(Map p62; 📞024-3926 3630; www.hanoi moment.vn; 101 P Hang Gai; ⊘8am-9pm) An oasis of classier Vietnamese souvenirs, including lacquerware and jewellery, amid the T-shirt overkill of nearby stores. Bamboo, stone and porcelain are also used to great effect.

Cua Hang Bach Hoa So 26
Clothing

(Map p58; 📞0989 877 793; www.fb.me/sohaimu-oisau26; 26 Đ Dao Duy Tu; ⊘10am-10pm) Come here to browse for hip vintage clothes – it's mostly American but there are some Vietnamese items too, including local designers who have refashioned old fabrics.

Mosaique
Homewares

(Map p62; 📞024-3971 3797; www.mosaique decoration.com; 6 P Ly Quoc Su; ⊘9am-8pm) Modern and chic updates of traditional lacquerware and silk. The ideal spot to pick up stylish cushion covers, linen and accessories.

Mekong+
Arts & Crafts

(Map p62; 📞024-3926 4831; https://me kong-plus.com; 13 P Hang Bac; ⊘8am-8pm) Beautiful quilts handcrafted by rural women working in a not-for-profit community-development program.

Craft Link
Arts & Crafts

(Map p58; 📞024-3733 6101; www.craftlink.com. vn; 43-51 P Van Mieu; ⊘9am-6pm) A not-for-profit organisation near the Temple of Literature that sells quality tribal handicrafts and weavings at fair-trade prices.

Mai Gallery
Art

(Map p62; 📞024-3938 0568, mobile 0936 368 367; www.maigallery-vietnam.com; 113 P Hang Bong; ⊘9am-7pm) Run by resident artist Mai, this is a good place to learn more about Vietnamese art before making a purchase.

⭐ ENTERTAINMENT

Binh Minh Jazz Club
Live Music

(Map p58; www.minhjazzvietnam.com; 1 P Trang Tien; ⊘performances 9pm-midnight) **FREE** This atmospheric venue tucked behind the Opera House is the place in Hanoi to catch live jazz. There's a full bar, food menu and high-quality gigs featuring father-and-son team Minh and Dac, plus other local and international jazz acts. Free admission means the small, smoky venue fills quickly, so get there early.

Thang Long Ca Tru Theatre
Live Music

(Map p62; 📞0122 326 6897; www.ca truthanglong.com; 28 P Hang Buom; 210,000d; ⊘8pm Thu & Sat) Concerts of traditional Vietnamese music are held in this intimate restored house in the Old Quarter. *Ca tru* is indigenous to the north of Vietnam, and concerts feature a selection of the 100 or so *ca tru* melodies. The art form has also been recognised as an endangered 'intangible cultural heritage' by Unesco.

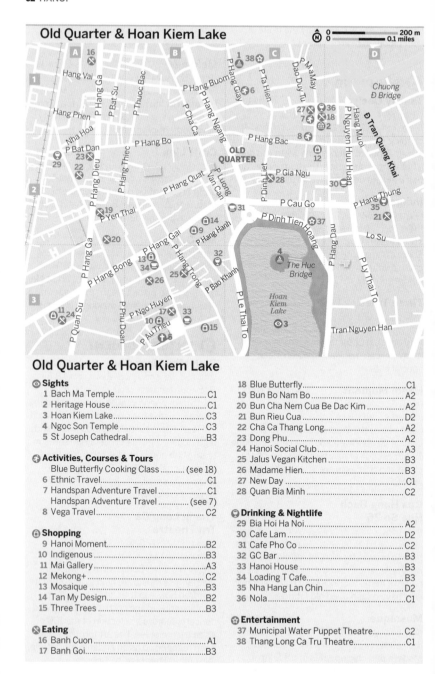

Old Quarter & Hoan Kiem Lake

Municipal Water Puppet Theatre
Theatre

(Map p62; ☑024-3824 9494; www.thanglong
waterpuppet.org; 57b P Dinh Tien Hoang;
adult/child 100,000/60,000d; ☺ 5 afternoon
performances daily, also 9.30am Sun) Water-
puppetry shows are a real treat for children.
Multilingual programs allow the audience to
read up on each vignette as it's performed.
Although there are multiple performances
daily, book well ahead, especially from
October to April.

EATING

Hanoi is an international city, and whatever
your budget or tastes, it's available here. If
you've just flown in, dig into the fragrantly
spiced local cuisine – the city's street food
is an essential experience.

Old Quarter

Bun Cha 34
Vietnamese $

(Map p58; ☑0948 361 971; 34 P Hang Than;
meals 35,000d; ☺8.30am-5pm; ☎) Best *bun
cha* in Vietnam? Many say 34 is up there.
No presidents have eaten at the plastic
tables, but you get perfectly moist chargrilled pork, zesty fresh herbs and delicious
broth to dip everything in. The *nem*
(seafood spring rolls) are great too. Aim for
midday for patties straight off the coals.

New Day
Vietnamese $

(Map p62; ☑024-3828 0315; http://newday
restaurant.com; 72 P Ma May; meals 50,000-
100,000d; ☺8am-late) Busy New Day attracts
locals, expats and travellers alike with its
broad menu. The eager staff always find
space for new diners, so look forward to
sharing a table with some like-minded fans
of Vietnamese food. It's not advertised,
but evening diners can point and choose
from dishes for a mixed plate for about
100,000d.

Quan Com Pho Co
Vietnamese $

(Map p58; ☑024-2216 4028; 16 Nguyen Sieu;
meals from 75,000d) This large, bustling restaurant attracts a mixed crowd for its long
menu of simple, good Vietnamese dishes

such as *ga nuong xa,* lemongrass chicken
and Hanoi *pho cuon,* steamed rice rolls
filled with mango, vegetables and shrimp.
The four-course set meals (from 119,000d)
are good value and can include surprisingly
tasty crème caramel. Choose the internal
leafy courtyard for some peace.

Blue Butterfly
Vietnamese $$

(Map p62; ☑024-3926 3845; http://blue
butterflyrestaurant.com; 69 P Ma May; meals
100,000-300,000d; ☺8am-10.30pm) Blue
Butterfly floats above its weight with the
lamp-lit dark, wood stylings of a heritage
house and a good-value menu of Viet-
namese classics. Staff offer knowledgable
suggestions and demonstrate how to tack-
le dishes such as *nem lui,* pork grilled on
lemongrass skewers, wrapped in rice paper
and dipped in peanut sauce. Set menus
(from 350,000d) are available.

Cha Ca Thang Long
Vietnamese $$

(Map p62; ☑024-3824 5115; www.chaca
thanglong.com; 19-31 P Duong Thanh; cha ca fish
meal 180,000d; ☺10am-3pm & 5-10pm) Bring
along your DIY cooking skills and grill your
own succulent fish with a little shrimp
paste and plenty of herbs. *Cha ca* is an
iconic Hanoi dish heavy on turmeric and
dill, and while another nearby more-famous
cha ca eatery gets all the tour-bus traffic,
the food here is actually better.

Dong Phu
Vietnamese $$

(Map p62; ☑091 870 9398; 12 Hang Dieu; meals
110,000-500,000d; ☺10am-2pm & 5-9.30pm;
☒☑) Dong Phu is a stunning restored
Vietnamese house that resembles an
art gallery lifted from an interior design
magazine. Classic Vietnamese dishes, like
mango salad with grilled prawns, look and
taste equally good, and are mild rather than
spicy. Try crab hotpot with sliced beef, and
for dessert, pandan mousse.

Around Hoan Kiem Lake

Jalus Vegan Kitchen
Vegan $

(Map p62; ☑024-3266 9730; 2nd fl, 46 Hang
Trong; meals 30,000-60,000d; ☺8am-10pm
Tue-Sun; ☒☎☑) Pull up a pine table at this

modern, hidden restaurant and try some delicious coconut and chia smoothies and veggie burgers, or pizza, quiche and ravioli made with vegan cheese. There are definite Vietnamese twists with lemongrass and spice, and sometimes special all-Vietnamese menus.

Hanoi Social Club   Cafe $$

(Map p62; ☏024-3938 2117; www.facebook.com/thehanoisocialclub; 6 Hoi Vu; meals 95,000-175,000d; ☺8am-11pm) On three funky levels with retro furniture, the Hanoi Social Club is the city's most cosmopolitan cafe and an artist hub. Dishes include potato fritters with chorizo for breakfast, and pasta, burgers and wraps for lunch or dinner. Vegetarian options feature a tasty mango curry, and the quiet laneway location is a good spot for an end-of-day coffee, beer or wine.

Madame Hien   Vietnamese $$$

(Map p62; ☏024-3938 1588; http://didiercorlou-hanoirestaurants.com; 15 Chan Cam; meals 100,000-350,000d, set menus from 397,000d; ☺11am-2pm & 5-10.30pm; 🛜) Housed in a restored 19th-century villa, Madame Hien is a tribute to French chef Didier Corlou's Vietnamese grandmother. Look forward to elegant versions of traditional Hanoi street food, with the '36 Streets' fixed menu (595,000d) an easygoing place to kick off your culinary tour of the city.

✖ West of the Old Quarter

Quan An Ngon   Vietnamese $

(Map p58; ☏024-3942 8162; http://quananngon.com.vn; 18 Phan Boi Chau; meals 70,000-150,000d; ☺7am-11pm) This branch of a number of small same-named kitchens turns out street-food specialities from across Vietnam. Try and visit just outside the busy lunch and dinner periods, or consider Quan An Ngon's newest branch in a lovely French villa just north of the **Old Quarter** (Map p58; ☏024-3734 9777; www.ngonhanoi.com.vn; 34 P Phan Đinh Phung; meals 70,000-150,000d; ☺11am-11pm).

Old Hanoi   Vietnamese $$

(Map p58; ☏024-3747 8337; www.oldhanoi.com; 4 Ton That Thiep; meals 90,000-179,000d; ☺10am-2pm & 5-10pm) This sophisticated eatery in a restored French-colonial villa has a pleasant casual courtyard outside and starched white tablecloths inside. Once host to celebrity chef Gordon Ramsay, it serves traditional Hanoian and Vietnamese specialities with aplomb; you'll enjoy the selection and find the best value for money if you dine in a group.

Koto   Cafe $$

(Nha Hang Koto Van Mieu; Map p58; ☏024-3747 0338; www.koto.com.au; 59 P Van Mieu; meals 120,000-160,000d; ☺7.30am-10pm, closed dinner Mon) Stunning four-storey modernist cafe-bar-restaurant overlooking the Temple of Literature, where the interior design has been taken very seriously, from the stylish seating to the fresh flowers by the till. Daily specials are chalked up on a blackboard, and the short menu has everything from excellent Vietnamese food to yummy pita wraps and beer-battered fish and chips.

✖ French Quarter

Bun Cha Huong Lien   Vietnamese $

(Map p58; 24 P Le Van Hu; meals to 90,000d; ☺10am-8pm) Bun Cha Huong Lien was launched into stardom thanks to Barack Obama, who dined here with celebrity chef Anthony Bourdain in May 2016. Customers fill the four storeys to sample the grilled-pork-and-noodle delicacy while staff call out 'Obama *bun cha!*' to passers-by. The 'Combo Obama' gets you a bowl of *bun cha,* fried seafood roll and Hanoi beer for US$3.80.

Moto-san Uber Noodle   Noodles $

(Map p58; ☏024-6680 9124; 4 P Ly Dao Thanh; meals 45,000-70,000d) Brainchild of Hanoi artist, journalist and designer Nguyen Qui Duc (of Tadioto fame), this wonderful noodle stall seats eight eager eaters. The menu is simple: miso, *shōyu* (soy) or *shio* (salty) ramen, and spicy *banh my thit ko* (stewed pork) sandwiches with killer hot sauce (optional) à la central Vietnam. Sake and beer are, of course, readily available.

Chim Sao   Vietnamese $$

(Map p58; ☑024-3976 0633; www.chimsao. com; 63-65 Ngo Hue; meals 45,000-120,000d; ☺11am-11pm; 🖍) Sit at tables downstairs or grab a more traditional spot on the floor upstairs and discover excellent Vietnamese food, with some dishes inspired by the ethnic minorities of Vietnam's north. Definite standouts are the hearty and robust sausages, zingy and fresh salads, and duck with star fruit (carambola). Even simple dishes are outstanding. Come with a group to sample the full menu.

La Badiane   International $$$

(Map p58; ☑024-3942 4509; www.labadiane-hanoi.com; 10 Nam Ngu; meals from 280,000d; ☺11.30am-2pm & 6-10pm Mon-Sat) This stylish bistro is set in a restored whitewashed French villa arrayed around a breezy central courtyard. French cuisine underpins the menu – La Badiane translates as 'star anise' – but Asian and Mediterranean flavours also feature. Menu highlights include sea-bass tagliatelle with smoked paprika, and prawn bisque with wasabi tomato bruschetta. Three-course lunches (385,000d) are excellent value, and there's an evening degustation (1,490,000d).

Other Areas

Maison de Tet Decor   Cafe $$

(☑0966 611 383; http://tet-lifestyle-collection. com; 156 Tua Hoa, Nghi Tam, Tay Ho; meals from 120,000d; ☺7am-10pm) Sumptuous, healthy and organic (when possible) whole foods are presented with aplomb in one of Hanoi's loveliest settings, an expansive, airy villa overlooking West Lake.

Tim Ho Wan   Dim Sum $$

(☑024-3333 1725; 36th fl, Lotte Tower, 54 P Lieu Giai, Ba Dinh; dim sum 69,000-95,000d) Do yourself a favour and reserve a window table at the Hanoi branch of this legendary Hong Kong dim sum chain, high above the city on the 36th floor of the Lotte Tower.

👍 Tour Hanoi

Get to grips with this Vietnamese metropolis by booking a cultural or foodie tour.

Hanoi Free Tour Guides (☑0988 979 174; http://hanoifreetourguides.com) There's no better way to experience the real Hanoi than with this not-for-profit social organisation run by a team of over 400 volunteer staff and guides comprising students and ex-students, speaking a multitude of languages. A variety of suggested tours are available, or work with your guide to tailor your own itinerary. Book online.

Sophie's Art Tour (☑0168 796 2575; www.sophiesarttour.com; tours from US$55) These fascinating tours are based on the lives of artists who studied, fought, witnessed and documented major changes in 20th- and 21st-century Vietnam, and will be appreciated not only by art lovers, but also by those who want to gain a deeper understanding of the complexities of Vietnam's unique history and culture.

Hanoi Street Food Tours (☑0904 517 074; www.streetfoodtourshanoi.blogspot. com.au; tours from US$75) There's a local company running tours under the same name, but we continue to recommend this pricier, private option, run by Van Cong Tu and Mark Lowerson, a couple of passionate Hanoi foodies. Whet your appetite with their individual social media photos. Tours can be customised to different interests.

Old Quarter (p40)
GRACETHANG2/SHUTTERSTOCK ©

From left: Thang Long Ca Tru Theatre (p61); Hanoi Social Club (p64); Quan An Ngon (p64)

Bring a friend or six and an empty stomach, and we guarantee you won't regret it.

The Kitchen
Cafe $$

(☎024-3719 2679; www.facebook.com/kitchen hanoi; 30 To Ngoc Van, Tay Ho; meals 100,000-210,000d; ☺7am-11pm Tue-Sun, to 3pm Mon; 🛜🍴👪) This Tay Ho terrace cafe with a Mexican tinge ticks all the right boxes: a mellow buzz and a creative, healthy menu of delicious sandwiches and salads sourced from organic ingredients. Also great for breakfast or a juice.

Pots 'n Pans
Fusion $$$

(Map p58; ☎024-3944 0204; www.potsnpans. vn; 57 P Bui Thi Xuan; meals 380,000-695,000d; ☺8am-11pm) In a chic modern space, Pots 'n Pans specialises in innovative fusion dishes blending Vietnamese and European influences. An excellent wine list partners with plenty of seafood dishes like crispy skin sea bass with black sesame noodles, wild mushrooms and tamarind-and-coconut sauce, and also rib-eye steak.

🍷 DRINKING & NIGHTLIFE

Tadioto
Bar

(Map p58; ☎024-6680 9124; www.fb.me/tadioto tongdan; 24b P Tong Dan; ☺8am-midnight) Nguyen Qui Duc's unofficial clubhouse for the underground art scene's latest incarnation is this dark and quirky colonial bar in the French Quarter. Obligatory red accents (seat covers, wrought-iron grill on the doors), reworkings of art deco furniture and plenty of recycled ironwork feature heavily. It attracts many well-dressed visitors. The highlight of the cool cocktail list is the sweet mojito.

Nola
Bar

(Map p62; 89 P Ma May; ☺9am-midnight) Retro furniture and art is mixed and matched in this bohemian, multi-level labyrinth tucked away from Ma May's tourist bustle. Pop in for a coffee and banana bread in a quiet section, or return after dark for one of Hanoi's best little bars.

PAUL QUAYLE/ALAMY STOCK PHOTO ©

Quan Ly   Bar

(Map p58; ☏024-3822 5276; 82 P Le Van Hu; ⏰10am-9pm) Owner Pham Xuan Ly has lived on this block since 1950, and now runs one of Hanoi's most traditional *ruou* (Vietnamese liquor) bars. Kick off with the ginseng one, and work your way up. An English-language menu makes it easy to choose, and there's also cheap beer and good Vietnamese food on offer.

Manzi Art Space   Bar

(Map p58; ☏024-3716 3397; www.facebook.com/manzihanoi; 14 Phan Huy Ich; ⏰cafe 9am-midnight, shop 10am-6pm) Part cool art gallery, part chic cafe and bar, Manzi is worth seeking out north of the Old Quarter. A restored French villa hosts diverse exhibitions of painting, sculpture and photography, and the compact courtyard garden is perfect for a cup of coffee or glass of wine. There's also a small shop selling works by contemporary Vietnamese artists.

GC Bar   Gay & Lesbian

(Map p62; ☏024-3825 0499; 7 P Ngo Bao Khanh; ⏰noon-midnight Sun-Thu, to 2am Fri & Sat) Hanoi's long-standing, only established gay bar, and unofficial LGBT HQ, might seem small and vanilla midweek, but it gets pumped on weekend nights. Reasonably priced drinks and chatty bar staff make it popular with a mixed local crowd and it's easy for gay visitors to drop by, especially those fond of playing pool. It's casual, so shorts and smoking indoors is common.

The Rooftop   Bar

(Map p58; ☏0913 706 966; http://therooftop.vn; 19th fl, Pacific Place, 83b P Ly Thuong Kiet; ⏰noon-midnight) For views of the city, pop in for an expensive beer or cocktail and enjoy the vista. It's very popular with a glittering array of Hanoi's bright young things, especially late in the evening when DJs play.

Summit Lounge   Bar

(Map p58; 20th fl, Sofitel Plaza, 1 Ð Thanh Nien; ⏰4.30pm-late) Enjoy fabulous views from

Ga Hà Nội train station

this 20th-floor lounge bar. Order a (pricey) cocktail or beer, grab a spot on the outside deck, and take in Truc Bach Lake and the city beyond.

GETTING THERE & AWAY

Hanoi's **Noi Bai International Airport** (HAN; ☑024-3827 1513; www.hanoiairportonline. com) is about 35km north of the city. The main **Hanoi train station** (Ga Hang Co, Train Station A; ☑024-3825 3949; 120 Đ Le Duan; ☺ticket office 7.30am-12.30pm & 1.30-7.30pm) serves southern destinations while **Tran Quy Cap Station** (Train

Station B; ☑024-3825 2628; P Tran Quy Cap; ☺ticket office 4-6am & 4-10pm) heads north to Lao Cai (for Sapa).

GETTING AROUND

Hanoi Taxi (☑024-3853 5353) and **Mai Linh** (☑024-3822 2666) are reliable taxis. Cyclo drivers are available but usually ask for more than taxis.

A metro system is under construction, and two lines should become operational in the near future.

VIETNAM STOCK PHOTOS/SHUTTERSTOCK ©

Where to Stay

Hanoi is one city where, if travelling on a budget, an extra US$10 to US$20 can make a big difference: splurge if you can. Almost all hotels include a generic buffet breakfast with some items cooked to order.

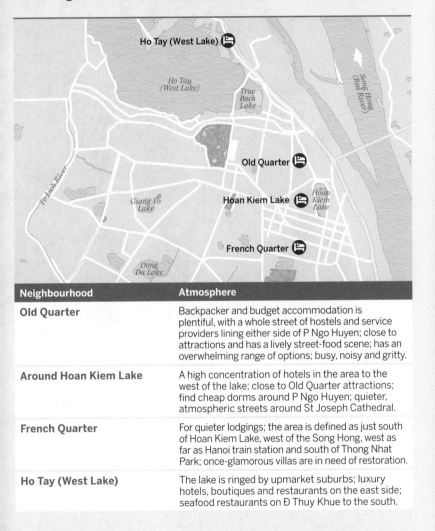

Neighbourhood	Atmosphere
Old Quarter	Backpacker and budget accommodation is plentiful, with a whole street of hostels and service providers lining either side of P Ngo Huyen; close to attractions and has a lively street-food scene; has an overwhelming range of options; busy, noisy and gritty.
Around Hoan Kiem Lake	A high concentration of hotels in the area to the west of the lake; close to Old Quarter attractions; find cheap dorms around P Ngo Huyen; quieter, atmospheric streets around St Joseph Cathedral.
French Quarter	For quieter lodgings; the area is defined as just south of Hoan Kiem Lake, west of the Song Hong, west as far as Hanoi train station and south of Thong Nhat Park; once-glamorous villas are in need of restoration.
Ho Tay (West Lake)	The lake is ringed by upmarket suburbs; luxury hotels, boutiques and restaurants on the east side; seafood restaurants on Đ Thuy Khue to the south.

HALONG BAY

Halong Bay at a Glance...

Majestic and mysterious, inspiring and imperious, Halong Bay's 2000 or more islands rise from the emerald waters of the Gulf of Tonkin. A Unesco World Heritage Site, this mystical seascape of limestone islets is breathtakingly beautiful. The islands are dotted with grottoes, many illuminated with Technicolour lighting effects. For a less touristy experience, head to nearby Lan Ha Bay or Bai Tu Long Bay.

Halong Bay attracts visitors year-round, with peak season between late May and early August. January to March is often cool and drizzly; the ensuing fog affects visibility, but adds eerie atmosphere.

Two Days in Halong Bay

Rather than attempt to tour Halong independently, it's far easier to book a tour from Hanoi. Prepare yourself for a long road trip: Halong City is over three hours away by bus. Once you're aboard your boat it's time to kick back and simply revel in the outstanding **karst island scenery** (p74), tour a **floating village** and pause for some kayaking and swimming.

Four Days in Halong Bay

Extend your stay with a couple of days in lovely **Cat Ba Island** (p78). Tour the **Cannon Fort** (p79) and **Hospital Cave** (p78) on the first morning and spend the afternoon on pretty **Cat Co Cove** (p78), then enjoy a seafood feast at **Vien Duong** (p81). The next day sign up for a boat tour of gorgeous **Lan Ha Bay** (p79), perhaps factoring in some rock climbing or kayaking.

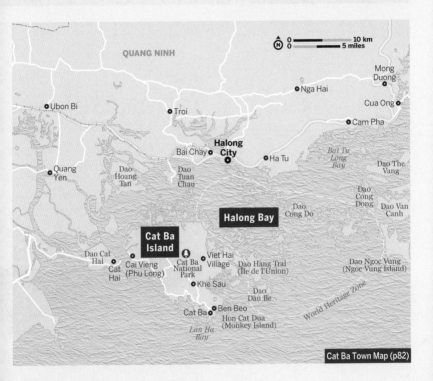

Arriving in Halong Bay

It's possible to join a tour in Halong City but it's far preferable to travel from Hanoi on a prearranged tour. Halong City is 160km from Hanoi; it takes three to four hours by road. Cat Ba Island can be accessed from either Hanoi or Haiphong.

Where to Stay

Aboard a boat in Halong Bay! Preferably on a traditional wooden junk if you have the resources. Otherwise Cat Ba Town has a good selection of hotels and guesthouses.

Cruising Halong Bay

The most popular way to experience Halong Bay's karst scenery is on a cruise. For many travellers this is an utterly memorable part of their trip to Vietnam.

Great For...

ℹ Need to Know

Tropical storms can occur between July and October and sailing trips can be cancelled.

★ **Top Tip**

Never contemplate a rushed day trip of Halong Bay; it's definitely worth at least one overnight stay.

Caves

Halong Bay's islands are peppered with caves, many now illuminated with cheesy technicolour lighting. Trinket-touting vendors are also part of the experience. Which of the caves you'll visit depends on certain factors, including the weather and the number of other boats in the vicinity.

Bai Tu Long National Park

The northeastern section of Halong Bay forms part of the **Bai Tu Long National Park** (100,000d). It's a stunning region not frequented by daytripping boats. The best way to experience Bai Tu Long's limestone-pinnacle-scattered scenery is on a cruise; try Hanoi-based outfit **Ethnic Travel** (Map p62; ☑024-3926 1951; www.ethnictravel.com.vn; 35 P Hang Giay; ⊗9am-6pm Mon-Sat, 10am-5pm Sun).

Kayaking

A kayak among the karsts is an option on most Halong Bay tours. Count on about an hour's paddling, often including negotiating your way through karst grottoes and around lagoons, or a vist to a **floating village** in the bay.

If you're really keen on kayaking, contact **Handspan Adventure Travel** in Hanoi or Blue Swimmer (p81) on Cat Ba Island, both of which run professionally organised trips and have qualified guides. Trips are operated in less-touristed Lan Ha Bay.

Choosing the Right Tour

Tours sold out of Hanoi start from a rock-bottom US$60 per person for a dodgy day trip, and can rise to around US$220 for two nights. For around US$110 to US$130,

Surprise Cave

you should get a worthwhile overnight cruise.

At the other end of the scale, cruising the karsts aboard a luxury Chinese-style junk is hard to beat. But be aware that paying top dollar doesn't necessarily compute into heading away from the crowds.

Most cruise-tours include return transport from Hanoi, Halong Bay entrance fees, and meals. A decent overnight tour usually includes kayaking. Drinks are extra.

This is one destination where it definitely pays to do your homework beforehand:

○ It can be a false economy to sign up for an ultra-cheapie tour. Spend a little more and enjoy the experience a whole lot more.

✗ Take a Break

All boats cruising the bay have well-stocked bars.

AEYPIX/SHUTTERSTOCK ©

○ At the very least, check basic on-board safety standards. Life jackets should be provided. If kayaking is included, make sure it's guided. Currents close to the karst formations are surprisingly strong. Accidents can occur when visitors are left to paddle off themselves.

○ Realise that most Halong Bay cruises follow a strict itinerary, with stops at caves often at the same time as other boats. On an overnight trip there's simply not the time to stray far from Halong City.

○ Make sure you know what you're paying for to avoid disappointment later. Many cruises are marketed as 'two-day' trips but are actually overnight tours, some involving less than 24 hours on board.

○ Ascertain in advance what the tour company's refund policy is if the cruise is cancelled due to bad weather.

Cruise operators to consider:

Cat Ba Ventures (p81) Overnight tours set out from Cat Ba Island and concentrate on the Lan Ha Bay area.

Handspan Adventure Travel (Map p62; ✆024-3926 2828; www.handspan.com; 78 P Ma May, Hanoi; overnight cruise d cabin from US$354; ✆9am-8pm) Operates the only true sailing ship on the bay; meander peacefully through the karsts without the constant hum of a diesel engine.

Indochina Sails (✆0982 042 426; www.indochinasails.com; overnight tour d cabin from US$440) Cruise Halong on a traditional junk with great viewing decks and cabins kitted out to a three-star standard.

Vega Travel (Map p62; ✆024-3926 2092; www.vegatravel.vn; cnr P Ma May & 24a P Hang Bac, Hanoi; overnight tour s/d cabin from US$130/240; ✆8am-8pm) Good-value overnight tours of Halong Bay, with comfortable cabins. Two-night tours also explore Lan Ha Bay and Cat Ba Island, including kayaking, cycling and hiking.

☑ Don't Miss

Halong at dawn is very special, an ethereal seascape tinged with steely grey light.

Floating villages off Cat Ba Island

TONKINPHOTOGRAPHY/SHUTTERSTOCK ©

Exploring Cat Ba Island

Rugged, craggy and jungle-clad Cat Ba is the largest island in Halong Bay. For climbers, kayakers and hikers it's the launching pad for a swag of sweat-inducing activities.

Great For...

ⓘ Need to Know

Cat Ba Town is quite tricky to reach; getting there involves travelling by boat and road.

Hospital Cave

This **cave** (40,000d; ◷7am-4.30pm) served both as a secret, bomb-proof hospital during the American War and as a safe house for VC leaders. Built between 1963 and 1965 (with assistance from China), this incredibly well-constructed three-storey feat of engineering was in constant use until 1975. The cave is about 10km north of Cat Ba Town on the road to Cat Ba National Park entrance.

It spans 17 rooms, including an old operating theatre and a huge natural cavern that was used as a cinema.

Cat Co Cove

A 10-minute walk southeast from Cat Ba Town, the three Cat Co Cove beaches boast the nearest sand to town, although rubbish in the water can be problematic some days.

Cai Vieng (Phu Long) • **Cat Ba Island** ◎
Cat Hai •
• Village
• Hospital Cave
World Heritage Zone
Cat Ba • Ben Beo

☑ Don't Miss

Hospital Cave is one of the most fascinating war sites in Vietnam.

✕ Take a Break

Good Bar (p83) always has a good vibe.

★ Top Tip

Other beaches on Cat Ba Island include Cai Vieng, Hong Xoai Be and Hong Xoai Lon.

Cat Co 3 is the closest, with a blink-and-you-miss-it sliver of sand. From there a walking trail, cut into the cliff, offering gorgeous sea views, winds its way to **Cat Co 1** dominated by a rather ugly resort, then onwards to the pretty white-sand swath of **Cat Co 2**.

Lan Ha Bay

Lying south and east of Cat Ba Town, the 300 or so karst islands and limestone outcrops of Lan Ha are just as beautiful as those of Halong Bay and have the additional attraction of numerous white-sand beaches.

Due to being a fair way from Halong City, not so many tourist boats venture here, meaning Lan Ha Bay has a more isolated appeal. Sailing and kayak trips here are best organised in Cat Ba Town.

Geologically, Lan Ha is an extension of Halong Bay but sits in a different province of Vietnam. Around 200 species of fish, 500 species of mollusc, 400 species of arthropod, and numerous hard and soft coral live in the waters here, while larger marine animals in the area include seals and dolphins.

Cannon Fort

For one of the best views in Vietnam – no, we're not kidding – head to **Cannon Fort** (40,000d; ☉sunrise-sunset) where there are astounding panoramas of Cat Ba Island's jungle-clad hills rolling down to colourful tangles of fishing boats in the harbour and out to the karst-punctuated sea beyond.

The entrance gate is a steep 10-minute walk from Cat Ba Town and from the gate it's another stiff 20-minute walk to the fort, or take a *xe om* from Cat Ba Town (15,000d).

Well-labelled paths guide visitors past underground tunnels, and two well-preserved gun emplacements, out to two viewpoints overlooking the island. There's even a cafe (with more great views from its terrace) and a tiny museum.

The tunnels and gun emplacements here were first installed by the Japanese in WWII, but were also utilised by the French and Vietnamese during subsequent conflicts.

SIGHTS

There are no real sights in Cat Ba Town, but several beaches and attractions are close by.

Cat Ba National Park National Park

(☏0225-216 350; 40,000d; ☺sunrise-sunset) Cat Ba's beautiful national park is home to 32 types of mammal, including most of the world's 65 remaining golden-headed langur, the world's most endangered primate. There are some good hiking trails here, including a hard-core 18km route up to a mountain summit.

To reach the **park headquarters** at Trung Trang, hop on the green QH public bus from the docks at Cat Ba Town (25,000d, 7am, 11am and 3pm), hire a *xe om* (around 80,000d one way) or rent a motorbike for the day.

Cat Ba Island Market Market

(☺6am-7pm) The market at the northern end of Cat Ba Town's harbour is a scruffy local affair with twitching crabs, jumbo shrimp and pyramids of fresh fruit.

🏂 ACTIVITIES

Cat Ba is a superb base for adventure sports – on the island, and in, on and over the water.

Boat trips around Lan Ha Bay are offered by nearly every hotel on Cat Ba Island. Typical prices start at around US$80 for overnight tours, but it is usually worth spending a bit more as we receive unfavourable feedback – cramped conditions and dodgy food – about some of these very low budget trips.

Asia Outdoors Climbing

(☏0225-368 8450; www.asiaoutdoors.com. vn; 229, Đ 1/4 Street, Cat Ba Town; half-/full-day climbing US$44/59; ☺8am-9pm) Climbing is Asia Outdoors' real expertise, with fully licensed and certified instructors leading trips; advanced climbers can hire gear here and talk shop. Also on offer are climbing and kayaking packages with an overnight on its boat (from US$90). It has also launched stand-up paddle-boarding (SUP) trips (US$36) and trekking excursions in the national park.

From left: Hiking in Cat Ba National Park; Lan Ha Bay (p79); *pho*

DALIUSPOSUS/SHUTTERSTOCK ©

JIMMI NGUYEN/SHUTTERSTOCK ©

Blue Swimmer
Adventure

(☑0915 063 737, 0225-368 8237; www.blue swimmersailing.com; Ben Beo Harbour; overnight sailing trip per person from US$190; ⏱8am-8pm) This environmentally conscious outfit was established by Vinh, one of the founders of respected tour operator Handspan Adventure Travel. Superb sailing and kayaking trips, trekking and mountain-biking excursions (some with overnight homestay accommodation) are offered. Enquire at the office at Ben Beo Harbour.

Cat Ba Ventures
Boating

(☑0225-388 8755, 0912 467 016; www.catba ventures.com; 223 Đ 1-4, Cat Ba Town; overnight boat tour per person from US$128; ⏱7.30am-8pm) Locally owned and operated company offering boat trips around Lan Ha and Halong Bays, one-day kayaking trips (US$29) and guided hikes in Cat Ba National Park. Excellent service from Mr Tung is reinforced by multiple reader recommendations. These guys are a font of knowledge on everything Cat Ba and a great source of information on onward transport options.

🍴 EATING

Yummy
International $

(7 Đ Nui Ngoc; meals from 40,000d; ⏱8am-10pm; 🍴) Tourist-oriented restaurant serving a vast menu of pan-Asian dishes – think Indian curries, *phat thai* and Vietnamese dishes – and backpacker staples, including some meat-free options. Capable rather than exceptional.

Phuong Nhung
Vietnamese $

(184 Đ 1-4; meals from 45,000d; ⏱7-10am) Bustling breakfast spot that's a popular place for a hearty bowl of *pho bo* (beef noodle soup) – just the thing you need before a day of climbing or kayaking.

Vien Duong
Vietnamese $$

(12 Đ Nui Ngoc; meals from 120,000d; ⏱11am-11pm) Justifiably one of the most popular of the seafood spots lining Đ Nui Ngoc, and often heaving with Vietnamese tourists diving into local crab, squid and steaming seafood hotpots. Definitely not the place to come if you're looking for a quiet night.

Cat Ba Town

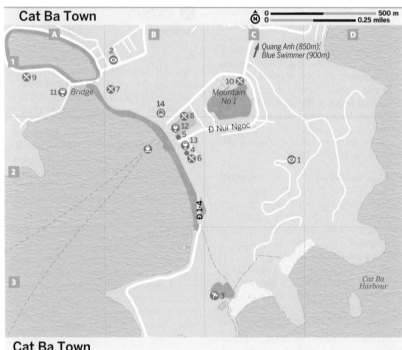

N
0 ———————— 500 m
0 ———————— 0.25 miles

Quang Anh (850m);
Blue Swimmer (900m)

Mountain
No 1

Đ Nui Ngoc

Đ 1-4

Bridge

Cat Ba
Harbour

Cat Ba Town

Quang Anh   Seafood $$

(☎0255-388 8485; Ben Beo Pier; meals from
200,000d) At this 'floating' fish-farm-meets-
restaurant at Ben Beo Pier, select your seafood from the pen and it will be grilled, fried
or steamed in no time. Prices go by weight
and type of seafood; you can eat your fill of
a selection of fish for around 200,000d per
person.

Green Mango   International $$

(☎0225-388 7151; Đ 1-4; meals 110,000-
220,000d; ☺8am-10pm; 🛜) With a menu
traipsing from steaks to seafood, and over
to Italy for pasta and pizza (with a small
selection of Asian dishes as well), Green
Mango is a decent dinner choice, with
friendly staff. It's also a chilled-out spot for
a glass of wine or cocktail.

Vietnam's Soul Food
Vietnamese $$

(📞0912 966 925; P Tung Dinh; meals from 120,000d; ⏰8am-10pm; 🍽) This TripAdvisor darling pulls the foreign crowd despite its overbearing service and overpriced and gentrified Vietnamese food. But it's a sensible choice for those spooked by eating at venues more authentic. Located 850m west of Cat Ba Town's pier.

🍷 DRINKING & NIGHTLIFE

Bia Hoi Stalls
Bar

(Đ 1-4; ⏰4-10pm) For a cheap and cheerful night out, not to mention pretty great views of Cat Ba Town's harbour, head to this strip of open-air *bia hoi* (draught beer) stalls.

Good Bar
Bar

(Noble House, Đ 1-4; ⏰noon-late) This upper-floor bar has a real vibe and goes on until late most nights. It comes fully equipped with pool tables and harbour views.

Oasis Bar
Bar

(Đ 1-4; ⏰noon-11pm; 📶) A free-use pool table, occasional karaoke, smiley staff and a location slap in the centre of the seafront strip make Oasis a popular spot to plonk yourself down for a beer or two.

ℹ️ GETTING THERE & AROUND

Departing from Hanoi's Luong Yen bus station, **Hoang Long** (📞0225-387 7224; http://hoanglongasia.com; Đ 1-4, Cat Ba Town; ⏰7.30am-6pm) operates an efficient bus-boat-bus combo to Cat Ba Town.

Bicycle and motorbike rentals are available from most Cat Ba hotels (both around US$5 per day). If you're heading out to the beaches or national park, pay the parking fee for security.

🧗 Climbing the Karsts

If you've ever been tempted to climb, Cat Ba Island is a superb place to go for it – the karst cliffs here offer exceptional climbing amid stunning scenery. Most climbers in Cat Ba are complete novices, but as the instruction is excellent, many leave completely bitten by the bug.

You don't need great upper-body strength to climb, as you actually use your legs far more. The karst limestone here is not too sharp and quite friendly on the hands, and as many of the routes are sheltered by natural overhangs that prevent the climbable portion of the rock from getting wet, climbing is almost always possible, rain or shine.

A few inexperienced locals may offer excursions to new arrivals on Cat Ba, but beginners should sign up with the experienced crew at Asia Outdoors (p80), who pioneered climbing here.

Climbing opportunities are located on walls inland on Cat Ba Island or out on beautiful Lan Ha Bay. You'll be kitted up with a harness and climbing shoes, given instruction and taught the fundamentals of the climbing and belaying techniques, then given a demonstration. Then it's over to you (with your climbing instructor talking you through each move and anchoring you, of course!). Most people are able to complete a couple of climbs at Hai Pai and Moody's Beach, which are both ideal for beginners.

Rock pillar and karst isles, Halong Bay
EFIRED/SHUTTERSTOCK ©

Hoang Lien Mountains (p91)

SAPA

Sapa at a Glance...

Established as a hill station by the French in 1922, Sapa today is the prime tourism centre in the northwest. Sapa is orientated to make the most of the spectacular views overlooking a plunging valley, with mountains towering above on all sides. Views of this epic scenery are often subdued by thick mist rolling across the peaks, but even when it's cloudy, local hill-tribe people fill the town with colour.

This is northern Vietnam's premier trekking base. The town of Sapa is undergoing a construction boom, but once you've stepped out into the lush fields you'll understand the region's real charm.

A Day in Sapa

Do some research first and choose an agency to sign up for a day hike. Enjoy a full day exploring minority villages and revelling in the views before returning to Sapa to a local-style meal at one of the **hotpot & roast piglet restaurants** (p92) and, for those with the stamina, drinks at **Cafe in the Clouds** (p94).

Two Days in Sapa

Check out the excellent **Sapa Museum** (p92) and **market** (p92) then consider an afternoon weaving workshop with textile specialists **Indigo Cat** (p92). Dine at the superb **Hill Station Signature Restaurant** (p94).

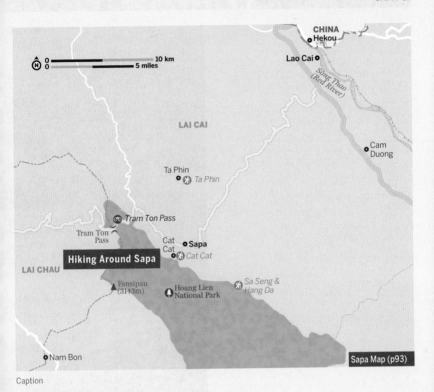

Caption

Arriving in Sapa

The gateway to Sapa is Lao Cai, 38km away via a well-maintained highway. Very regular minibuses connect the two towns.

There's a good train service between Hanoi and Lao Cai too.

Where to Stay

Construction, touts and tourists mean that staying in Sapa itself can be a hectic experience, and we advise visitors to stay outside the centre.

A few kilometres out of town the landscape is mountainous, beautiful and rural.

Rice terraces near Sapa

Hiking Around Sapa

The verdant, dramatic countryside around Sapa features cascading rice terraces, muddy trails and tiny hill-tribe villages.

Great For...

ⓘ Need to Know

Most hill-tribe villages have admission fees from 20,000d to 40,000d.

★ **Top Tip**

Note many hotels raise rates on Fridays and Saturdays with the weekend influx of domestic tourists.

You won't step too far out of your hotel in Sapa before being accosted with offers to guide you on hikes.

For longer treks with overnight stays in villages, it's important to hire someone who knows the terrain and culture. We recommend using minority guides, as this offers them a means of making a living. Note it's illegal to stay overnight in villages that are not officially recognised as homestays. Ignoring this could cause significant problems for your hosts and yourself.

Guided Tours

Many visitors arrive on tour packages prearranged in Hanoi but there's a couple of standout local operators in town that are well worth looking into.

As well as hiking tours, many companies offer more culturally focused trips such as community-based tours to the nearby Hmong village of **Sin Chai**, with an overnight in the village to learn about textiles or music. Other popular communities to visit include the Giay village of **Ta Van** and the Hmong village of **Matra**.

Excellent local company **Sapa O'Chau** (☎0214-377 1166; www.sapaochau.org; 8 Đ Thac Bac; ⊙6.30am-6.30pm) ✔ offers day walks (from US$30), longer homestay treks (from US$60), Bac Ha market trips and Fanispan hikes. It also runs culturally immersive tours that focus on handicrafts and farmstays. Profits provide training to Hmong children in a learning centre.

Run by a group of savvy and knowledgable Hmong women, **Sapa Sisters** (☎0214-773 388; www.sapasisters.com; Sapa Graceful Hotel, 9 Đ Phan Si; ⊙7am-5pm) offers fully customised private day hikes (from

Hmong market vendors, Sapa

US$37) and longer village homestay treks (from US$86). Excellent English is spoken, and some French.

Hikes

Sa Seng & Hang Da

For spectacular valley views (if the mist and cloud gods relent), try this beautiful **hike** along a high ridge east of Sapa through the Black Hmong settlements of Sa Seng and Hang Da down to the Ta Van River, where you can get transport back to Sapa.

Ta Phin

A very popular **hike** (admission 20,000d) from Sapa is to Ta Phin village (about

> ✕ **Take a Break**
> Check out Cong Ca Phe (p94) for a beer or a coffee.

MARTINHO SMART/SHUTTERSTOCK ©

10km from Sapa), home to Red Dzao. Most people take a taxi (around 200,000d) to a starting point about 8km from Sapa, and then make a 14km loop through the area, passing through Black Hmong and Red Dzao villages.

Cat Cat

The nearest village within walking distance is **Cat Cat** (70,000d), 3km south of Sapa. It's beautiful and the consistent souvenir soft sell doesn't spoil it for most visitors. It's a steep and beautiful hike down, and there are plenty of *xe om* for the return uphill journey.

Fansipan

Surrounding Sapa are the Hoang Lien Mountains, dubbed the Tonkinese Alps by the French. These mountains include the often-cloud-obscured Fansipan (3143m), Vietnam's highest peak. Fansipan is accessible year-round to sensibly equipped trekkers in good shape with a guide, but don't underestimate the challenge. It is very wet, and can be perilously slippery and generally cold.

Fansipan's wild, lonesome beauty has been somewhat shattered with the opening of a 6282m-long cable car (return adult/child 600,000/400,000d, from 6.30am to 4.30pm), taking people across the Muong Hoa Valley and up to the summit in 15 minutes where a new complex of shops awaits. A taxi here is a little over 100,000d.

For the full satisfaction of earning that view, the summit of Fansipan is 19km by foot from Sapa. The terrain is rough and adverse weather is frequent. Through local operators, count on an all-inclusive rate of around US$150 per person for a couple, US$125 per person for a group of four, and US$100 per person for the sensible maximum group size of six.

> ☑ **Don't Miss**
> Sapa Market (p92) is a full-on assault on the senses and also has good food stalls.

◉ SIGHTS

Sapa Museum — Museum
(103 P Cau May; ⊘7.30-11.30am & 1.30-5pm)
FREE Excellent showcase of the history
and ethnology of the Sapa area, including
the colonial times of the French. Dusty
exhibitions demonstrate the differences
between the various ethnic minority people
of the area, so it's definitely worth a quick
visit when you first arrive in town, even if
some descriptions are too faded to read.
Located above a handicrafts shop behind
the **Tourist Information Center** (☑0214-
387 3239; www.sapa-tourism.com; 103 Đ Xuan
Vien; ⊘7.30-11.30am & 1.30-5.30pm).

Sapa Market — Market
(Đ Ngu Chi Son; ⊘6am-2pm) Unfortunately
turfed out of central Sapa, and now in a
purpose-built modern building near the bus
station, Sapa Market is still a hive of colourful activity outside with fresh produce,
a butcher's section not for the squeamish
and hill-tribe people from surrounding
villages heading here most days to sell
handicrafts. Saturday is the busiest day.

Sapa Church — Church
(Đ Ham Rong; ⊘Mass from 6am Sun) Sapa's
small stone church was built by the French.
It's only open for Mass on Sunday and on
certain evenings for prayers. It also func-
tions as a landmark in the centre of town.

Tram Ton Pass — Viewpoint
The road between Sapa and Lai Chau
crosses the Tram Ton Pass on the northern
side of Fansipan, 15km from Sapa. At
1900m this is Vietnam's highest mountain
pass, and acts as a dividing line between
two weather fronts. The lookout points here
have fantastic views – and lots of stalls
selling souvenirs. Most people also stop
at 100m-high **Thac Bac** (Silver Waterfall),
12km from Sapa.

On the Sapa side it's often cold and
foggy, but drop a few hundred metres onto
the Lai Chau side and it can be sunny and
warm. Surprisingly, Sapa is the coldest
place in Vietnam, but Lai Chau can be one
of the warmest.

☺ ACTIVITIES

Hill Station
Signature Restaurant — Cooking
(☑0214-887 112; 37 Đ Phan Si; per person US$29;
⊘9am-noon) Excellent three-hour cooking
classes with an English-speaking Hmong
chef starting with a 30-minute market tour
and featuring five local dishes, including
homemade tofu, smoked buffalo and
Hmong-style black pudding, as well as tasting local rice wine. Book the evening before.

Indigo Cat — Art
(☑0982 403 647; www.facebook.com/indigo
catsapa; 46 Đ Phan Si; class 350,000d; ⊘9am-
7pm) Craft shop Indigo Cat runs afternoon
workshops where you can learn traditional
Hmong weaving and embroidery skills.
Workshops take place in the village of
Ta Ven. Call into the lovely Sapa shop for
details.

🔒 SHOPPING

Indigo Cat — Arts & Crafts
(www.facebook.com/indigocatsapa; 46 Đ Phan Si;
⊘9am-7pm) This Hmong-owned handicrafts
shop offers a wonderful selection of interesting local crafts, including bags, clothing,
pillows and belts. Many items have hip
design touches unique to the store and the
set-price labels are a relief if you have hag-
gling fatigue. Co-owner Pang speaks good
English and her kids are real charmers.

✖ EATING

Hotpot & Roast
Piglet Restaurants — Vietnamese $
(Đ Xuan Vien; meals from 50,000d; ⊘11am-11pm)
This strip is home to several similar places
serving Vietnamese-style *lau* (hotpot; meat
stew cooked with local vegetables, cabbage
and mushroom) and roast piglet (a speciality of Sapa; look for the rotisserie grills).

Sapa O'Chau — Cafe $
(www.sapaochau.org; 8 Đ Thac Bac; snacks from
40,000d; ⊘6.30am-6.30pm; 🛜) Don't miss

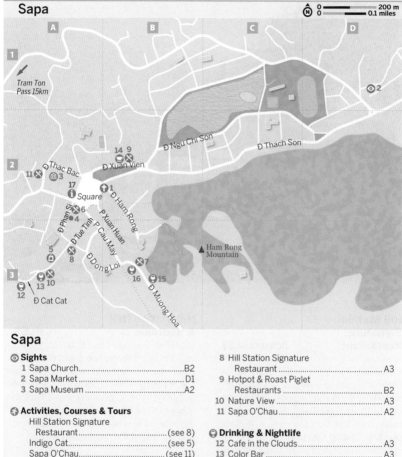

Sapa

⊚ Sights

✛ Activities, Courses & Tours

🔒 Shopping

✕ Eating

🍸 Drinking & Nightlife

ℹ Information

warming up with a cup of ginger tea sweetened with Sapa mountain honey at this simple cafe attached to the Sapa O'Chau tour company. Also does good breakfasts and a few simple snacks and light meals.

Co Lich   Vietnamese $

(Đ Phan Si; meals from 70,000đ; ☺noon-11pm)
This rowdy place brings all the local faves – grilled skewers, roast piglet, dried beef, hotpot – together in one venue. Pull up a pew at one of the simple tables and tuck in.

Cafe near Sapa

Hill Station Signature Restaurant
Vietnamese $$

(www.thehillstation.com; 37 Đ Phan Si; meals from 150,000d; ⊙7am-11pm; ❄🛜🖊) A showcase of Hmong cuisine with cool Zen decor and superb views. Dishes include flash-cooked pork with lime, ash-baked trout in banana leaves, and traditional Hmong-style black pudding. Tasting sets of local rice and corn wine are also of interest to curious travelling foodies. Don't miss trying the delicate rainbow-trout rice-paper rolls; think of them as 'Sapa sushi'.

Nature View
Vietnamese $$

(51 Đ Phan Si; meals from 90,000d; ⊙8am-10pm; 🛜🖊) You've got to love the photos of the owner's kids on the walls at this friendly spot with great valley views. Look forward to decent Vietnamese and European food and just maybe Sapa's best fruit smoothies. Those who aren't fans of tofu should try the sizzling tofu with lemongrass and be converted. Don't worry – it's not all vegetarian food.

Hill Station Deli & Boutique
Cafe $$

(7 Đ Muong Hoa; meals from 125,000d; ⊙7am-10.30pm; ❄🛜) With cheese and charcuterie plates, pork terrine and local smoked trout, the Hill Station Deli & Boutique is a stylish addition to the Sapa dining scene. Factor in some of Sapa's best coffee and an interesting array of international beers and wines, and you've got the most cosmopolitan option in town.

🍷 DRINKING & NIGHTLIFE

Cong Ca Phe
Cafe

(Đ Xuan Vien; ⊙7am-11pm; 🛜) Sapa is home to a branch of everybody's favourite communist/retro-themed coffee shop. A selection of beers and occasional live performances mean that it also doubles neatly as a bar.

Cafe in the Clouds
Beer Garden

(☎0214-377 1011; 60 Đ Phan Si; ⊙6am-11pm; 🛜) The large terrace of this bar is a great corner of Sapa (and the planet) to pause and ponder the valley or, often, the wan-

> *...a great corner of Sapa (and the planet) to pause and ponder the valley...*

dering mist at eye level. The crisp air must come with lofty prices? Actually drinks are priced very reasonably, plus wi-fi is zippy for logging in to electronic clouds. The food isn't bad either.

Color Bar   Bar

(56 Đ Phan Si; ☺noon-11pm; 🛜) Owned by a Hanoi artist, this atmospheric spot ticks all the boxes with reggae, table football, *shisha* and ice-cold Bia Lao Cai. A great refuelling option on the steep walk up from Cat Cat village.

Mountain Bar & Pub   Bar

(2 Đ Muong Hoa; ☺noon-11pm; 🛜) Dangerously strong cocktails, cold beer and ultra-competitive games of table-football conspire to make this Sapa's go-to place for a great night out. Even if it's freezing outside, a *shisha* beside the open fire will soon perk up the chilliest of travellers. Try the warm apple wine for some highland bliss.

Hmong Sisters   Bar

(📱0915 042 366; 31 Đ Muong Hoa; ☺4pm-late; 🛜) This spacious bar with pool tables and an open fire has pretty decent music, but can feel a bit sparse if it's a quiet night. Bar prices are reasonable, though, so it's always worth checking out.

ⓘ GETTING THERE & AWAY

The gateway to Sapa is Lao Cai, 38km away. Minibuses (30,000d, 30 minutes) leave every half-hour between 6am and 6pm, from a bus stop near Sapa Church.

👪 A Hmong Future

Inherent in Sapa's burgeoning prosperity is cultural change for the hill-tribe people.

Traditionally, the Hmong have been employees of Vietnamese-owned trekking companies, restaurants and accommodation, with many Hmong children kept out of school to sell handicrafts or act as trekking guides, often walking up to 10km daily from their villages to Sapa to earn money. A new generation, though, is now focused on securing a more independent and positive future for their people.

Sapa O'Chau (p90), meaning 'thank you Sapa' in the Hmong language, is focused on providing training and opportunities to Hmong children. The organisation is run by former handicraft peddler Shu Tan, who created the Sapa O'Chau Learning Centre, a live-in school where up to 20 Hmong children can learn English and Vietnamese. The organisation also runs excellent walks and treks.

Traditional Hmong dwelling, Sapa
PRADEEP_KMPK14/SHUTTERSTOCK ©

PHONG NHA-KE BANG NATIONAL PARK

Phong Nha-Ke Bang National Park at a Glance...

A Unesco World Heritage Site, remarkable Phong Nha-Ke Bang National Park contains the oldest karst mountains in Asia. Riddled with hundreds of cave systems, many of extraordinary scale and length, and spectacular underground rivers, it's a speleologist's heaven on earth.

Above ground, most of the mountainous national park is near-pristine tropical evergreen jungle, with more than 90% being primary forest. A few years ago Phong Nha was seldom visited but the region is changing fast. Son Trach is the nearest village, with a growing range of accommodation and eating options, and excellent tour operators.

One Day in Phong Nha-Ke Bang National Park

Book ahead for an early morning tour of stunning **Paradise Cave** (p103), part of a simply colossal cave system. In the afternoon head over to **Hang Toi** (p102) for more caving shenanigans, this time with the added bonus of ziplining, kayaking, swimming and a mud bath. In the evening, chill at **D-Arts Zone** (p104) in Son Trach.

Two Days in Phong Nha-Ke Bang National Park

Book ahead for a terrific one-day tour of **Tu Lan Cave**, run exclusively by **Oxalis** (p104). The trip includes jungle trekking past karst mountains, spectacular swimming through a wonderful river cave and a barbecue lunch beside a waterfall. In the evening enjoy a meal at the **Bamboo Cafe** (p105) then drinks at **Jungle Bar** (p105).

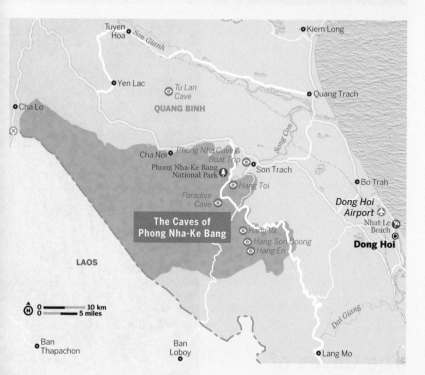

Arriving in Phong Nha-Ke Bang National Park

The coastal town of Dong Hoi is the main gateway to both Phong Nha and Son Trach town, and has the nearest airport and train station. Hotels organise lifts in private cars to/from Dong Hoi (500,000d).

Where to Stay

Son Trach town has simple local hotels (all charging around 350,000d), a hostel and a few midrange options. Other hotels and rural lodges are scattered in the countryside around Son Trach. Some travellers base themselves in Dong Hoi and travel to Phong Nha on day trips.

Paradise Cave (p103)

The Caves of Phong Nha-Ke Bang

Serious exploration of this extraordinary national park only began in the 1990s. Since then some astonishing cave systems have been discovered, including the world's largest cave, Hang Son Doong.

Great For...

ⓘ Need to Know

Officially you are not allowed to hike inside the **national park** (☎052-367 7021; http://phongnhakebang.vn/en) ✎ without a licensed tour operator.

★ **Top Tip**

Overnight caving tours for Tu Lan, Hang Va and Hang En should be booked in advance.

Tu Lan Cave

The **Tu Lan cave** (www.oxalis.com.vn; 2-day tours per person 5,500,000d; ⊘Nov–mid-Sep) trip begins with a countryside hike then a swim (with headlamps and life jackets) through two spectacular river caves before emerging in an idyllic valley. Then there's more hiking through dense forest to a 'beach' where rivers merge that's an ideal campsite. There's more wonderful swimming here in vast caverns. Moderate fitness levels are necessary. Tu Lan is 65km north of Son Trach and can only be visited on a guided tour.

Hang En

This gigantic **cave** (per person 1,100,000d; ⊘late Dec-Aug) is very close to Hang Son Doong, and featured in the same National Geographic photographic spread in 2011. Getting here involves a trek through dense jungle, valleys and the Ban Doong minority village, a very remote tribal settlement (with no electricity or roads). You stay overnight in the cave or a minority village. Tours can be booked via Oxalis and local accommodation.

Hang Toi

Incorporating an above-water zipline, followed by a swim into the cave and then exploration of a pitch-black passageway of oozing mud, it's little wonder **Hang Toi** (Dark Cave; per person 350,000d) is the cave experience you've probably already heard about from other travellers. On exiting the cave, a leisurely kayak paddle heads to a jetty where there are more into-the-water zipline thrills to be had. The Dark Cave

Phong Nha Cave

can be visited independently or on tours booked with local accommodation.

Paradise Cave

Surrounded by forested karst peaks, this **remarkable cave system** (Thien Dong; adult/child under 1.3m 250,000/125,000d; ☺7.30am-4.30pm) extends for 31km, though most people only visit the first kilometre. The scale is breathtaking, as wooden staircases descend into a cathedral-like space with colossal stalagmites and glimmering stalactites. Get here early to beat the crowds, as during peak times (early afternoon), tour guides shepherd groups using megaphones. Paradise Cave is about 14km southwest of Son Trach. Electric buggies (per person one way/return 15,000/25,000d) ferry visitors from the car park to the entrance.

XUAN HUONG HO/SHUTTERSTOCK ©

Phong Nha Cave & Boat Trip

The spectacular boat trip through **Phong Nha Cave** (adult/child under 1.3m 150,000/25,000d, boat up to 14 people 320,000d; ☺7am-4pm) is an enjoyable, though touristy, experience beginning in Son Trach village. Boats cruise along past buffalo, limestone peaks and church steeples to the cave's gaping mouth. The engine is then cut and the boats are negotiated silently through cavern after garishly illuminated cavern. On the return leg there's the option to climb (via 330 steps) up to the mountainside **Tien Son Cave** (80,000d) with the remains of 9th-century Cham altars.

Hang Va

Discovered in 2012, and opened to visitors in 2015, **Hang Va** (www.oxalis.com.vn; per person 1,200,000d; ☺Feb-Aug) is explored on a two-day/one-night excursion that travels firstly along an underground river in Hang Nuoc Nut. Tours overnight in a jungle camp at the entrance to Hang Va, where the cave's highlight is a spectacular stalagmite field partly submerged in crystalline waters. Ropes and harnesses are used extensively.

Hang Son Doong

Ho Khanh, a hunter, stumbled across gargantuan Hang Son Doong (Mountain River Cave) in the early 1990s, but the sheer scale and majesty of the principal cavern (more than 5km long, 200m high and, in some places, 150m wide) was only confirmed as the world's biggest cave when British explorers returned with him in 2009.

Hang Son Doong is one of the most spectacular sights in Southeast Asia (some stalagmites are up to 80m high). The only specialist operator permitted to lead tours here is Son Trach–based Oxalis (p104).

Son Doong is no day-trip destination: it's in an extremely remote area and the only way to visit is by booking a four-day expedition, costing US$3000 per person.

JEJIM/GETTY IMAGES ©

Phong Nha-Ke Bang National Park

> *...unquestionably the expert
> in caving and trekking...*

🎯 TOURS

Oxalis Adventure Tours   Adventure
(☎0232-367 7678; www.oxalis.com.vn; Son
Trach; ⊙7.30am-noon & 1.30-5.30pm Mon-Sat)
Oxalis is unquestionably *the* expert in
caving and trekking expeditions, and is
the only outfit licensed to conduct tours
to Hang Son Doong. Staff are all fluent
English speakers, and trained by world-
renowned British cavers Howard and Deb
Limbert.

Phong Nha
Farmstay Tours   Adventure
(☎0232-367 5135; www.phong-nha-cave.com;
Cu Nam) Phong Nha Farmstay's popular National Park Tour (per person 1,350,000d)
incorporates the Ho Chi Minh Trail with Paradise Cave and Hang Toi; there's also the
option of negotiating the recently opened
Tra Ang Cave. Ask about exciting cus-

tomised tours (per person 2,500,000d),
bouncing around in the farmstay's vintage
Ural motorbike and sidecar.

Jungle Boss Trekking   Hiking
(☎0917 800 805; www.jungle-boss.com;
Phong Nha village, Son Trach; per person from
1,350,000d) Dzung ('Jungle Boss') is an
experienced guide to the area. He speaks
excellent English and runs one- and two-
day tours around the Ho Chi Minh Trail and
the Abandoned Valley area of the national
park.

Hai's Eco Tours   Hiking
(☎0962 606 844; www.ecophongnha.com;
Bamboo Cafe, Son Trach; per person 1,450,000d)
Interesting day tours combining hiking in
the jungle – you'll need to be relatively fit –
with a visit to Phong Nha's Wildlife Rescue
and Rehabilitation Centre.

❌ EATING

D-Arts Zone   Vietnamese, Barbecue $
(www.facebook.com/dartphongnha; Son
Trach; meals 50,000-90,000d; ⊙7am-10pm)

Vintage jazz and blues often feature at this interesting spot co-owned by an artist and an architect. Menu highlights include good salads and spicy northern Vietnamese sausage infused with smoke from the restaurant's barbecue grill. The barbecue duck is also good. Sit out front at the rustic wooden tables and watch what's happening along Son Trach's main street.

Bamboo Cafe
Cafe $

(www.phong-nha-bamboo-cafe.com; Son Trach; meals 40,000-80,000d; ☺7am-10.30pm; 🐾🚲) This laid-back haven on Son Trach's main drag has colourful decor, and well-priced food and drink, including excellent fresh fruit smoothies and varied vegetarian options.

Pub with Cold Beer
Barbecue $

(Bong Lai valley; meals from 50,000d; ☺10am-sunset) Up a dirt track in the middle of nowhere (but well signposted), this spot owned by a farming family does what it says on the tin – the beer is ice cold. Hungry? Order roast chicken with peanut sauce (all ingredients are farm-fresh). A kilo of perfectly grilled chicken is around 300,000d. Volleyball and river tubing are other lazy days distractions.

Capture Vietnam
Cafe $

(📞0164 515 3869; www.facebook.com/capturevietnam; Son Trach; snacks & meals 60,000-200,000d; ☺8am-10pm) This cafe has espresso coffee, homestyle baking, and interesting Western and Vietnamese meals. Bagels with smoked salmon, good pizza and Mediterranean-style antipasto all add up to the area's most cosmopolitan spot. There's also an attached deli section selling local souvenirs – try the Phong Nha beef jerky – and takeaway beer, wine and cider.

The Best Spit Roast Pork & Noodle Shop in the World (probably...)
Vietnamese $

(Son Trach; meals 40,000-50,000d; ☺7am-4pm) Also probably the longest name of any

restaurant in Vietnam, and excellent grilled pork paired with noodles, baguettes or rice. Get ready to smell this place well before you see it as you're wandering Son Trach's sleepy main street.

🍸 DRINKING & NIGHTLIFE

Bomb Crater Bar
Bar

(📞0163 943 1690; www.bombcraterbar.com; Cu Lac village) Ride a bike 3km from Son Trach to this riverside spot for cold beers, robust gin and tonics, and tasty Vietnamese snacks. Lying in a hammock, kayaking on the river, or chilling with the bar's resident water buffalo are all added attractions at this great place for a sundowner drink. And yes, there is a 1970s bomb crater just nearby.

Jungle Bar
Bar

(Son Trach; ☺7am-midnight; 📞) The in-house bar/cafe at **Easy Tiger** (📞0232-367 7844; www.easytigerphongnha.com; dm 160,000d; ❄@🐾🏊) is the most happening place in Son Trach, with cheap beer, pool tables, and live music a few nights a week. Add to the growing display of national flags if you're feeling patriotic. There's loads of local information on hand, even if you're not staying at Easy Tiger.

ℹ️ GETTING THERE & AWAY

Son Trach town is 50km northwest of Dong Hoi. Phong Nha-Ke Bang National Park abuts Son Trach. Hotels can organise cars from Dong Hoi (500,000d).

ℹ️ GETTING AROUND

Bicycling is recommended to explore Phong Nha's rural back roads; Easy Tiger rents bikes and can supply a handy map.

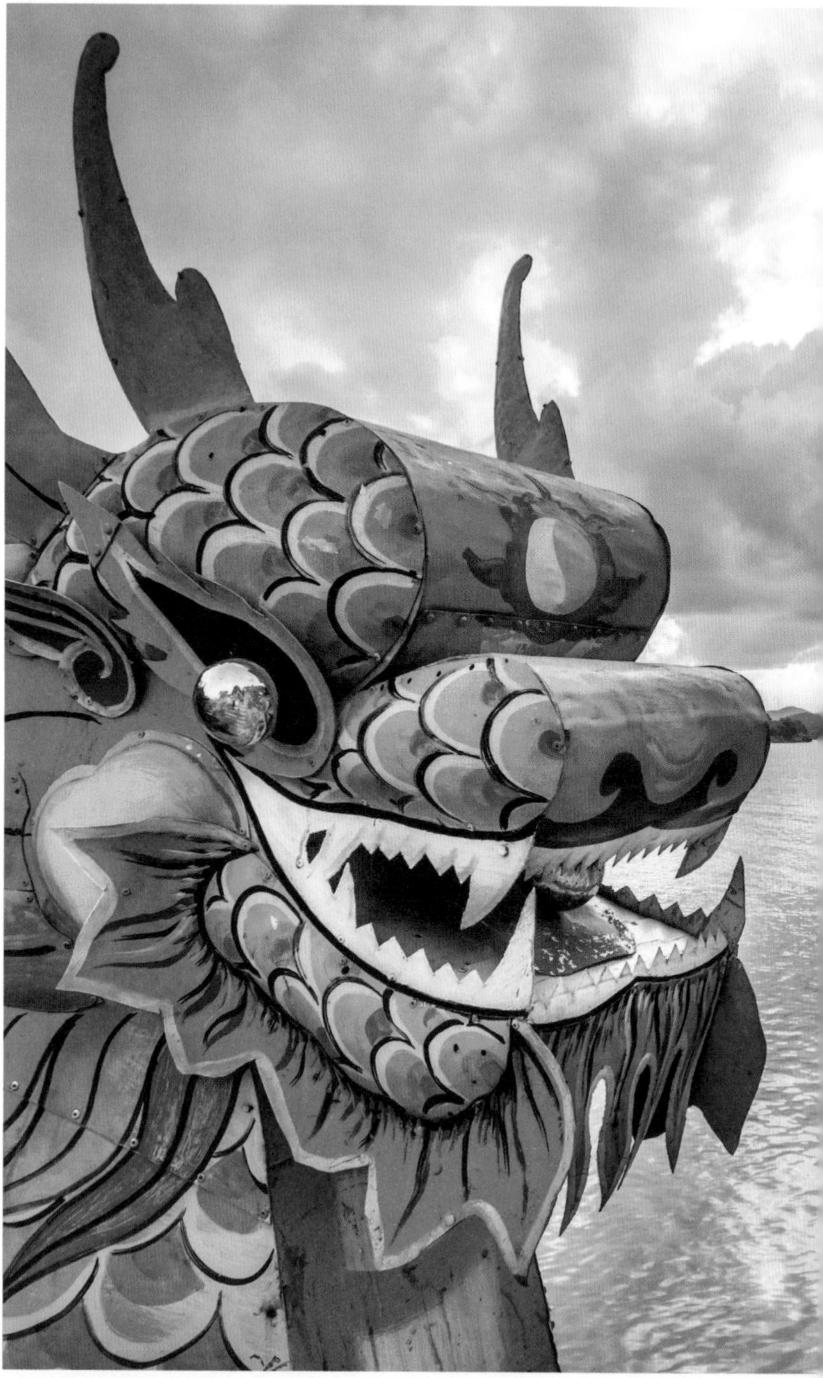

CHRISTIAN WITTMANN/SHUTTERSTOCK ©

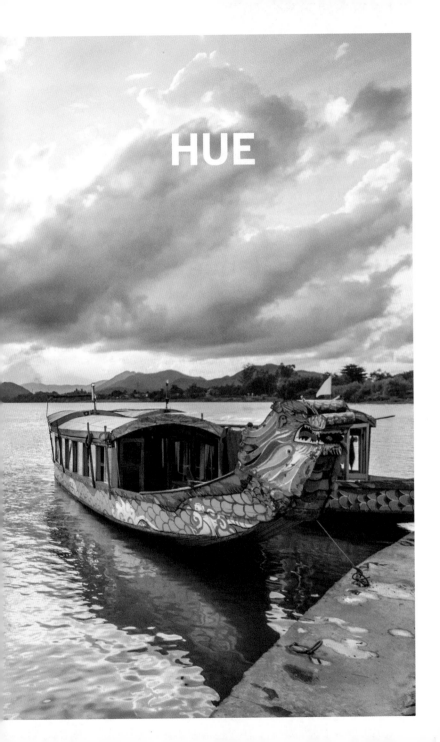

HUE

In This Chapter

Hue at a Glance...

Hue (pronounced 'hway'), the deeply evocative capital of the Nguyen emperors, still resonates with the glories of imperial Vietnam, even though many of its finest buildings were destroyed during the American War. Hue owes its charm partly to its location on the Perfume River – picturesque on a clear day, atmospheric even in less flattering weather. Today the city blends new and old as sleek modern hotels tower over crumbling century-old Citadel walls.

A few touts are a minor hassle, and Hue remains a tranquil, conservative city with just the right concentration of nightlife.

A Day in Hue

Head straight for the **Imperial Enclosure** (p110) taking in key temples such as Thai **To Mieu Temple Complex** (p114) and important sights like the **Halls of the Mandarins** (p113). In the late afternoon, wander the lanes off Hung Vuong and sample outstanding local cuisine at **Hanh Restaurant** (p126).

Two Days in Hue

On day two, book a Perfume River tour to the impressive emperors' tombs and pagodas. Return to town to browse boutiques such as **Spiral Foundation Healing the Wounded Heart Center** (p125) before a memorable dinner at **Les Jardins de la Carambole** (p128).

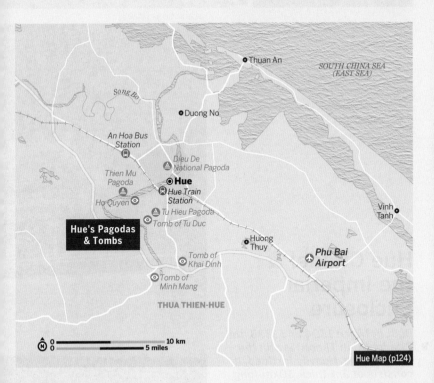

SOUTH CHINA SEA
(EAST SEA)

Thuan An

Song Bo

Duong No

An Hoa Bus
Station

Dieu De
National Pagoda

Thien Mu
Pagoda

Hue

Hue Train
Station

Ho Quyen

Tu Hieu Pagoda

Vinh
Tanh

Tomb of Tu Duc

**Hue's Pagodas
& Tombs**

Huong
Thuy

*Phu Bai
Airport*

Tomb of
Khai Dinh

Tomb of
Minh Mang

THUA THIEN-HUE

0 — 10 km
0 — 5 miles

Hue Map (p124)

Arriving in Hue

Hue's Phu Bai Airport is 14km southeast
of the city. Metered taxis cost about
240,000d to the centre.

The main bus station, 4km southeast
of the centre, has connections south to
Danang (for Hoi An). An Hoa bus station
serves northern destinations.

The Hue train station is at the south-
western end of Le Loi.

Where to Stay

The main hotel enclave is between Le
Loi and Vo Thi Sau, and other good options are along Nguyen Cong Tru. You'll
also find luxury hotels on the beach,
around 7km east of the centre, and on
the western fringes of town.

Entrance to Hue Citadel

Hue Citadel & the Imperial Enclosure

Built between 1804 and 1833, the Citadel (Kinh Thanh) is still the heart of Hue. Heavily fortified, it consists of 2m-thick, 10km-long walls, a moat and 10 gateways.

Great For...

❶ Need to Know

adult/child 150,000/30,000d; ⏲7am-5.30pm, to 10pm mid-Apr– mid-Sep

★ **Top Tip**

Note that if you're planning on also visiting the Royal Tombs, combination tickets including the Citadel and the tombs are available.

Imperial Enclosure

The Imperial Enclosure is a citadel-within-a-citadel, housing the emperor's residence, temples and palaces and the main buildings of state within 6m-high, 2.5km-long walls. What's left is only a fraction of the original – the enclosure was badly bombed during the French and American wars, and only 20 of its 148 buildings survived. This is a fascinating site easily worth half a day, but poor signage can make navigation a bit difficult. Restoration and reconstruction is ongoing.

Expect a lot of broken masonry, rubble, cracked tiling and weeds as you work your way around. Nevertheless it's enjoyable as a leisurely stroll and some of the less-visited areas are highly atmospheric. There are little cafes and souvenir stands dotted around.

It's best to approach the sights starting from Ngo Mon Gate and moving anticlockwise around the enclosure.

Ngo Mon Gate

The principal entrance to the Imperial Enclosure is Ngo Mon Gate, which faces the Flag Tower. The central passageway with its yellow doors was reserved for the use of the emperor, as was the bridge across the lotus pond. Others had to use the gates to either side and the paths around the pond. On top of the gate is Ngu Phung (Belvedere of the Five Phoenixes); on its upper level is a huge drum and bell.

The emperor appeared here on important occasions, most notably for the promulgation of the lunar calendar. On 30 August 1945, the Nguyen dynasty ended

Hue Citadel

here when Emperor Bao Dai abdicated to a delegation sent by Ho Chi Minh.

Thai Hoa Palace

This **palace** (Palace of Supreme Harmony), dating from 1803, is a spacious hall with an ornate timber roof supported by 80 carved and lacquered columns. It was used for the emperor's official receptions and important ceremonies. On state occasions the emperor sat on his elevated throne, facing visitors entering via the Ngo Mon Gate. No photos are permitted, but be sure to see the impressive audio-visual display, which gives an excellent overview of the entire

> ☑ **Don't Miss**
>
> The impressive audio-visual display in the Thai Hoa Palace, which gives excellent historical context.

LUCIANO MORTULA - LGM/SHUTTERSTOCK ©

Citadel, its architecture and the historical context.

Halls of the Mandarins

Located immediately behind Thai Hoa Palace, on either side of a courtyard, these halls were used by mandarins as offices and to prepare for court ceremonies.

The hall on the right showcases fascinating old photographs (including boy-king Vua Duya Tan's coronation), gilded Buddha statues and assorted imperial curios. Behind the courtyard are the ruins of the Can Chanh Palace, where two wonderful long galleries, painted in gleaming scarlet lacquer have been reconstructed.

Emperor's Reading Room

The exquisite (though crumbling) little two-storey **Emperor's Reading Room** (Royal Library; Thai Binh Lau) was the only part of the Forbidden Purple City to escape damage during the French reoccupation of Hue in 1947.

The Gaudi-esque, yin-yang roof mosaics outside are in stark contrast to the sombre, recently renovated interior, the circular hallway of which you can now walk around on the small ground level. The exterior features poems by Emperor Khai Dinh on either side, and three Chinese characters that translate as 'Emperor's Reading Room'.

Royal Theatre

The **Royal Theatre** (Duyen Thi Duong; ☑054-351 4989; www.nhanhac.com.vn; performances 200,000d; ☺performances 10.40am & 3.40pm), begun in 1826 and later home to the National Conservatory of Music, has been rebuilt on its former foundations. Cultural performances here last 45 minutes.

> ✕ **Take a Break**
>
> Just outside the Dien Tho Residence a pleasure pavilion above a lily pond has been transformed into a cafe.

Co Ha Gardens

Occupying the northeast corner of the Imperial Enclosure, these delightful **gardens** (Royal Gardens) were developed by the first four emperors of the Nguyen dynasty but fell into disrepair. They've been beautifully recreated in the last few years, and are dotted with little gazebo-style pavilions and ponds. This is one of the most peaceful spots in the entire Citadel. The latest section to be discovered, excavated and restored was completed in early 2017.

Forbidden Purple City

In the very centre of the Imperial Enclosure, there's almost nothing left of the once-magnificent **Forbidden Purple City** (Tu Cam Thanh). This was a citadel-within-a-citadel-within-a-citadel and was reserved solely for the personal use of the emperor – the only servants allowed into this compound were eunuchs who would pose no threat to the royal concubines. The Forbidden Purple City was almost entirely destroyed in the wars, and its crumbling remains are now overgrown with weeds.

Dien Tho Residence

The stunning, partially ruined Dien Tho Residence (1804) once comprised the apartments and audience hall of the Queen Mothers of the Nguyen dynasty. The audience hall houses an exhibition of photos illustrating its former use, and there is a display of embroidered royal garments.

To Mieu Temple Complex

Taking up the southwest corner of the Imperial Enclosure, this highly impressive walled complex has been beautifully restored. The imposing three-tiered **Hien Lam Pavilion** sits on the south side of the complex; it dates from 1824. On the other side of a courtyard is the solemn **To Mieu Temple**, housing shrines to each of the emperors, topped by their photos. Between these two temples are **Nine Dynastic Urns** (dinh), cast between 1835 and 1836, each dedicated to one Nguyen sovereign.

About 2m in height and weighing 1900kg to 2600kg each, the urns symbolise the power and stability of the Nguyen throne. The central urn, also the largest and most ornate, is dedicated to dynasty founder Gia Long. Also in the courtyard are two dragons, trapped in what look like red phone boxes.

On the north side of the complex, a gate leads into a small walled enclosure that houses the **Hung To Mieu Temple**, a reconstruction of the 1804 original, built to honour Gia Long's parents.

Forbidden Purple City

Nine Holy Cannons

Located just inside the Citadel ramparts, near the gates to either side of the Flag Tower, are the Nine Holy Cannons (1804), symbolic protectors of the palace and kingdom. Commissioned by Emperor Gia Long, they were never intended to be fired. The four cannons near **Ngan Gate** represent the four seasons, while the five cannons next to **Quang Duc Gate** represent the five elements: metal, wood, water, fire and earth.

Each brass cannon is 5m long and weighs about 10 tonnes.

Imperial Nights

Starting in 2017, from mid-April to mid-September the Citadel was open until 10pm, and visitors could enjoy a nightly program of dance and cultural performances. At the time of writing, evening openings were only being trialled however, so check with your accommodation for the latest information. Visiting at night is an excellent option as it is cooler, and the spectacular lighting showcases the best of the historic complex.

☑ **Don't Miss**

An island on Tang Tau Lake is occupied by the small Ngoc Huong Pagoda.

CHRISTIAN WITTMANN/SHUTTERSTOCK ©

Hue's Imperial Enclosure

EXPLORING THE SITE

An incongruous combination of meticulously restored palaces and pagodas, ruins and rubble, the Imperial Enclosure is approached from the south through the outer walls of the Citadel. It's best to tackle the site as a walking tour, winding your way around the structures in an anticlockwise direction.

You'll pass directly through the monumental ❶ **Ngo Mon Gateway** where the ticket office is located. This dramatic approach quickens the pulse and adds to the sense of occasion as you enter this citadel-within-a-citadel. Directly ahead is the ❷ **Thai Hoa Palace** where the emperor would greet offical visitors from his elevated throne. Continuing north you'll step across a small courtyard to the twin ❸ **Halls of the Mandarins**, where mandarins once had their offices and prepared for ceremonial occasions.

To the northeast is the Royal Theatre, where traditional dance performances are held several times daily. Next you'll be able to get a glimpse of the Emperor's Reading Room built by Thieu Tri and used as a place of retreat. Just east of here are the lovely Co Ha Gardens. Wander their pathways, dotted with hundreds of bonsai trees and potted plants, which have been recently restored.

Guarding the far north of the complex is the Tu Vo Phuong Pavilion, from where you can follow a moat to the Truong San residence and then loop back south via the ❹ **Dien Tho Residence** and finally view the beautifully restored temple compound of To Mieu, perhaps the most rewarding part of the entire enclosure to visit, including its fabulous ❺ **Nine Dynastic Urns**.

TOP TIPS

➡ Allow half a day to explore the Citadel.

➡ Drink vendors are dotted around the site, but the best places to take a break are the delightful Co Ha Gardens, the Tu Vo Phuong Pavilion and the Dien Tho Residence (the latter two also serve food).

Dien Tho Residence
This pretty corner of the complex, with its low structures and pond, was the residence of many Queen Mothers. The earliest structures here date from 1804.

Tu Vo Phuong Pavilion

Truong San Residence

④

To Mieu Temple Complex

Nine Dynastic Urns
These colossal bronze urns were commissioned by Emperor Minh Mang and cast between 1835 and 1836. They're embellished with decorative elements including landscapes, rivers, flowers and animals.

Tu Vo Phuong Pavilion

The two-storey Tu Vo Phuong Pavilion, elevated above a moat, was once a defense bastion for the northern part of the Imperial Enclosure. It combines both European and Vietnamese architectural styles (note the elaborate roof dragons).

Halls of the Mandarins

Unesco-sponsored conservation work is ongoing in the eastern hall here to preserve the elaborate ceiling and wall murals.

Emperor's Reading Room

Co Ha Gardens

Royal Theatre

③

②

①

⑤

Ngo Mon Gateway

A huge, grandiose structure that guards the main approach to the Imperial Enclosure, this gateway has a fortified lower level and a more architecturally elaborate upper part. It dates from 1833.

Thai Hoa Palace

Be sure to check out this palace's incredible ironwood columns, painted in 12 coats of brilliant scarlet and gold lacquer. The structure was saved from collapse by restoration work in the 1990s.

Tomb of Khai Dinh

DMHA/SHUTTERSTOCK ©

Perfume River Tombs

South of Hue are the extravagant mausoleums of the rulers of the Nguyen dynasty (1802–1945), spread out close to the banks of the Perfume River between 2km and 16km south of the city.

Great For...

☑ Don't Miss

At the Tomb of Tu Duc, a Stele Pavilion shelters a 20-tonne stone tablet; Tu Duc drafted the inscriptions himself.

Tomb of Minh Mang

This majestic **tomb** (adult/child 150,000/30,000d) is renowned for its architecture and sublime forest setting. The tomb was planned during Minh Mang's reign (1820–40) but built by his successor, Thieu Tri.

The **Honour Courtyard** is reached via three gates on the eastern side of the wall. Three granite staircases lead from the courtyard to the square **Stele Pavilion** (Dinh Vuong). **Sung An Temple**, which is dedicated to Minh Mang and his empress, is reached via three terraces and the rebuilt **Hien Duc Gate**.

Tomb of Tu Duc

This **tomb** (adult/child 150,000/30,000d), constructed between 1864 and 1867, is the most popular and impressive of the royal

Stone soldier, Tomb of Minh Mang

STEFANO BARZELLOTTI/SHUTTERSTOCK ©

mausoleums. Emperor Tu Duc designed it himself to use before and after his death. The enormous expense of the tomb and the forced labour used in its construction spawned a coup plot that was discovered and suppressed. Tu Duc's tomb is 5km south of Hue on Van Nien Hill in Duong Xuan Thuong village.

Tomb of Khai Dinh

This hillside **monument** (adult/child 150,000/30,000đ) is a synthesis of Vietnamese and European elements. Most of the tomb's grandiose exterior is covered in blackened concrete, creating an unexpectedly Gothic air, while the interiors resemble an explosion of colourful mosaic. Khai Dinh was the penultimate emperor of Vietnam, from 1916 to 1925, and widely seen as a puppet of the French. The construction of his flamboyant tomb took 11 years.

Tomb of Thieu Tri

The only royal tomb not enclosed by a wall, the monument of Thieu Tri (built 1848) has a similar floor plan to his father Minh Mang's tomb, but is substantially smaller. The tomb is about 7km from Hue.

Vinh Moc Tunnels

JE.JIM/GETTY IMAGES ©

Day Trip: The DMZ

Most of the bases and bunkers have long vanished, but the strip of land on either side of the Ben Hai River is still known by its American War moniker: the DMZ.

Great For...

☑ **Don't Miss**

The museum at Khe Sanh Combat Base has a compelling collection of American War artifacts.

From 1954 to 1975 the DMZ acted as a buffer between the North and the South. Ironically, it became one of the most militarised areas in the world, forming what *Time* magazine called 'a running sore'. Other sites including Hamburger Hill, Rockpile, Camp Carroll and the Truong Son National Cemetery can be added to bespoke tours.

Vinh Moc Tunnels

A highly impressive complex of tunnels, **Vinh Moc** (30,000d; ⊘7am-4.30pm) is the remains of a coastal North Vietnamese village that literally went underground in response to unremitting American bombing. More than 90 families disappeared into three levels of tunnels running for almost 2km, and continued to live and work while

Hien Luong Bridge, Ben Hai River

NIELS COETERMANS/SHUTTERSTOCK ©

bombs rained down around them. Most of the tunnels are open to visitors.

Khe Sanh Combat Base

The site of the most famous siege of the American War, the USA's **Khe Sanh Combat Base** (museum 20,000d; ⊙7am-5pm) was never overrun, but saw the bloodiest battle of the war. About 500 Americans, 10,000 North Vietnamese troops and uncounted civilian bystanders died around this remote highland base. Today the site is occupied by a small museum, which contains some fascinating old photographs, plus a few reconstructed bunkers and American aircraft.

Ben Hai River

Once the border between North and South Vietnam, the southern bank of **Ben Hai River** (museum 20,000d; ⊙7am-4.30pm) now has a grandiose reunification monument, its stylised palm leaves oddly resembling missiles. Ben Hai's northern bank is dominated by a reconstructed flag tower and small museum full of war mementoes.

Tours

Standard tours (around US$15 for a group day trip) can be arranged in Hue. For a superior experience, explore the DMZ independently. Reckon on US$120 for a car and expert guide.

◉ SIGHTS

Most of Hue's principal sights lie within the moats of its Citadel. Other museums and pagodas are dotted around the city. The royal tombs are south of Hue.

Thien Mu Pagoda   Buddhist Temple

FREE Built on a hill overlooking the Perfume River, 4km southwest of the Citadel, this pagoda is an icon of Vietnam and as potent a symbol of Hue as the Citadel. The 21m-high octagonal tower, **Thap Phuoc Duyen**, was constructed under the reign of Emperor Thieu Tri in 1844. Each of its seven storeys is dedicated to a *manushi-buddha* (a Buddha that appeared in human form). Visit in the morning before tour groups show up.

Thien Mu Pagoda was originally founded in 1601 by Nguyen Hoang, governor of Thuan Hoa province. Over the centuries its buildings have been destroyed and rebuilt

> *...Thien Mu Pagoda is...as potent a symbol of Hue as the Citadel...*

From left: Golden dragon statue; Thien Mu Pagoda; Mosaic, Tomb of Khai Dinh (p119); Tomb of Minh Mang (p118)

several times. Since the 1960s it has been a flashpoint of political demonstrations.

To the right of the tower is a pavilion containing a stele dating from 1715. It's set on the back of a massive marble turtle, a symbol of longevity. To the left of the tower is another six-sided pavilion, this one sheltering an enormous bell (1710), weighing 2052kg and audible from 10km away.

The temple itself is a humble building in the inner courtyard, past the triple-gated entrance where three statues of Buddhist guardians stand at the alert. In the main sanctuary behind the bronze laughing Buddha are three statues: A Di Da, the Buddha of the Past; Thich Ca, the historical Buddha (Sakyamuni); and Di Lac Buddha, the Buddha of the Future.

Ho Quyen   Historic Site

FREE Wildly overgrown but evocative, Ho Quyen was built in 1830 for the royal pastime of watching elephants and tigers face off in combat. The tigers (and leopards) were usually relieved of their claws and teeth so that the elephants – a symbol of the emperor's power – triumphed every

OLESKAUS/SHUTTERSTOCK ©

GWENGOAT/GETTY IMAGES ©

time. Climb up grassy ramparts and imagine the scene in the old arena – the last fight was held in 1904.

Tu Hieu Pagoda   Buddhist Temple

FREE Nestled in a pine forest, this popular pagoda was built in 1843 and later co-opted by eunuchs from the Citadel. Today 70 monks reside at Tu Hieu; they welcome visitors to the twin temples (one dedicated to Cong Duc, the other to Buddha). Listen to their chanting daily at 4.30am, 10am, noon, 4pm and 7pm. Tu Hieu Pagoda is about 5km from the centre of Hue, on the way to the tomb of Tu Duc (p118).

Dieu De National Pagoda   Buddhist Temple

(Quoc Tu Dieu De; 102 Đ Bach Dang) FREE Overlooking Dong Ba Canal, this pagoda was built under Emperor Thieu Tri's rule (1841–47) and is famous for its four low towers, one either side of the gate and two flanking the sanctuary. The pavilions on either side of the main sanctuary entrance contain the 18 La Ha, whose rank is just below that of Bodhisattva, and the eight Kim Cang, protectors of Buddha. In the back

row of the main dais is Thich Ca Buddha, flanked by two assistants.

Royal Fine Arts Museum   Museum

(150 Đ Nguyen Hue; ⊙6.30am-5.30pm summer, 7am-5pm winter) FREE This recently renovated museum is located in the baroque-influenced An Dinh Palace, commissioned by Emperor Khai Dinh in 1918 and full of elaborate murals, floral motifs and trompe l'œil details. Emperor Bao Dai lived here with his family after abdicating in 1945. Inside, you'll find some outstanding ceramics, paintings, furniture, silverware, porcelain and royal clothing, though information is a little lacking.

⊙ TOURS

Many sights around Hue, including Thien Mu Pagoda and several of the Royal Tombs, can be reached by boat via the Perfume River.

Most hotels and travellers' cafes offer shared day tours from US$5 to US$20 per person. Better ones start with a morning

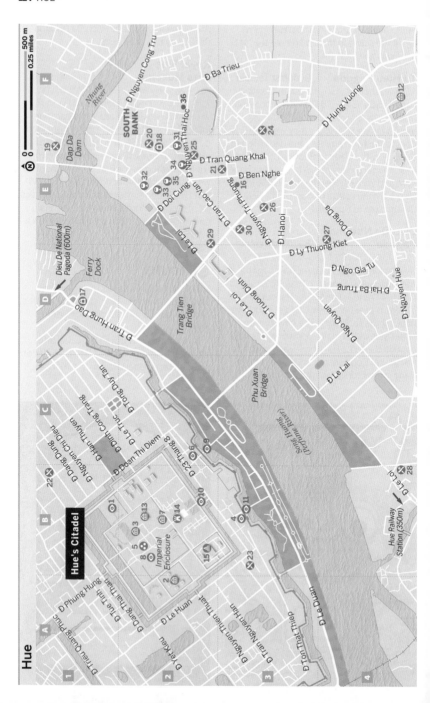

Hue

Hue's Citadel

SOUTH BANK

Nhung River

Dap Da Dam

Dieu De National Pagoda (600m)

Ferry Dock

Đ Trần Hưng Đạo

Trang Tien Bridge

Phu Xuan Bridge

Sông Hương (Perfume River)

Hue Railway Station (350m)

Đ Le Loi

Đ Nguyen Cong Tru

Đ Ba Trieu

Đ Hung Vuong

Đ Trần Quang Khải

Đ Nguyen Thai Hoc

Đ Ben Nghe

Đ Hanoi

Đ Ly Thuong Kiet

Đ Nguyen Tri Phuong

Đ Tran Cao Van

Đ Doi Cung

Đ Le Loi

Đ Truong Dinh

Đ Ngo Gia Tu

Đ Hai Ba Trung

Đ Ngo Quyen

Đ Nguyen Hue

Đ Dong Da

Đ Le Lai

Đ Tue Tinh

Đ Phung Hung

Đ Dang That Than

Đ Nguyen Thien Thuat

Đ Tran Nguyen Han

Đ Tran Hung Dao

Đ Ton That Thiep

Đ Le Duan

Đ Le Huan

Đ Dang Dung

Đ Nguyen Chi Dieu

Đ Han Thuyen

Đ Dinh Cong Trang

Đ Le Truc

Đ Trong Duy Tan

Đ 23 Thang 8

Đ Doan Thi Diem

Đ Tieu Quang Phuc

Đ Yet Kieu

Imperial Enclosure

500 m
0.25 miles

Hue

river cruise, stopping at pagodas and temples, then after lunch a minibus travels to the main tombs before returning to Hue. On the cheaper options you'll often have to hire a motorbike to get from the moorings to the tombs, or walk in tropical heat.

Tran Van Thinh
Tours

(✆0905 731 537; www.tranvanthinhtours.com; half-day tours per person from US$15) Knowledgable local motorbike guide who can arrange local city tours and explorations of the royal tombs. Thinh is a long-time resident of Hue and speaks excellent English.

Hue Adventures
Tours

(✆0905 771 602; www.hueadventures.com; 44 Đ Nguyen Tri Phuong) Well-regarded motorbike and jeep tours around Hue and also motorbike transfers from Hue to Hoi An, the DMZ and Phong Nha.

Stop & Go Café
Driving

(✆0234-382 7051; www.stopandgo-hue.com; 3 Đ Hung Vuong) Personalised motorbike and

car tours. A full-day DMZ car tour guided by a Vietnamese vet costs around US$30 per person for four people, representing a good deal. Guided trips to Hoi An stopping at beaches are also recommended. Note, there are similarly named, unrelated businesses at other addresses. Also has a travellers' cafe with good food.

Hue Flavor
Food & Drink

(✆0905 937 006; www.hueflavor.com; per person US$49) Excellent street-food tours exploring the delights of Hue cuisine. Transport is by *cyclo* and around 15 different dishes are sampled across four hours.

⊙ SHOPPING

Spiral Foundation Healing the Wounded Heart Center
Arts & Crafts

(✆0234-381 7643; www.spiralfoundation.org; 23 Đ Vo Thi Sau; ⊗8am-10pm) Generating cash from trash, this shop stocks lovely handicrafts – such as quirky bags made

From left: *Banh beo*; Dong Ba Market; Vegetarian *pho*

from plastic, and picture frames made from recycled beer cans – all crafted by artists with disabilities. Profits aid heart surgery for children in need. Also has a tea room.

Dong Ba Market   Market

(Đ Tran Hung Dao; ⊙6.30am-8pm) Just north of Trang Tien Bridge, this is Hue's largest market, selling anything and everything.

🗙 EATING

We have the famed fussy eater Emperor Tu Duc to thank for the culinary variety of Hue. Vegetarian food has a long tradition in Hue; stalls in Dong Ba Market serve it on the first and 15th days of the lunar month. Hue also has great street food.

Hanh Restaurant   Vietnamese $

(☑0905 520 512; 11 Pho Duc Chinh; meals 30,000-100,000d; ⊙10am-9pm) Newbies to Hue specialities, start at this busy restaurant. Order the five-dish set menu (120,000d) for a speedy lesson of *banh khoai* (savoury prawn pancakes), *banh beo* (steamed rice cakes topped with shrimp and spring onions), and divine *nem*

lui (grilled pork on lemongrass skewers) wrapped in rice paper and herbs. Ask the patient staff how to devour everything.

Nook Cafe
& Bar   Vietnamese, Cafe $

(☑0935 069 741; www.facebook.com/nookcafe barhue; 7/34 Đ Nguyen Tri Phuong; meals 50,000-120,000d; ⊙8am-10pm; 🛜☑) Tucked away near a tangle of cheaper accommodation and travel agencies, Nook's breezy upstairs location is a good spot for well-executed Vietnamese dishes and Western comfort food like veggie burgers and toasted sandwiches. Top marks for the quirky decor, good music and refreshing and rejuvenating fresh juices and smoothies too.

Quan Bun
Bo Hue   Vietnamese $

(17 Đ Ly Thuong Kiet; meals from 35,000d; ⊙6am-2pm) Excellent spot for a hearty bowl of *bun bo Hue*, the city's signature noodle dish combining tender beef, vermicelli and lemongrass. Next door at number 19, Ly Thuong Kiet is equally good. Both sell out by early afternoon.

DAOLEDUC/GETTY IMAGES ©

Quan Tai Phu   Vietnamese $

(2 Đ Dien Bien Phu; meals 20,000-30,000d; ☺9am-9pm) Our favourite spot for Hue's famous *bun thit nuong* – grilled pork with vermicelli and a forest of fresh herbs. Don't forget a hearty dollop of the special peanut sauce.

Hang Me Me   Vietnamese $

(16 Đ Vo Thi Sau; meals from 40,000d; ☺8am-11pm; 🖉) A top, unfussy spot to try Hue's dizzying menu of royal rice cakes. Serving portions are pretty big, so rustle up a few friends to try the different variations. Our favourite is the *banh beo*, perfect little mouthfuls topped with spring onions and dried shrimp.

Com Hen   Vietnamese $

(17 Đ Han Mac Tu; meals from 10,000d; ☺7am-11pm) Tuck into bowls of rice *(com hen)* or noodles *(bun hen)* combining fresh herbs and tasty local clams from a nearby island in the middle of the Perfume River. Servings are fairly small, so maybe have a bowl of each.

Lien Hoa   Vegetarian $

(🖉054-381 2456; 3 Đ Le Quy Don; meals 50,000-80,000d; ☺6.30am-9pm; 🖉) No-nonsense Viet vegetarian restaurant renowned for filling food at bargain prices. Fresh *banh beo*, noodle dishes, crispy fried jackfruit and aubergine with ginger all deliver. The menu has very rough English translations to help you order (staff speak little or no English).

Stop & Go Café   International $

(www.stopandgo-hue.com; 3 Đ Hung Vuong; meals 35,000-90,000d; ☺7am-10pm; 🖀) Atmospheric little place with decent Vietnamese and backpacker fare: *banh beo*, beef noodle soup, tacos, pizza and pasta, and filling Western breakfasts. It's worth dropping by for the excellent travel information.

Hong Mai   Vietnamese $

(110 Đ Dinh Tien Toang; snacks from 20,000d; ☺11am-8pm) After visiting the Citadel, try this excellent Vietnamese eatery for superior versions of two local street food classics. The *banh khoai* (rice crêpes filled with pork and shrimp) are crammed with bean sprouts, and the *nem lui* (minced pork

grilled on lemongrass sticks) go perfectly with a chilled Huda lager. Closing time can be somewhat flexible so go for lunch.

Les Jardins de
la Carambole   French Fusion $$

(📞0234-354 8815; www.lesjardinsdelacarambole.com; 32 Đ Dang Tran Con; meals 120,000-300,000d; ☺7am-11pm; 🛜) A memorable dining experience, this classy French restaurant occupies a gorgeous colonial-style building in the Citadel quarter. The menu majors in Gallic classics, and a Vietnamese set menu popular with groups. Add a lengthy wine list and informed service and it's just the place for a romantic meal – arrive by *cyclo* and it's easy to roll back the years to Indochine times.

...this classy French restaurant occupies a gorgeous colonial-style building...

Ta.ke   Japanese $$

(34 Đ Tran Cao Van; meals 70,000-220,000d; ☺10.30am-10pm; ❄) An authentic Japanese restaurant with tasteful furnishings including lanterns and calligraphy, and a winsome menu with sushi, tempura and yakitori dishes. The air-conditioned interior is a calming haven away from Hue's increasingly busy streets.

Little Italy   Italian $$

(📞054-382 6928; www.littleitalyhue.com; 10 Đ Nguyen Thai Hoc; meals 59,000-139,000d; ☺8am-10pm; ❄) Large trattoria with a decent line-up of Italian favourites (pasta, calzoni, pizzas and seafood), a choice of beers and a palatable Sicilian house wine.

🍷 DRINKING & NIGHTLIFE

Ta Vet   Bar

(📞0914 833 679; 11 Đ Vo Thi Sau; ☺6.30am-1am; 🛜) One part beer bar and one part cafe, this spacious spot with rustic wooden furniture a short walk from Hue's backpacker strip is a good location to meet younger English-speaking locals. There's a decent

Hue shop fronts

beer selection beyond the usual suspects, and the Vietnamese food is also affordable and tasty.

Sirius   Bar
(www.moonlighthue.com; 20 Đ Pham Ngu Lao; ☺10am-10pm) Outdoors, on the 15th floor of the **Moonlight Hotel** (🖉054-397 9797; www.moonlighthue.com; 20 Đ Pham Ngu Lao; r US$60-80, ste US$120-150; 😀❄@📶🏊), Sirius is the best place in town for sunset drinks. Combine BBQ snacks (beef, squid, prawns; from 60,000d) and a few beers or a cocktail and view the arrival of dusk on the Perfume River.

Why Not? Bar   Bar
(🖉0903 583 812; www.whynot.com.vn; 26 Pham Ngu Lao; ☺7am-midnight; 📶) With a pool table, good cocktails and food, and a popular street-front terrace, the Cowboy-themed Why Not? is a perennial favourite along Hue's PNL backpacker way. Upstairs there's good dorm and private room accommodation so you won't have to move far at the end of the night.

DMZ Travel   Bar
(www.dmz.com.vn; 60 Đ Le Loi; ☺7am-1am; 📶) Ever-popular bar near the river with a free pool table, cold Huda beer, cocktails (try a watermelon mojito) and antics most nights. Also serves Western and local food till midnight, smoothies and juices. Happy hour is 3pm to 8pm. Check out the upside-down map of the DMZ – complete with a US chopper – on the ceiling of the bar.

Also has a tour desk that can organise budget boat trips along the Perfume River, DMZ tours and tickets to Laos.

Brown Eyes   Bar
(Đ Chu Van An; ☺5pm-late; 📶) This late-night bar features a good blend of locals and traveller revellers. DJs drive the dance floor with R 'n' B, hip hop and house anthems, and staff rally the troops with free shots.

ℹ️ INFORMATION

Sinh Tourist (🖉0234-384 5022; www.thesinh tourist.vn; 37 Đ Nguyen Thai Hoc; ☺6.30am-8.30pm) Books Open-Tour buses, and buses to Laos and many other destinations in Vietnam.

ℹ️ GETTING THERE & AROUND

There are several daily flights to both Hanoi and Ho Chi Minh City.

The main bus station, 4km southeast of the centre, has connections to Danang and south. An Hoa bus station, northwest of the Citadel, serves northern destinations.

For Phong Nha (around 135,000d, five hours), the Hung Thanh Open-Tour bus leaves 49 Chu Van An at 4.30pm, and the Tan Nha bus leaves from the Why Not? Bar on Pham Ngu Lao around 6.30am.

Trains leave Hue train station on Đ Le Loi to points north and south (including Danang).

Hotels rent bicycles for around US$3 per day and a car with driver from US$50.

My Khe Beach, Danang

A Night in Danang

Danang is changing fast. For decades it was something of a provincial backwater but this city now boasts a spectacular riverfront spanned by stunning new bridges and a booming beach zone.

Great For...

ℹ Need to Know

The riverfront is perfect for a stroll, replete with bars, cafes and restaurants.

★ **Top Tip**

To/from Hoi An it's cheaper to fix a taxi price (reckon on 400,000d) without using the meter.

The city may be upwardly mobile but conventional sightseeing spots are few.

Sights

Dragon Bridge
Bridge

(Cau Rong; ⊘24hr) **FREE** Welcome to the biggest show in town every Saturday and Sunday night. At 9pm, this impressive dragon sculpture spouts fire and water from its head near the Han River's eastern bank. The best observation spots are the cafes lining the eastern bank to the north of the bridge; boat trips taking in the action also depart from Đ Bach Dang on the river's western bank.

Museum of Cham
Sculpture
Museum

(Bao Tang; 1 Đ Trung Nu Vuong; 40,000d; ⊘7am-5pm) This fine, small museum has the world's largest collection of Cham artefacts, housed in buildings marrying French-colonial architecture with Cham elements. It displays more than 300 pieces including altars, *lingas*, garudas, apsaras, Ganeshes and images of Shiva, Brahma and Vishnu, all dating from the 5th to 15th centuries. Explanations are slim.

Tours

Danang Food Tour
Food & Drink

(www.danangfoodtour.com; per person US$45) Excellent morning and evening explorations of the local food scene by passionate foodies.

Danang Free
Walking Tour
Walking

(✆0905 631 419; www.danangfreewalkingtour.com; 108 Đ Bach Dang; ⊘9am & 3pm) Run by

Dragon Bridge

local English-speaking students, these walking tours are a good introduction to the city. Maybe also sign up for one of the other (paid) specialised tours. Book ahead.

Eating & Drinking

Quan Com Hue Ngon   Vietnamese $

(65 Đ Tran Quoc Toan; meals 60,000-100,000d; ⊙3-9pm) Fab barbecue place, all charcoal smoke and sizzling meats, where you grill your own. There's a street terrace, and the welcoming English-speaking owner will help with the menu.

> ☑ **Don't Miss**
> Danang's fire-spewing Dragon Bridge symbolises the city's resurgence.

Fatfish   Fusion $$

(☏0236-394 5707; www.fatfishdanang.com; 439 Đ Tran Hung Dao; meals 110,000-330,000d; ⊙11am-10pm; 🛜) This stylish restaurant and lounge bar is leading the eating and drinking charge across the river on the Han's eastern shore. Innovative Asian fusion dishes, pizza and wood-fired barbecue all partner with flavour-packed craft beers from Ho Chi Minh City's Pasteur Street Brewing (p223).

Waterfront   International $$

(☏0236-384 3373; www.waterfrontdanang.com; 150-152 Đ Bach Dang; meals 150,000-350,000d; ⊙9am-11pm; ❄🛜🍸) A riverfront lounge and restaurant that gets everything right on every level. It works as a stylish bar for a chilled glass of New Zealand sauvignon blanc or an imported beer, and also as a destination restaurant for a memorable meal (book the terrace deck for a stunning river vista).

TANG TRUNG KIEN/SHUTTERSTOCK ©

> ✗ **Take a Break**
> Enjoy a chilled glass of wine in classy Waterfront.

Thu Bon River and the Old Town (p138)

HOI AN

Hoi An at a Glance...

Graceful, historic Hoi An is Vietnam's most atmospheric and delightful town. Once a major port, it features the grand architecture and beguiling riverside setting that befits its heritage, but the 21st-century curses of traffic and pollution are almost entirely absent.

The Old Town boasts an incredible legacy of tottering merchant houses, Chinese temples and ancient tea warehouses. Travel a few kilometres further – there are some superb bicycle, motorbike and boat trips – and swathes of central Vietnam's most captivating scenery and beaches are within easy reach.

Two Days in Hoi An

Spend the entire day in the **Old Town** (p138), taking in its remarkable sights including the emblematic **Japanese Covered Bridge** (p141), **Assembly Hall of the Fujian Chinese Congregation** (p142) and **Tan Ky House** (p141). On day two book a bicycle, scooter or motorbike tour to explore the glorious hinterland around Hoi An, hit the beach at An Bang then eat at **Cargo Club** (p157).

Four Days in Hoi An

Book a morning trip to the impressive nearby Cham ruins of **My Son** (p146), then return to Hoi An for a gorgeous lunch of local specialities at **Sea Shell** (p157). In the afternoon, take in some of the lesser-known temples and museums. On day four, sign up for a cooking course, then treat yourself to a spa treatment before a memorable dinner at **Hill Station** (p156).

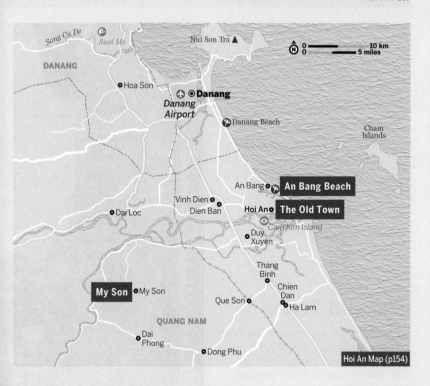

Song Cu De

Suoi Mo

Nui Son Tra ▲

DANANG

Hoa Son

Danang
Danang
Airport

Danang Beach

Cham
Islands

An Bang○ **An Bang Beach**

Vinh Dien○
Dien Ban
Dai Loc○

Hoi An○ **The Old Town**

Cam Kim Island

Duy
Xuyen

Thang
Binh

My Son ○My Son

Chien
Dan
Que Son○ ○Ha Lam

QUANG NAM

Dai
Phong

○Dong Phu

○ 0 ___ 10 km
○ 0 ___ 5 miles

Hoi An Map (p154)

Arriving in Hoi An

Danang airport is a 45-minute drive
from Hoi An; taxis charge 400,000d.

Very few intercity buses stop in Hoi An.
Most travellers use open-tour buses.

The nearest train station is in Danang.

Sleeping

Hoi An has good-value accommodation
in all price categories. There are only
a couple of hotels in the Old Town, but
many budget and midrange places are
spread out to the northwest.

Many luxury hotels are a few kilometres
from town by the coast but all offer
shuttle-bus transfers.

An Bang beach also has lots of good
options.

The Old Town

By Unesco decree, more than 800 historic buildings in Hoi An have been preserved, so much of the Old Town looks as it did several centuries ago.

Great For...

Đ Phan Chu Trinh
Japanese Covered Bridge
Assembly Hall of the Fujian Chinese Congregation
Assembly
Assembly Hall of the Hainan
Quan Cong Temple
Tan Ky House
Đ Nguyen Thai Hoc
Đ Bach Dang
Đ Nguyen Phuc Chu
Thu Bon River

ℹ️ Need to Know

An Old Town ticket (120,000d, valid 10 days) allows access to five different heritage attractions.

★ **Top Tip**

Visitors should dress modestly as some of the old houses are still private homes.

A Historic Port

From the 2nd to the 10th centuries, Hoi An was a busy seaport of the Champa kingdom. After the 15th century Hoi An – known as Faifoo to Western traders – was one of Southeast Asia's major ports. Chinese, Japanese, Dutch, Portuguese, Spanish, Indian, Filipino, Indonesian, Thai, French, British and American ships came to call, and the town's warehouses teemed with treasures: high-grade silk, fabrics, paper, porcelain, areca nuts, pepper, Chinese medicines, elephant tusks, beeswax, mother-of-pearl and lacquer.

Japanese, Chinese & Western Influences

The Japanese ceased coming to Hoi An after 1637 (when the Japanese government forbade contact with the outside world), but the Chinese lingered. The Chinese who settled in Hoi An identified themselves according to their province of origin. Each community built its own assembly hall, known as *hoi quan* in Vietnamese, for social gatherings, meetings and celebrations.

Under French rule, Hoi An served as an administrative centre. It was virtually untouched in the American War, thanks to the cooperation of both sides. The town was declared a Unesco World Heritage Site in 1999.

Surviving Architecture

The historic buildings of Hoi An not only survived the 20th century's wars, they also retained features of traditional architecture rarely seen today. As they have been for centuries, some shopfronts are shuttered

Japanese Covered Bridge

at night with horizontal planks inserted into grooves that cut into the columns that support the roof.

Some roofs are made up of thousands of brick-coloured *am* (yin) and *duong* (yang) roof tiles – so called because of the way the alternating rows of concave and convex tiles fit snugly together.

A number of Hoi An's houses have round pieces of wood with an *am-duong* symbol in the middle surrounded by a spiral design over the doorway. These *mat cua* (door

Entering the Buildings

The Old Town has dozens of historic structures, of which 22 are open to visitors and require an Old Town ticket (sold at numerous booths) for admission.

RICHIE CHAN/SHUTTERSTOCK ©

eyes) are supposed to protect the residents from harm.

Hoi An's historic structures are gradually being sensitively restored. Strict rules govern the colour that houses can be painted and the signs that can be used.

Japanese Covered Bridge

This beautiful little **structure** (Cau Nhat Ban; admission by Old Town ticket; ⊙24hr) is emblematic of Hoi An. A bridge was first constructed here in the 1590s by the Japanese community to link them with the Chinese quarters. Over the centuries the ornamentation has remained relatively faithful to the original design. The French flattened out the roadway for cars, but the original arched shape was restored in 1986.

The bridge is due for a complete removal for repair, so check it's still there before you travel, if making a special trip.

Phung Hung Old House

Just a few steps down from the Japanese Covered Bridge, this old **house** (4 Đ Nguyen Thi Minh Khai; admission by Old Town ticket; ⊙8am-7pm) has a wide, welcoming entrance hall decorated with exquisite lanterns, wall hangings and embroidery. You can walk out on to a balcony and there's also an impressive suspended altar.

Tan Ky House

Built two centuries ago by an ethnically Vietnamese family, this gem of a **house** (101 Đ Nguyen Thai Hoc; admission by Old Town ticket; ⊙8am-noon & 2-4.30pm) has been lovingly preserved through seven generations. Look out for signs of Japanese and Chinese influences on the architecture. Japanese elements include the ceiling (in the sitting area), which is supported by three

Touring the Sites

Short guided tours of the old houses tend to be efficient, if a tad perfunctory. All four museums are small with basic displays and limited information.

progressively shorter beams, one on top of the other. Under the crab-shell ceiling are carvings of crossed sabres wrapped in silk ribbon. The sabres symbolise force, the silk represents flexibility.

The interior is brightened by a beautiful detail: Chinese poems written in inlaid mother-of-pearl hang from some of the columns that hold up the roof. The Chinese characters on these 150-year-old panels are formed entirely of birds gracefully portrayed in various positions of flight.

Assembly Hall of the Fujian Chinese Congregation

Originally a traditional **assembly hall** (Phuc Kien Hoi Quan; opposite 35 Đ Tran Phu; admission by Old Town ticket; ⊗7am-5.30pm) ✐, this structure was later transformed into a temple for the worship of Thien Hau, a deity from Fujian province. The green-tiled triple gateway dates from 1975. The mural on the right-hand wall depicts Thien Hau, her way lit by lantern light as she crosses a stormy sea to rescue a foundering ship. Opposite is a mural of the heads of the six Fujian families who fled from China to Hoi An in the 17th century.

In the last chamber, the central altar contains seated figures of the heads of the six Fujian families. The smaller figures below them represent their successors as clan leaders. Behind the altar on the right are three fairies and smaller figures representing the 12 *ba mu* (midwives), each of whom teaches newborns a different skill necessary for the first year of life: smiling, sucking and so forth. Childless couples often come here to pray for offspring and leave fresh fruit as offerings.

Tran Family Chapel

Built for worshipping family ancestors, this **chapel** (21 Đ Le Loi; admission by Old Town ticket; ⊗7.30am-noon & 2-5.30pm) dates back to 1802. It was commissioned by Tran Tu, one of the clan who ascended to the rank of mandarin and served as an ambassador to China. His picture is to the right of the chapel. The architecture of the building reflects the influence of Chinese (the 'turtle' style roof), Japanese (triple beam) and vernacular (look out for the bow-and-arrow detailing) styles.

Quan Cong Temple

Founded in 1653, this small **temple** (Chua Ong; 24 Đ Tran Phu; admission by Old Town ticket; ⊗8am-5pm) is dedicated to Quan Cong, an esteemed Chinese general who is worshipped as a symbol of loyalty, sincerity, integrity and justice. His partially gilded statue, made of papiermâché on a wooden frame, is on the central altar at the back of the sanctuary. When someone makes an offering to the portly looking Quan Cong, the caretaker solemnly strikes a bronze bowl that makes a bell-like sound.

Assembly Hall of the Hainan Chinese Congregation

Assembly Hall of the Hainan Chinese Congregation

Built in 1851, this assembly hall is a memorial to 108 merchants from Hainan Island who were mistaken for pirates and killed in Quang Nam province in 1851. The elaborate dais contains plaques to their memory. In front of the central altar is a fine gilded woodcarving of Chinese court life.

Phuoc Lam Pagoda

This **pagoda** (Thon 2a, Cam Ha; ⏱8am-5pm) (founded in the mid-17th century) is associated with An Thiem, a Vietnamese prodigy and monk from the age of eight. When he was 18, he volunteered for the army so his brothers could escape the draft; he eventually rose to the rank of general. Later he

returned to the monkhood, but to atone for his sins of war he volunteered to clean the Hoi An market for 20 years, then joined this pagoda as its head monk.

❶ Did You Know?

It's not just individual buildings that have survived – it's whole streetscapes. This is particularly true around Đ Tran Phu and waterside promenade Đ Bach Dang.

★ Top Tip

Hoi An floods most years after storms during the monsoon months (September to December).

RICHIE CHAN/SHUTTERSTOCK ©

Morning Glory Cooking School

NEIL SETCHFIELD/ALAMY STOCK PHOTO ©

Cooking Courses

Hoi An has become a mecca for Vietnamese cooking courses, with many locals and restaurants offering classes.

Great For

☑ **Don't Miss**

Tasting the local specialities in the Old Town before trying to recreate them yourself.

Green Bamboo Cooking School

Directed by Van, a charming local chef and English speaker, these **courses** (☑0905 815 600; www.greenbamboo-hoian.com; 21 Đ Truong Minh Hung, Cam An; per person US$45) are more personalised than most. Groups are limited to a maximum of 10, and take place in Van's spacious kitchen.

Red Bridge Cooking School

At this **school** (☑0235-393 3222; www.visit hoian.com/redbridge/cookingschool.html; Thon 4, Cam Thanh; per person US$33-55), going to class involves a relaxing 4km cruise down the river. There are half-day and full-day courses, both of which include market visits.

ⓘ Need to Know

Courses start at US$20 per person.

✕ Take a Break

Sample your own delicious creations.

★ Top Tip

Excellent foodie tours run by **Eat Hoi An** (Coconut Tours; ☏0905 411 184; www. eathoian.com; 37 Đ Phan Chau Trinh; per person US$45) and **Taste of Hoi An** (☏0905 382 783; www.tasteofhoian.com; per person US$65) taking in street food and village visits are also very popular.

A Hoi An Taster

Hoi An is a culinary hotbed and there are some unique dishes you should be sure to sample.

○ 'White rose' or *banh vac* is an incredibly delicate, subtly-flavoured shrimp dumpling topped with crispy onions.

○ *Banh bao* is another steamed dumpling, this time with minced pork or chicken, onions, eggs and mushrooms that's said to be derived from Chinese dim sum.

○ *Cao lau* is an amazing dish – Japanese-style noodles seasoned with herbs, salad greens and bean sprouts and served with slices of roast pork.

○ *Hoanh thanh* (fried wonton) is another local speciality.

○ *Banh xeo* are crispy savoury pancakes rolled with herbs in fresh rice paper.

Herbs & Spices

Excellent **classes** (☏0235-393 6868; www. herbsandspicesvn.com; 2/6 Đ Le Loi; per person US$35-58; ⊙10.30am, 4.30pm & 8pm) with three different menu options, and smaller more hands-on groups than some other cookery classes.

Morning Glory Cooking School

This is the **cooking course** (☏0510-224 1555; www.msvy-tastevietnam.com; 106 Đ Nguyen Thai Hoc; half-day courses US$25-32) that launched Hoi An cooking courses. It's directed by Trinh Diem Vy, owner of several restaurants in town, or one of her protégés. Classes can have up to 30 people.

ROMAS_PHOTO/SHUTTESTOCK ©

Day Trip: My Son

The site of Vietnam's most extensive Cham remains, My Son enjoys an enchanting setting in a lush forested valley 55km west of Hoi An.

Great For...

☑ **Don't Miss**

Buildings D1 and D2 (once meditation halls) now house small displays of Cham sculpture.

History

My Son was once the most important intellectual and religious centre of the kingdom of Champa. It became a religious centre under King Bhadravarman in the late 4th century and was continuously occupied until the 13th century.

My Son was rediscovered in the late 19th century by the French, who restored parts of the complex, but American bombing later devastated the temples.

Today it is a Unesco World Heritage Site.

Exploring the Site

Group A   Hindu Temple

Group A was almost completely destroyed by US bombs. According to locals, the massive **A1**, considered the most important monument at My Son, remained impervious to aerial bombing and was intentionally

CHONLAWUT/SHUTTERSTOCK ©

ⓘ Need to Know

150,000d; ⊗6.30am-4pm

✕ Take a Break

There are snacks and drinks for sale around the site's entrance.

★ Top Tip

'Sunrise' trips do not mean you'll see the first ray of morning light, but they do beat the crowds.

in Danang, used to stand. Note the motifs, characteristic of the 8th century, carved into the brickwork of the exterior walls. With the massive bomb crater in front of this group, it's amazing that anything's still standing.

My Son Museum   Museum

(admission with entrance ticket; ⊗6.30am-4pm) My Son's impressive museum has many statues from the site and information about how the temples were constructed, the carvings and statues and architecture. Cham culture, religion and way of life are also explained.

Getting There & Away

My Son is best visited on a tour. Hotels in Hoi An arrange day trips to My Son (US$8 to US$15). Most minibuses depart at 8am and return between 1pm and 2pm. For the boat-ride option on the return leg, add an extra hour.

finished off by a helicopter-borne sapper team. All that remains today is a pile of collapsed brick walls.

Group B   Hindu Temple

The main *kalan* (sanctuary), **B1**, was dedicated to Bhadresvara, which is a contraction of the name of King Bhadravarman, who built the first temple at My Son, combined with '-esvara', which means Shiva. The first building on this site was erected in the 4th century, destroyed in the 6th century and rebuilt in the 7th century. Only the 11th-century base, made of large sandstone blocks, remains.

Group C   Hindu Temple

The 8th-century **C1** was used to worship Shiva, portrayed here in human form. Inside is an altar where a statue of Shiva, now in the Museum of Cham Sculpture (p132)

Cycling outside Hoi An

LAHIRU RANASINGHE/SHUTTERSTOCK ©

Tours Around Hoi An

The quintessentially Vietnamese countryside around Hoi An begs to be explored. Two-wheeled tours are very popular, as are paddle-boarding, kayaking and boat trips to the idyllic Cham Islands.

Great For...

☑ Don't Miss

Testing your two-wheel prowess on a motorbike tour around idyllic back roads.

Motorbike & Jeep

Quite possibly the most fun and stylish way to explore around Hoi An, **Vespa Adventures** (☑0938 500 997; www.vespaadventures. com; 134 Đ Tran Cao Van; per person $US69-80) offers the opportunity to ride pillion on classic retro two-wheelers. **Hoi An Jeep Adventures** (☑0905 101 930; www. vietnamjeeps.com; 54 Đ Hung Vuong; per person from US$96) offers half- to three-day trips in classic US army jeeps taking in everything from Monkey Mountain, the Hai Van Pass, Danang street food, and the Co Tu village of Bho Hoong. **Hoi An Motorbike Adventures** (☑0905 101 930; www.motorbike tours-hoian.com; 54 Đ Hung Vuong) specialises in tours on cult Minsk motorbikes. The guides really know the terrain and the trips make use of beautiful back roads and riverside tracks.

the river: you can fish, paddle a basket boat or learn about wet rice planting.

Explore the waterways around Hoi An with **SUP Monkey** (☑0125 593 1463; www.supmonkey.net; 250 Đ Cua Dai; per person US$30-120). Options include a sunrise tour starting at An Bang Beach.

Cham Islands

A breathtaking cluster of granite islands, set in aquamarine seas, around 15km directly offshore from Hoi An, the Cham Islands make a fine excursion.

Day trips, diving or snorkelling the reefs, and overnight stays are possible. The diving is not world class, but can be intriguing.

Blue Coral Diving (☑0235-627 9297; www.divehoian.com; 33 Đ Trung Hung Dao) is a friendly, professional outfit with a good dive boat and additional speedboat. Snorkelling trips are US$45 and there are PADI courses too. **Cham Island Diving Center** (☑0235-391 0782; www.vietnamscubadiving.com; 88 Đ Nguyen Thai Hoc; snorkelling day trips US$44, overnight snorkelling/diving trips US$82/112) is run by a friendly, experienced team and has the mantra 'no troubles, make bubbles'. They've a large boat and also a speedboat for zippy transfers. Also runs overnight trips to the Chams.

Bicycle

Phat Tire Ventures (☑0235-653 9839; www.ptv-vietnam.com; 80 Le Hong Phong; per person from US$39) offers a terrific mountain bike trip to the My Son ruins that takes in country lanes and temple visits. **Grasshopper Adventures** (☑0932 034 286; www.grasshopperadventures.com; 62 Đ Hai Ba Trung; per person US$37-47) runs highly recommended biking tours on very well-maintained bikes. Ride around the fringes of Hoi An with students on a **Hoi An Free Tour** (☑0961 278 730; www.hoianfreetour.com; 591 Đ Hai Ba Trung) **FREE**. You get to meet the locals and see village life, they get to practise their English.

Boat, SUP & Kayak

Jack Tran Tours (☑0914 082 850; www.jacktrantours.com; Phuoc Hai village; adult/child from 1,000,000/500,000đ) runs boat trips along

Day Trip: An Bang Beach

An Bang is one of Vietnam's most happening and enjoyable beaches. Inland from a fabulous stretch of golden sand there's a cluster of cool cafe-restaurants.

Great For...

☑ Don't Miss

The beach scene at daybreak when fishermen return to the shore with their catches.

An Bang's star is on the rise and it's become the key expat hang-out in Central Vietnam.

It's easy to see the beach's appeal. There's a wonderful broad strip of fine sand to enjoy, and an enormous horizon with only the distant Cham Islands interrupting the seaside symmetry.

Beachside Dining & Drinks

DeckHouse

An Bang's most cosmopolitan oceanfront eating and drinking **option** (www.thedeck houseanbang.com; meals 80,000-180,000d; ⏲7am-10.30pm) includes beachy decor with rustic timber, private cabanas, and a menu stretching from local flavours through to burgers and fresh seafood. The cocktail and wine list is equally eclectic, and there's often good craft beers from Hanoi's Fur-

❶ Need to Know

An Bang is just 3km from central Hoi An; most visitors cycle here.

✖ Take a Break

Sound of Silence is one of central Vietnam's best cafes.

★ Top Tip

In summer locals flock to the beach, but between 10am and 4pm An Bang is always quite tranquil.

brew on tap. Check the Facebook page for occasional DJs and live music.

Salt Pub & Restaurant

Located beachfront on the quiet side of the An Bang strip, this relaxed **place** (www.saltpubhoian.com; Ð Nguyen Phan Vinh; meals 120,000-180,000d; ☯8am-11pm) offers craft beers on tap, espresso coffee and a tempting choice of Western and Vietnamese breakfasts and meals (try the pulled-pork burger). There's an ocean-facing terrace and stylish interior.

Soul Kitchen

An oceanfront **restaurant** (☏0906 440 320; www.soulkitchen.sitew.com; meals 90,000-180,000d; ☯10am-10pm Tue-Sun, to 6pm Mon; 🛜) with a grassy garden and thatched dining area where the daily menu could

include tuna carpaccio, seafood salad or calamari. There's good wine, strong cocktails, and live music from 7pm from Wednesday to Sunday.

Sound of Silence

An Bang's best **spot** (www.facebook.com/soundofsilencecoffee; coffee from 25,000d; ☯7am-5pm; 🛜) for a coffee, Sound of Silence combines a rustic garden setting, ocean views and the best barista skills in the village. Fresh coconuts and crêpes crammed with tropical fruit are other distractions while you wonder about going for a swim.

Family Friendly

There's an expanding accommodation scene in An Bang with stylish holiday rental houses making a fine alternative for families and friends travelling together. The area is much quieter in the winter months.

⊙ SIGHTS

Assembly Hall of the Chaozhou Chinese Congregation
Historic Building

(Trieu Chau Hoi Quan; opposite 157 Đ Nguyen Duy Hieu; admission by Old Town ticket; ⊘8am-5pm) Built in 1752, the highlights in this congregational hall are the gleaming woodcarvings on the beams, walls and altar – absolutely stunning in their intricacy. You could stand here for hours to unravel the stories, but if you're just popping by quickly, look for the carvings on the doors in front of the altar of two Chinese women wearing their hair in an unexpectedly Japanese style.

Cam Kim Island
Island

The master woodcarvers who crafted the intricate detail adorning Hoi An's public buildings and the historic homes of the town's merchants came from Kim Bong village on Cam Kim Island. Most of the woodcarvings on sale in Hoi An are produced here.

Boats to the island leave from the boat landing at Đ Bach Dang in Hoi An (35,000d, 30 minutes). The village and island, quite rural in character, are fun to explore by bicycle for a day.

Museum of Trading Ceramics
Museum

(80 Đ Tran Phu; admission by Old Town ticket; ⊘7am-5.30pm) Occupies a restored wooden house and contains a small collection of artefacts from all over Asia, with oddities from as far afield as Egypt. While this reveals that Hoi An had some rather impressive trading links, it takes an expert's eye to appreciate the display. The exhibition on the restoration of Hoi An's old houses provides a useful crash course in Old Town architecture.

Quan Thang House
Historic Building

(77 Đ Tran Phu; admission by Old Town ticket; ⊘7am-5pm) This house is three centuries old and was built by a Chinese captain. As usual, the architecture includes Japanese and Chinese elements. There are some especially fine carvings of peacocks and

Assembly Hall of the Fujian Chinese Congregation (p142)

RAFAL CICHAWA/SHUTTERSTOCK ©

flowers on the teak walls of the rooms around the courtyard, on the roof beams and under the crab-shell roof (in the salon beside the courtyard).

Museum of Sa Huynh Culture & Museum of the Revolution
Museum

(149 Đ Tran Phu; admission by Old Town ticket; ⊘7am-5.30pm) On the lower floor you'll find stone, bronze, gold, glass and agate jewellery, assorted ceramic fragments and burial jars dating from the early Dong Son civilisation of Sa Huynh. The upper floor's revolution museum was closed at the time of research.

Chinese All-Community Assembly Hall
Historic Building

(Chua Ba; 64 Đ Tran Phu; ⊘8am-5pm) **FREE** Founded in 1773, this assembly hall was used by Fujian, Cantonese, Hainanese, Chaozhou and Hakka congregations in Hoi An. To the right of the entrance are portraits of Chinese resistance heroes in Vietnam who died during WWII. The well-restored main temple is a total assault on the senses, with great smoking incense spirals, demonic-looking deities, dragons and lashings of red lacquer – it's dedicated to Thien Hau.

🟢 ACTIVITIES
Nomad Yoga
Yoga

(⌨0122 718 4604; www.nomadyogahoian.com; 6 Le Hong Phong; single class 150,000d, 1-week unlimited classes 700,000d) ✿ Classes are either held in a peaceful studio location surrounded by rice fields or on An Bang beach. Check the online schedule. Spa treatments and healing programs are also available, and the on-site cafe specialises in natural foods, tasty breakfast bowls and juice detox programs.

Palmarosa
Spa

(⌨0235-393 3999; www.palmarosaspa.vn; 48 Ba Trieu; massages & treatments from 220,000d; ⊘10am-9pm) This highly professional spa offers massages (including Thai and Swed-

 Professional Photo Tour

Experienced and newbie photographers are both catered for on the **Hoi An Photo Tour** (⌨0905 671 898; www.hoianphototour.com; 42 Đ Phan Boi Chau; per person from US$45) coordinated by professional cameraman Etienne Bossot. Sunrise and sunset tours are most popular, harnessing Hoi An's delicate light for images of fisherfolk and rice paddies.

The Old Town (p138)
MEOGIAPHOTO/GETTY IMAGES ©

ish), scrubs and facials, as well as hand and foot care.

Ba Le Beauty Salon
Spa

(⌨0905 226 974; www.balewellbeautysalon. com; 45-11 Đ Tran Hung Dao; ⊘9am-7pm) Ba Le is run by a fluent English-speaker, who has trained in the UK, and offers inexpensive threading, waxing, facials, manicures and pedicures.

🛒 SHOPPING
Hoi An has a history of flogging goods to international visitors, and today's residents haven't lost their commercial edge. Clothes are the biggest lure: Hoi An has long been known for fabric production.

Hoi An has over a dozen art galleries too and woodcarvings are a local speciality: head to Cam Nam village and Cam Kim Island for these.

Reaching Out
Souvenirs, Clothing

(www.reachingoutvietnam.com; 103 Đ Nguyen Thai Hoc; ⊘8.30pm-9.30pm Mon-Fri, 9.30am-

Hoi An

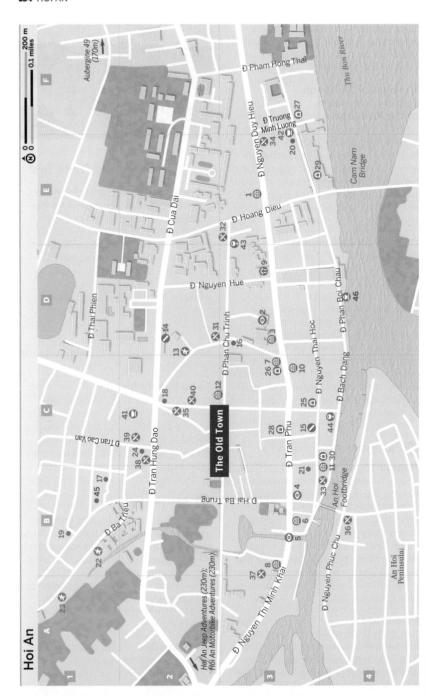

The Old Town

Hoi An Jeep Adventures (230m);
Hoi An Motorbike Adventures (230m)

Aubergine 49
(170m)

Đ Pham Hong Thai

Thu Bon River

Cam Nam
Bridge

An Hoi
Peninsula

An Hoi
Footbridge

0   200 m
0   0.1 miles

Hoi An

◎ Sights

◎ Activities, Courses & Tours

◎ Shopping

◎ Eating

◎ Drinking & Nightlife

◎ Information

◎ Transport

8.30pm Sat & Sun) ✿ Excellent fair-trade gift shop that stocks good-quality silk scarves, clothes, jewellery, hand-painted Vietnamese hats, handmade toys and teddy bears. The shop employs and supports artisans with disabilities, and staff are happy to show visitors through the workshop.

Villagecraft Planet   Arts & Crafts

(www.facebook.com/villagecraftplanet; 59 Đ Phan Boi Chau; ◷10am-6pm) ✿ Shop here for interesting homewares and fashion, often using natural hemp and indigo, and crafted incorporating fair-trade practices by the Hmong, Black Thai and Lolo ethnic minority people in the north of Vietnam.

March Gallery   Art

(✆0122 377 9074; www.marchgallery-hoian.com; 25 Đ Phan Boi Chau; ◷10am-8pm) Owned by British expat artist Bridget March, this new gallery showcases her work – mainly poignant watercolours and whimsical sketches – and a slowly expanding range of work from other Hoi An resident artists. Styles include fine lacquer paintings, but there is an affordable range of well-priced souvenir pieces and artisan jewellery as well.

Metiseko   Clothing

(✆0235-392 9278; www.metiseko.com; 140-42 Đ Tran Phu; ◷8.30am-9.30pm) ✿ Winners of a Sustainable Development award, this eco-minded store stocks gorgeous clothing (including kids' wear), accessories, and homewares such as cushions using natural silk and organic cotton. It is certified to use the Organic Contents Standards label, and the company sources natural twill and

Shantung and Habutai silk from within
Vietnam

Avana
Clothing

(www.hoiandesign.com; 57 Đ Le Loi; ⊙8am-
9.30pm) Stylish boutique run by a European
fashion designer that stocks fab off-the-
peg dresses, blouses, shoes and accessories (including great hats and bags).

Yaly
Clothing

(⎙0235-391 0474; www.yalycouture.com; 47
Đ Nguyen Thai Hoc; ⊙8am-9pm) Hoi An is
bustling with tailors; get something made
to order at this popular shop offering some
of the best service with several branches
around town.

You can also order additional clothing
online once you get home.

Lotus
Jewellery
Fashion & Accessories

(www.lotusjewellery-hoian.com; 82 Đ Tran Phu;
⊙8am-10pm) Very affordable and attractive
hand-crafted pieces loosely modelled on
butterflies, dragonflies, Vietnamese sam-
pans, conical hats and Chinese symbols.

⊗ EATING

The beauty of Hoi An is that you can snag
a spectacular cheap meal at the central
market and in casual eateries – or you can
splash out on a fine-dining experience.

Banh Mi Phuong
Vietnamese $

(2b Đ Phan Chu Trinh; banh mi 20,000-30,000d)
What makes the *banh mi* at this cramped
joint draw the crowds? It's the dense,
chewy bread, the freshness of the greens
and the generous serves of *thit nuong*
(chargrilled pork), beef or other meat that
seals the deal. A celebrity-chef endorse-
ment helps too.

Streets
Vietnamese $

(⎙0235-391 1949; www.streetsinternational.org;
17 Đ Le Loi; mains 80,000-165,000d; ⊙8am-10pm)
Do the meals taste exceptional here because Streets is for a good cause? Perhaps
it helps to know that the staff are disadvantaged youths trained up in hospitality, but
the textbook-good *cao lau* and white-rose
dumplings deserve an A+ regardless. Although endlessly busy, it's a comfortable, if
warm, spot to linger with a cocktail too.

From left: Yaly; Cargo Club; *Banh mi* at Banh Mi Phuong

Pheva Chocolate   Sweets $

(☑0235-392 5260; www.phevaworld.com; 74 Đ Tran Hung Dao; chocolate from 50,000d; ⊗8am-7pm) Excellent artisan chocolate crafted from organic and free-trade cacao from Vietnam's southern Ben Tre province. The dark chocolate spiked with Phu Quoc peppercorns is especially good.

Hill Station   International $$

(☑0235-629 2999; www.thehillstation.com; 321 Đ Nguyen Duy Hieu; platters 160,000-275,000d, mains 100,000-165,000d; ⊗7.30am-10.30pm; 🛜) With a superb location in one of Hoi An's most interesting historic mansions, the Hill Station is ideal for a drink and snack after a busy day. Relax in the heritage armchairs and partner craft beer or wine with shared plates of Sapa charcuterie and Dalat cheeseboards. More robust are interesting pasta dishes and Euro classics like *coq au vin*.

Cargo Club   International $$

(☑0235-391 1227; www.msvy-tastevietnam. com/cargo-club; 107 Đ Nguyen Thai Hoc; meals 70,000-160,000d; ⊗8am-11pm; 🛜) Remark-able cafe-restaurant serving Vietnamese and Western food, with a terrific riverside location (the upper terrace has stunning views). A relaxing day here munching your way around the menu would be a day well spent. The breakfasts are legendary (try the eggs Benedict), the patisserie and cakes are superb, and fine-dining dishes and good cocktails also deliver.

Sea Shell   French, Seafood $$

(119 Đ Tran Cao Van; meals 90,000d; ⊗noon-9pm) Shaded by a decades-old banyan tree, Sea Shell is a flavour-packed offshoot of Nu Eatery in Hoi An's Old Town. Try snacks like tempura prawn rolls and turmeric catfish wraps, or mains like spicy pork noodles with a refreshing calamari and green apple salad. A decent wine list covers Australia, France, Italy and South Africa.

Aubergine 49   Fusion $$

(www.hoian-aubergine49.com; 49a Đ Ly Thai Tho; 3-course menu 495,000d; ⊗6-10pm Mon-Sat) Three-course menus for 495,000d per person are a fine reason to taxi around five minutes north of central Hoi An to

Hoi An speciality *cao lau*

this stylish restaurant crafting interesting fusion combinations of Asian and Western cuisine. There are also à la carte options and a decent wine list; menu standouts include stuffed squid and roast quail.

Little Menu   Vietnamese $$

(www.thelittlemenu.com; 12 Đ Le Loi; meals 60,000-150,000d; ☺9.30am-11pm; 🐿) 🍃 English-speaking owner Son is a fantastic host at this popular little restaurant with an open kitchen and short menu – try the fish in banana leaf or duck spring rolls, which feature on the set menu (225,000d). Almost all of the ingredients are strictly local from around Hoi An.

Bale Well   Vietnamese $$

(45-51 Đ Tran Cao Van; meals 150,000d; ☺11.30am-10pm) Down a little alley near the famous well, this local place is renowned for one dish: barbecued pork, served up satay-style, which you then combine with fresh greens and herbs to create your own fresh spring roll. A global reputation means it can get very busy.

Mango Mango   Fusion $$$

(☑0235-391 0839; www.themangomango.com; 45 Đ Nguyen Phuc Chu, An Hoi; meals US$18-23; ☺7am-10pm; 🐿) Celebrity chef Duc Tran's most beautiful Hoi An restaurant enjoys a prime riverside plot and puts a global spin on Vietnamese cuisine, with fresh, unexpected combinations. Perhaps at times the flavour matches are just a little too out there, but the cocktails are some of the best in town, especially with an after dark view of the river.

🍸 DRINKING & NIGHTLIFE

Espresso Station   Cafe

(☑0905 691 164; www.facebook.com/the espressostation; 28/2 Đ Tran Hung Dao; coffee 30,000-50,000d; ☺7.30am-5pm; 🐿) A slice of Melbourne-style coffee culture – albeit in a heritage Hoi An residence – the Espresso Station is where to go for the best flat whites and cold brew coffees in town. There's a compact food menu with granola, muesli and sandwiches; relaxing in the arty courtyard is where you'll want to be.

QUYNH ANH NGUYEN/GETTY IMAGES/MOMENT RF ©

Tap House   Craft Beer
(📞0235-391 0333; www.facebook.com/tap-tap-house-hoi-an-925846390887804/; 3 Đ Phan Chau Trinh; ⊗8am-10pm Mon-Sat, noon-10pm Sun) Craft beers from around Vietnam are the tasty attraction at this new Hoi An bar, but don't be surprised if you linger for the tasty charcuterie and cheeseboards as well.

Mia Coffee House   Cafe
(www.facebook.com/miacoffeehouse; 20 Đ Phan Boi Chau; ⊗8am-5pm) One of our favourite spots for an espresso, latte or cappuccino, and good food including grilled *panini* sandwiches and hearty baguettes. Mia's own coffee blend sourced from Dalat arabica beans is the standout brew, and be sure to try the coffee *affogato*, a delicious blend of dessert and hot beverage.

Dive Bar   Bar
(88 Đ Nguyen Thai Hoc; ⊗8am-midnight; 🛜) A top bar option in Hoi An with a great vibe thanks to the welcoming service, contemporary electronic tunes and sofas for lounging. There's also a cocktail garden and bar at the rear, a pool table and pub grub.

White Marble   Bar
(www.visithoian.com; 99 Đ Le Loi; ⊗11am-11pm; 🛜) This wine-bar-cum-restaurant in historic premises has an unmatched selection of wines; many are available by the glass. Lunch and dinner tasting menus cost US$16, and the corner location is a great place to watch the world go by.

ℹ️ INFORMATION

Sinh Tourist (📞0235-386 3948; www.thesinh tourist.vn; 587 Đ Hai Ba Trung; ⊗6am-10pm) Books reputable open-tour buses.

ℹ️ GETTING THERE & AWAY

The closest airport is 45 minutes away in Danang.

Taxis cost approximately 400,000d to Danang. A trip in a car to Hue starts at US$100.

ℹ️ GETTING AROUND

Hoi An is best explored on foot; the Old Town is compact and highly walkable. To go further afield, rent a bicycle (25,000d per day). Reckon on about 90,000d for a taxi to An Bang beach.

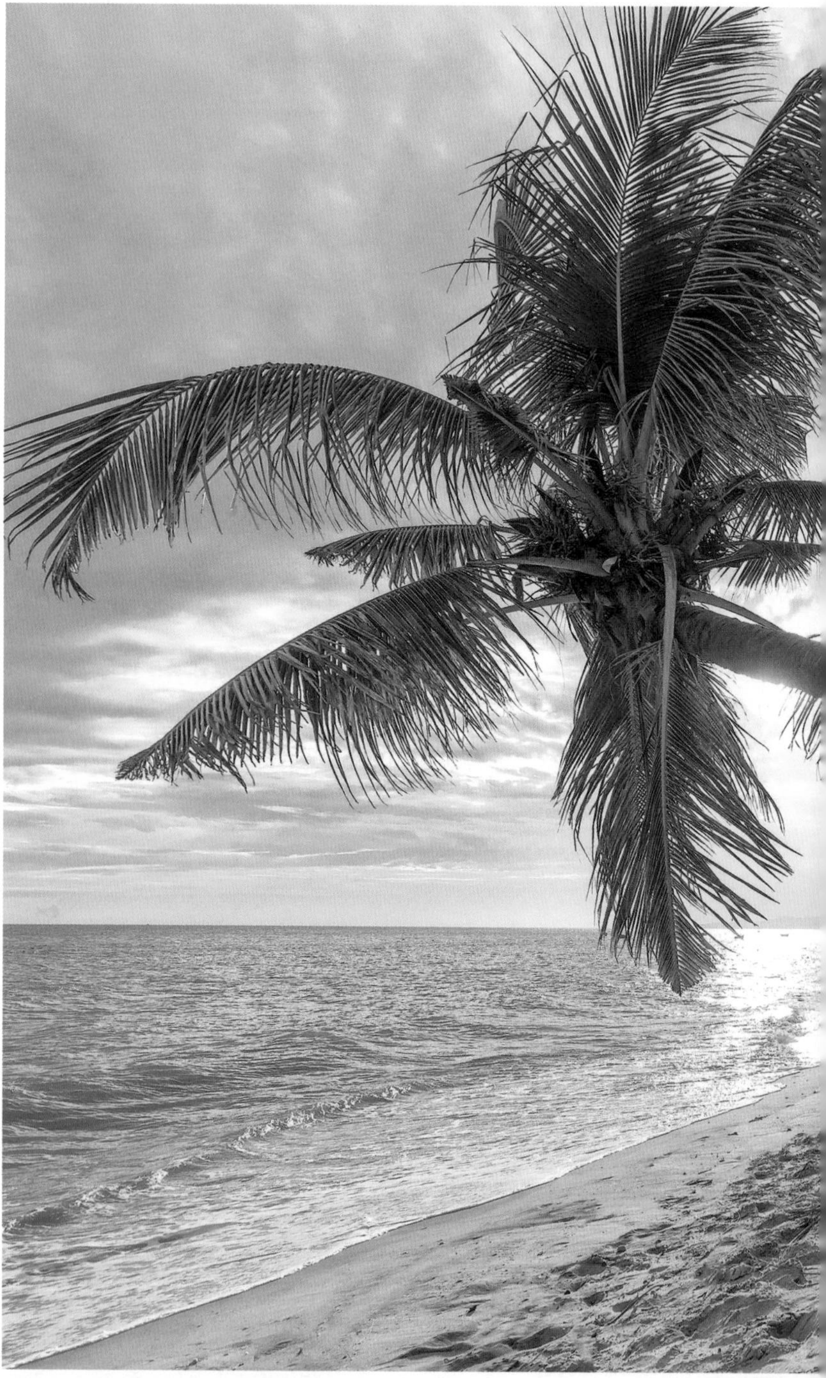
THOAI/SHUTTERSTOCK ©

MUI NE

Mui Ne at a Glance...

Once upon a time, Mui Ne was an isolated stretch of beach where pioneering travellers camped on the sand. Times have changed and it's now an established beach resort. Mui Ne has moved upmarket, as more exclusive places open their doors, complemented by swish restaurants, but there is still a (kite) surfer vibe to the town. Sailing, windsurfing and hot-air ballooning are also popular.

A Day in Mui Ne

Book a sunrise trip to see the region's famous **sand dunes** (p166) then enjoy some beach time on Mui Ne's lovely sands. In the late afternoon drop by the **Po Shanu Cham Towers** (p166), indulge in an early evening massage at **Xanh Spa** (p167), then head to **Dong Vui Food Court** (p167) for drinks and dinner.

Two Days in Mui Ne

The next day sign up for a windsurfing, sailing or cooking course followed by a visit to the **Fairy Spring** (p166). After dark enjoy a memorable meal in the acclaimed shoreside **Sandals** (p169) restaurant then hit **Joe's Cafe** (p169) for live music and beers.

BIN THUAN

Song La Nga

Luong Son

Bac Binh

Nga Ba Gop

Ma Lam

Sand Dunes

Ap Thien Ai

Xa Muong Man

Phan Thiet

Po Shanu Cham Towers

Mui Ne

Mui Ne Beach

Ham Thuan Nam

Phu Sung

Ham Minh

Ta Cu Mountain (688m)

SOUTH CHINA SEA (EAST SEA)

Tan Hai

Van Ke

0 ——— 10 km
0 ——— 5 miles

Mui Ne Map (p168)

Arriving in Mui Ne

There's no airport, and the nearest train station is in Phan Thiet, so most visitors arrive by road via bus or private transport.

Mui Ne has good bus links to Ho Chi Minh City. For Nha Trang and points north catch an open-tour bus.

Sleeping

Most midrange and top-end accommodation is either right on the long coastal road or just off it, with a few good-value places in the hills behind town. Budget places tend to be on the back streets. Wherever you are, you won't be far from the beach.

Mui Ne Beach

HEMIS/ALAMY STOCK PHOTO ©

Sports & Activities

For kite- and windsurfers, late October to late April is peak season when gales blow. There's also some surf, good sailing, a decent local golf course and hot-air ballooning.

Great For...

☑ **Don't Miss**

For a fun hour or so check out Tropical Minigolf Mui Ne (p167).

Mui Ne is the adrenaline capital of southern Vietnam. There's no scuba-diving or snorkelling to speak of, but when Nha Trang and Hoi An get the rains, Mui Ne gets the waves. Surf's up from August to December.

Kitesurfing has really taken off and the infinite horizon is often obscured by dozens of kites flapping in the wind.

If this all sounds too much like hard work, you can simply lounge around on the beach, watching others take the strain, or perhaps book a hot-air balloon trip.

Boating

One of Southeast Asia's best sailing schools, **Manta Sail Training Centre** (☑0908 400 108; http://mantasailing.org; 108 Đ Huynh Thuc Khang; sailing instruction per hour US$66) offers instruction and training (from beginner to advanced racing). Speak to

them about wakeboarding (US$100 per hour), SUP rentals (US$10 per hour) and boat tours. They also have budget rooms available right by the beach.

Ballooning

Mui Ne Hot Air Balloon (☑0120 853 6828; www.vietnamballoons.com; from US$136), the first hot-air balloon experience in Vietnam, is a professionally run, European-owned operation that sees you either soaring over the spectacular white sand dunes and desert lakes east of Mui Ne, or alternatively over the bustling fishing harbour of Phan Thiet. Prepare yourself for a magical flight at sunrise.

Kitesurfing & Surfing

One of Mui Ne's best-regarded kite schools, **Surfpoint Kiteboarding School** (☑0167 342 2136; www.surfpoint-vietnam.com; 52a Đ Nguyen Dinh Chieu; 5hr course incl all gear US$250; ☺7am-6pm) offers a three-hour starter course for US$150. Surfing lessons on soft boards are also offered (from US$50) when waves permit.

Mui Ne's original kitesurfing school, **Jibes** (☑0252-384 7405; www.jibesbeachclub.com; 84-90 Đ Nguyen Dinh Chieu; ☺7.30am-6pm) offers instruction (US$60 per hour) and rents gear including windsurfs (US$55 per day), SUPs (US$20 per half-day), surfboards, kitesurfs and kayaks.

◎ SIGHTS & ACTIVITIES

Sand Dunes   Beach

Mui Ne is famous for its enormous red and white sand dunes. The 'red dunes' *(doi hong)* are convenient to Hai Long, but the 'white dunes' *(doi cat trang)* 24km northeast are the more impressive – the near-constant oceanic winds sculpt the pale yellow sands into wonderful Sahar-aesque formations. But as this is Vietnam (not deepest Mali) there's little chance of experiencing the silence of the desert.

Prepare yourself for the hard sell as children press you to hire a plastic sledge to ride the dunes. Unless you're supermodel-light, it can be tricky to travel for more than a few metres this way.

Quad bikes and dune buggies also destroy the peace. Bizarrely, ostrich riding is offered as an activity, but we don't rec-ommend it due to animal-cruelty concerns. Expect some litter too; periodically there's a clean-up, but the tide of plastic keeps returning.

If you're booking a sand dune tour, be careful to agree on an itinerary, preferably in writing. We hear complaints, particularly about 'sunset tours' that cut short with the sun high in the sky.

Po Shanu
Cham Towers   Hindu Site

(Km 5; 10,000d; ⊘7.30-11.30am & 1-4.30pm) Around 6km west of Mui Ne, these Cham towers occupy a hillside with sweeping views of nearby Phan Thiet and a cemetery filled with candy-like tombstones. Dating from the 9th century, this complex consists of the ruins of three towers, none of which are in very good shape. There's a small pagoda on site too.

Fairy Spring   River

(Suoi Tien) This stream flows through a patch of dunes and past some interesting sand and rock formations. It's a pleasant walk wading from the sea up the creek to its source, a spring. You can do the trek barefoot, but if you're heading out into the big sand dunes after, you'll need proper footwear. Expect some trash and souvenir stands along the way.

From left: Mui Ne's sand dunes; Po Shanu Cham Towers; Fairy Spring

Tropical Minigolf
Mui Ne   Minigolf

(www.minigolfmuine.com; 97 Đ Nguyen Dinh
Chieu; 1 round 100,000-120,000d; ⊙10am-11pm)
This attractive shady crazy golf course
is dotted with craggy rock formations to
challenge your putting skills. There's a bar
and restaurant here too.

Botanica Spa   Spa

(☑094 887 7203; 83b Đ Nguyen Dinh Chieu;
1hr massage from 300,000d; ⊙noon-midnight)
Down a little lane, this good-value spa is
perfect for a soothing massage, treatment,
manicure or pedicure. The Vietnamese and
Thai massages are excellent.

Xanh Spa   Spa

(☑062-384 7440; www.miamuine.com; 24 Đ
Nguyen Dinh Chieu; 1hr massage from 710,000d)
Located in the Mia Resort, this gorgeous
upmarket spa offers the full gamut of
massages, facials (from 600,000d), body
treatments (try an Aloe Vera Body Soothe),
steam sessions, wraps and manicures
and pedicures. Essential oils and natural
products are used.

⊗ EATING

Dong Vui
Food Court   Food Hall $

(www.facebook.com/FoodCourtDongVui; 246
Đ Nguyen Dinh Chieu; meals 30,000-170,000d;
⊙5-11pm) A brilliant new concept, this
attractive open-air food court has loads of
independently-run cook stations offering
everything from Punjabi cuisine to paella,
German sausages and Thai curries – plus
plenty of Vietnamese options. Just grab a
seat and order what you fancy. There's also
great craft beer on tap and live music some
weekends. Located on the eastern side of
the strip.

Sindbad   Middle Eastern $

(www.sindbad.vn; 233 Đ Nguyen Dinh Chieu;
meals 50,000-110,000d; ⊙11am-1am; 🛜)
Always busy, Sindbad serves tasty,
great-value Greek cuisine including mean
shawarma (beef or chicken doner kebabs),
shish kebabs and great salads (Greek, Italian, garden). For a feast, order the Mediterranean Delight, which includes lots of mini
plates including hummus and bruschetta.

ACHI4OS/SHUTTERSTOCK ©

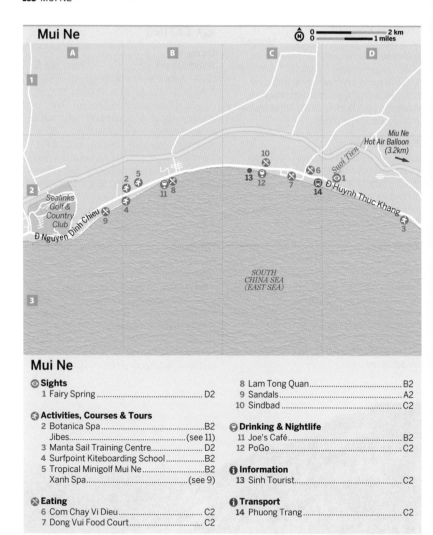

Mui Ne

Com Chay Vi Dieu
Vegetarian $

(15B Đ Huynh Thuc Khang; meals 25,000d; ◷7am-9pm; 🍴) A simple roadside place perfect for inexpensive Vietnamese vegetarian dishes (curries, noodle soup and fried rice dishes); it also serves great smoothies (20,000d). It's opposite the Eiffel Tower of the Little Paris resort. Almost no English is spoken.

Lam Tong Quan
Vietnamese, Seafood $

(92 Đ Nguyen Dinh Chieu; meals 40,000-140,000d; ◷7.30am-10pm) This no-frills seafront place has tables by the shore (and some shelter if it's raining). There's a wide choice of dishes including lots of seafood (try the crab or steamed fish). However, expect service that's surly verging on rude. Very little English is spoken.

Sandals   International $$

(📞0252-384 7440; www.miamuine.com; Mia
Resort, 24 Đ Nguyen Dinh Chieu; meals 120,000-
370,000d; 🕗7am-10pm; 🛜) For a memorable
meal in Mui Ne head straight to Sandals,
located at Mia Resort. It's particularly
romantic at night, with tables set around
the shoreside pool and subtle lighting. The
menu is superb, with everything from sea-
food platters to perfectly seasoned grilled
meat dishes. There's a great choice of wine
by the glass, and craft beers too.

🍺 DRINKING & NIGHTLIFE

PoGo   Bar

(📞0912 000 751; www.thepogobar.com; 138 Đ
Nguyen Dinh Chieu; 🕗8.30am-2am) This casual
bar has a great beachfront location, day
beds for lounging, DJs on weekends and
regular movie nights. Staff are very friendly;
happy hour runs from 6pm to 8pm.

Joe's Café   Bar

(http://joescafemuine.com; 86 Đ Nguyen Dinh
Chieu; 🕗7am-1am; 🛜) This very popular
pub-like place has live music (every night at
7.30pm) and a gregarious vibe. During the
day it's a good place to hang too with seats
set under a giant mango tree, magazines
to browse, pool table and an extensive food
menu.

ℹ️ INFORMATION

Sinh Tourist (📞098 925 8060; www.thesinh
tourist.vn; 144 Đ Nguyen Dinh Chieu; 🕗7am-
10pm) Operates open-tour buses to HCMC, Nha
Trang and Dalat and has a computerised booking
system.

ℹ️ GETTING THERE & AWAY

Open-tour buses are the most convenient
option for Mui Ne. Several companies have daily
services to/from HCMC (110,000d to 135,000d,
six hours), Nha Trang (from 112,000d, 5½ hours)
and Dalat (125,000d, four hours).

Phuong Trang (http://futabus.vn; 97 Đ Nguyen
Dinh Chieu) Very regular buses between Mui Ne
and Ho Chi Minh City.

ℹ️ GETTING AROUND

Mai Linh (📞0252-389 8989) operates reliable
metered taxis, although call ahead to book later
in the evening.

Love Valley, Dalat

DALAT

In This Chapter

Dalat at a Glance...

This is Vietnam's alter ego: the weather is springlike cool instead of tropical hot, the town is dotted with elegant French-colonial villas rather than stark socialist architecture, and the farms are thick with strawberries and flowers, not rice.

Dalat is small enough to remain charming and its countryside is blessed with lakes, waterfalls, evergreen forests and gardens. The town is a big draw for domestic tourists, for whom it's a honeymoon capital. For travellers the moderate climate is ideal for adrenaline-fuelled activities – mountain biking, forest hiking, canyoning and climbing.

A Day in Dalat

Head straight for the **Hang Nga Crazy House** (p178) and marvel at its kitsch eccentricity, and then take in the **King Palace** (p178). In the afternoon book a toy train ride from the **Crémaillère Railway Station** (p179), and finish off with a stroll around **Xuan Huong Lake** and a meal at **Le Rabelais** (p181).

Two Days in Dalat

Sign up with a recommended **adventure tour specialist** (p176) for a day's trekking, mountain biking, kayaking, canyoning, abseiling or rock climbing. Or just explore the region's waterfalls by taxi if you're not feeling that active. If there's time in the late afternoon, catch the **cable car** (p179) to the Truc Lam Pagoda. Make for the **Escape Bar** (p182) in the evening for live music.

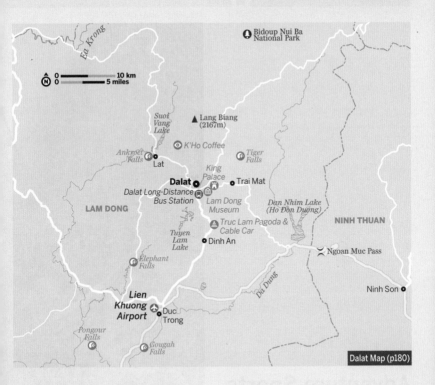

Arriving in Dalat

Dalat airport (30km from town) has daily flights to Ho Chi Minh City, Hanoi, Danang and other cities.

Very efficient and regular bus services link Dalat with HCMC from the central terminal 1.5km south of Xuan Huong Lake. Other cities including Danang are also covered.

Sleeping

Hotels and guesthouses are scattered around town and in the hills beyond.

Many budget places are located in the streets north of Hoa Binh Square.

Abseiling Datanla Falls (p179)

Adventure Sports

Dalat is Vietnam's highland adventure sports mecca, offering mountain biking and hiking, canyoning and rock climbing, white-water rafting, kayaking and motorbiking trips.

Compare prices, but make sure that you're comfortable with all the equipment and safety procedures.

Great For...

☑ **Don't Miss**

The thrill of riding (like the locals) on two wheels is an essential Vietnam experience.

ℹ Need to Know

Stick to the recommended tour operators listed, as accidents have occurred with unlicensed guides.

Tour Operators

Phat Tire Ventures

A highly professional and experienced **operator** (☏063-382 9422; www.ptv-vietnam. com; 109 Đ Nguyen Van Troi; ⊘8am-7pm) with mountain-biking trips from US$49, trekking from US$39, kayaking from US$39, canyoning (US$75) and rappelling (US$57), and white-water rafting (US$67) in the rainy season. Multiday cycling trips are available and it also ventures into Cat Tien National Park.

Groovy Gecko Adventure Tours

Long-running **agency** (☏0263-383 6521; www.groovygeckotours.net; 65 Đ Truong Cong Dinh; ⊘7.30am-8.30pm) that offers a unique (for Dalat) canyoning adventure that includes abseiling down a remote 65m waterfall (US$55). Also does mountain bike

trips (from US$28) and day treks (from US$28), as well as a one-day downhill cycle to Nha Trang (US$75).

Pine Track Adventures

Run by an enthusiastic and experienced local team, **Pine Track Adventures** (☏0263-383 1916; www.pinetrackadventures.com; 72b Đ Truong Cong Dinh; ⊘8am-8.30pm) offers canyoning (from US$55), white-water rafting (US$60), trekking (from US$35), biking (from US$41) and some excellent multisport packages. A seven-day bike tour from Dalat to Hoi An is US$595.

Mountain Biking & Cycling

There's excellent biking around Dalat, which is ringed by hills and mountains. Trails run through pine forests and offer magnificent views.

Bidoup Nui Ba National Park

Road cycling is also highly rewarding, with light traffic and sublime vistas. The routes to Nha Trang (one day including some rafting) and Mui Ne (two days) are wildly popular and involve some serious descents.

Canyoning

A dramatic day out at the Datanla canyon involves negotiating several waterfalls using ropes and rappelling and a natural water slide. Only book this trip with the experienced operators we recommend.

White-Water Rafting & Kayaking

White-water rafting the Da Don river through remote terrain and taking in Class II and III

> **✗ Take a Break**
> Check out the Dalat Train Cafe (p181) for snacks, meals and drinks in a classic colonial-era carriage.

JOEL WHALTON/SHUTTERSTOCK ©

rapids makes a fine day trip. Some operators offer combined hiking and rafting trips.

Motorbiking

For many travellers, the highlight of their trip in Vietnam is an off-the-beaten-track motorcycle tour with an 'Easy Rider'. Rider-guides can be found in hotels and cafes in Dalat. Read testimonials from past clients. Check the bike over. Discuss the route in detail – for scenery, the highways that link Dalat to Mui Ne and Nha Trang are wonderful. Rates start at US$30 or so for a day tour, or US$50 to US$75 per day for longer journeys.

Trekking

From day hikes through jungle rich with bird life to extended trekking trips through tribal villages and over rolling hills and along lonely ridges, there's a fine choice of walks from Dalat. Troops of monkeys are sometimes encountered on some hikes.

Bidoup Nui Ba National Park

Occupying a densely forested highland plateau, this little-visited national park encompasses evergreen and coniferous woodlands, bamboo groves and grasslands at altitudes between 650m and 2288m. It is also home to various primates, black bears and the vampire flying frog. The park is 50km north of Dalat and most people visit on motorbike tours. English-speaking staff can be elusive. There are plans to make it more foreigner-friendly in the future.

Bidoup Nui Ba has 96 endemic plants, including the Dalat pine, and nearly 300 species of orchids.

The pleasant 3.5km trail from the visitor centre to a waterfall only fringes the national park; to penetrate deep inside Bidoup Nui Ba consider other options, which include ascents of Lang Biang and Bidoup mountains. Permits and a guide are needed and you'll camp overnight.

> **★ Top Tip**
> If considering an 'Easy Rider' motorbike trip, test-drive the rider first before committing.

⊙ SIGHTS

Hang Nga
Crazy House   Architecture

(☎0263-382 2070; 3 Đ Huynh Thuc Khang; 50,000d; ⊗8.30am-7pm Mon-Fri) A free-wheeling architectural exploration of surrealism, Hang Nga Crazy House is a joyously designed, outrageously artistic private home. Imagine sculptured rooms connected by superslim bridges rising out of a tangle of greenery, an excess of cascading lava-flow-like shapes, wild colours, spiderweb windows and an almost-organic quality to it all, with the swooping hand rails resembling jungle vines. Think of Gaudí and Tolkien dropping acid together.

The brainchild of owner Mrs Dang Viet Nga, the Crazy House has been an imaginative work in progress since 1990. Hang Nga, as she's known locally, has a PhD in architecture from Moscow and has designed a number of other buildings around Dalat.

Hang Nga started the Crazy House project to entice people back to nature and although it's becoming more outlandish every year, she's not likely to have any trouble with the authorities. Her father, Truong Chinh, succeeded Ho Chi Minh as Vietnam's second president from 1981 until his death in 1988. There's a shrine to him in the ground-floor lounge.

A note of caution for those with young kids: the Crazy House's maze of precarious tunnels, high walkways with low guard rails and steep ladders are not at all child-safe.

King Palace   Palace

(Dinh 1; ☎0263-358 0558; Hung Vuong; adult/child 30,000/10,000d; ⊗7am-5pm) Tastefully revamped, the main palace of Bao Dai, Vietnam's last emperor, beckons visitors with its beautiful tree-lined avenue and a surprisingly modest but attractive royal residence. It was home to Bao Dai and his family until they went into exile in France in 1954. The house was subsequently taken over by then Prime Minister Ngo Dinh Diem.

> *A free-wheeling architectural exploration of surrealism...*

Hang Nga Crazy House

BULGN/SHUTTERSTOCK ©

K'Ho Coffee
Farm

(📞0989 722 184; www.khocoffee.com; Lat Village; ⊗by appointment 8am-4pm Mon-Sat) 🍴 This coffee farm has been in the family of Rolan since the 1860s. It's part of a K'Ho coffee-growing cooperative that ensures that profits are directly supporting the K'Ho minority farmers. The beans are Arabica, including varieties grown in Africa, which are rarely found in Vietnam even though it's the world's second-biggest coffee producer.

Crémaillère
Railway Station
Historic Building

(Ga Da Lat; 1 Đ Quang Trung; 5000d; ⊗6.30am-5pm) From Dalat's wonderful art-deco train station you can ride one of the nine scheduled trains that run to Trai Mat (return 108,000d, 30 minutes) daily between 6.55am and 4.39pm; a minimum of 25 passengers required.

A *crémaillère* (cog railway) linking Dalat and Thap Cham from 1928 to 1964 was closed due to VC attacks. A Japanese steam train is on display, and the classy waiting room retains a colonial feel.

Truc Lam Pagoda
& Cable Car
Buddhist Temple

(Ho Tuyen Lam; cable car one way/return adult 60,000/80,000d, child 30,000/40,000d; ⊗cable car 7.30-11.30am & 1.30-5pm) The Truc Lam Pagoda enjoys a hilltop setting and has splendid gardens. It's an active monastery, though the grounds frequently teem with tour groups. Be sure to arrive by cable car (the terminus is 3km south of the centre, up a short road next to the long-distance bus station), which soars over majestic pine forests.

Lam Dong Museum
Museum

(📞0263-381 2624; 4 Đ Hung Vuong; 15,000d; ⊗7.30-11.30am & 1.30-4.30pm Mon-Sat) This hillside museum is a stampede through Dalat's history, with a side trip into the natural history section, complete with outrageously bad taxidermy (look out for the angry wildcats!), and plenty of propaganda.

 Waterfalls Around Dalat

Dalat's waterfalls are obviously at their gushing best in the wet season but still flow when it's dry. Most tend to focus on commerce rather than nature – Prenn and Cam Ly Falls are two to avoid.

An uneven and sometimes hazardous path heads down to **Elephant Falls** (Thac Voi; 20,000d; ⊗7.30am-5pm), which are best seen from below. The falls are near Nam Ban village, 30km west of Dalat.

Datanla Falls (adult/child 30,000/10,000d, bobsled ride one way/return 30,000/50,000d) are 7km southeast of Dalat off Hwy 20. It's a nice walk through the rainforest and a steep hike downhill to the falls. You can also take a fun bobsled-rollercoaster ride down (and back up) a winding elevated track. On weekends expect crowds and loud music.

Dambri Falls (adult/child 150,000/100,000d; ⊗7am-5pm), 75km from Dalat, are the tallest falls (90m) in the area – walking down to feel the spray from the bottom is divine. You can take the elevator-like vertical cable car back up.

Elephant Falls
ALDARINHO/SHUTTERSTOCK ©

🎫 TOURS
Dalat Happy Tours
Food & Drink

(📞0163 654 6450; www.dalathappytours.com; street-food tour US$4) After all the active exertions around Dalat, replenish your calories by going on an entertaining nightly

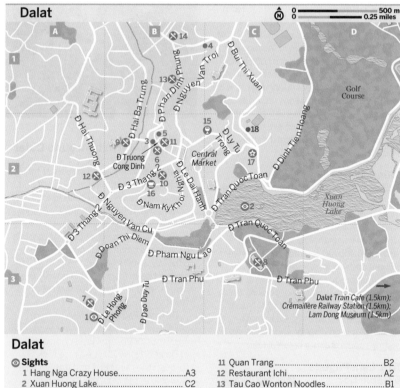

Dalat

street-food tour with friendly Lao. Food costs are not included.

⊗ EATING

Tau Cao Wonton Noodles
Noodles $

(217 Đ Phan Dinh Phung; noodles 35,000-40,000d; ⊙6am-8pm) This humble eatery is famed throughout Dalat and is always heaving with locals, who come for the noodle wonton soup. It's served with thin slices of pork on top and a sprinkling of mincemeat. Add chilli, lime and bean sprouts to taste and you're good to go. Classic Asian street eats are served here. No English is spoken.

Trong Dong   Vietnamese $

(☑0263-382 1889; 220 Đ Phan Dinh Phung; meals 75,000-150,000d; ⊙11am-3pm & 5-9pm; 🛜) Intimate restaurant run by a very hospitable team where the creative menu includes spins on Vietnamese delights such as shrimp paste on a sugar-cane stick, beef wrapped in *la lut* leaf, and fiery lemongrass and chilli squid.

Oz Burgers   Burgers $

(☑0902 475 923; 61 Đ Ba Thang Hai; meals 70,000-180,000d; ⊙11am-2pm & 5.30-9pm Wed-Mon) Packed out every night with backpackers, Asian tourists and even a few locals, this Australian-run joint serves up delicious burgers on wooden platters, along with fries and imported beers. Various set meal options are available, but they all involve burgers.

Quan Trang   Vietnamese $

(☑0263-382 5043; 15 Tang Bat Ho; dishes 50,000d; ⊙1.30-7pm) Love it or hate it, the local speciality *banh uot long ga* here is among the best, so you can decide for yourself. The rice noodles are saucy not soupy, the liver easy to avoid in the bowl (if you hate it) and the fresh shredded chicken, herbs and chilli lift the dish. Delicious – people certainly aren't here for the plastic decor.

Goc Ha Thanh   Vietnamese $

(☑0263-355 3369; 53 Đ Truong Cong Dinh; meals 65,000-105,000d; ⊙10am-10pm; 🛜🖋) Casual, popular, foreigner-friendly place with bamboo furnishings run by a welcoming Hanoi couple. Strong on dishes such as coconut curry, hotpots, clay pots, tofu stir-fries and noodles. Plenty of vegetarian options.

One More Cafe   Cafe $

(☑0129 934 1835; 77 Đ Hai Ba Trung; meals 85,000-110,000d; ⊙8am-9pm, closed Wed; 🛜🖋) Comfy chairs to sink into, eclectic-lined peach walls and a glass display full of cakes greet you at this cosy, Aussie-owned cafe. The menu offers up Western classics: burgers, pasta, sandwiches and salads, as well as a recommended all-day breakfast. Fine for a coffee, tea or smoothie too.

Le Chalet Dalat   Vietnamese $$

(☑0263-382 8886; 6 Huynh Thuc Khang; meals 79,000-230,000d; ⊙7am-10pm; 🛜) Strategically located almost opposite Dalat's most popular tourist sight, Hang Nga Crazy House (p178), this semi-open-air, artfully decorated bistro makes a fine lunch stop. The menu ranges across the Vietnamese classics with healthy soups and rice and noodle dishes. Good coffee and smoothies as well. There's live music Wednesday, Friday and Sunday evenings.

Restaurant Ichi   Japanese $$

(☑0263-355 5098; 1 Đ Hoang Dieu; sushi 30,000-130,000d, meals from 160,000d; ⊙5.30-10pm Tue-Sun, closed every 2nd Tue) Dalat's only truly genuine Japanese restaurant is compact, with subdued lighting and jazz in the background. Spicy tuna rolls, chicken yakitori and tempura are all fantastic, the bento boxes are a bargain and there's even *natto* (fermented soybeans) for aficionados. Perch in front of the bar (with extensive whisky offerings from around the world) to watch sushi-master Tomo at work.

Dalat Train Cafe   International $$

(☑0263-381 6365; www.dalattrainvilla.com; 1 Đ Quang Trung; mains 79,000-159,000d; ⊙8am-10pm; 🛜🖋) Calling all trainspotters! Don't miss the opportunity to step inside this lovingly resorted French-era railway carriage for a meal in a unique setting, surrounded by images of trains worldwide. The blue-cheese burger, spicy tofu and veggie lasagne are all sound choices. From Dalat Train Station, turn right, walk up the hill, look for the sign on the left.

Le Rabelais   French $$$

(☑0263-382 5444; www.royaldl.com; 12 Đ Tran Phu; meals 400,000-1,600,000d; ⊙7am-10pm) The signature restaurant at the Dalat Palace is *the* colonial-style destination with the grandest of dining rooms and a spectacular terrace that looks down to the lake shore.

Dalat Train Cafe (p181)

> *Caffeine fiends will want to head to this unique mix of a coffee shop, farm and factory...*

Set dinner menus (1,300,000-1,700,000d) offer the full monty. Otherwise, treat yourself to flawless à la carte dishes, such as seared duck breast with orange or roast rack of lamb.

🍸 DRINKING & NIGHTLIFE

Escape Bar   Live Music
(Basement, Muong Thanh Hotel, 4 Ð Phan Boi Chau; ⊙4pm-midnight; 🛜) Outstanding live-music bar, owned by blues guitarist Curtis King who performs here nightly with a rotating band (from 9.15pm). Expect covers of Hendrix, the Eagles, the Doors and other classics, but the improvisation is such that the tunes take on lives of their own; travelling musicians are welcome to jam. The bar's decor, all 1970s chic, suits the sonics perfectly.

La Viet Coffee   Coffee
(📞0263-398 1189; www.facebook.com/coffee laviet; 200 Ð Nguyen Cong Tru; ⊙7.30am-9.30pm; 🛜) Caffeine fiends will want to head to this unique mix of a coffee shop, farm and factory. Housed in a warehouse-like building with industrial design touches, and surrounded outside by coffee plants, you can either sip the excellent brews on offer at a table, or go on a tour of the facility and have the coffee production process explained to you.

100 Roofs Café   Bar
(Duong Len Trang; 📞0263-837 518; 57 Ð Phan Boi Chau; ⊙8am-midnight; 🛜) This is a surreal drinking experience. The owners claim Gandalf and his hobbit friends have drunk here, and this dim labyrinth of rooms with multiple nooks and crannies and art and sculptures that range from the cool to the kitsch does resemble a Middle Earth location. A cheap happy hour and Wonderland-like rooftop garden add to the fun.

An Cafe Cafe

(☎0975 735 521; www.ancafe.vn; 63bis Ba Thang Hai; ⊗7am-10pm; 🛜) Perched high above the street, this cafe feels like a hip treehouse. Sip good lattes, healthy juices and smoothies or artichoke tea at the wood-chic booths inside or on garden bench swings outside. If you tire of people-watching, there are crayons and paper for doodling, and an atrium filled with coffee beans for sniffing.

ℹ️ INFORMATION

Sinh Tourist (☎0263-382 2663; www.thesinhtourist.vn; 22 Ð Bui Thi Xuan; ⊗8am-7pm) Reliable tours, including city sightseeing trips, and open-tour bus bookings.

ℹ️ GETTING THERE & AROUND

There are regular flights with Vietnam Airlines, VietJet Air and Jetstar to Danang, Hanoi and HCMC.

Lien Khuong Airport is 30km south of Dalat. Vietnam Airlines offers shuttle-bus transfers or a taxi is 170,000d to 200,000d.

Dalat is a major stop for open-tour buses. Sinh Tourist has daily buses to Mui Ne, Nha Trang and HCMC.

For reliable taxis try **Mai Linh** (☎0263-352 1111; www.mailinh.vn).

 **French Hill Station**

Home to hill tribes for centuries, 'Da Lat' means 'river of the Lat tribe' in their language. The city was established in 1912 and quickly became fashionable with Europeans – at one point during the French colonial period, some 20% of Dalat's population was foreign, and grand villas remain scattered around the city.

During the American War, Dalat was spared by the tacit agreement of all parties concerned. Indeed, it seems that while South Vietnamese soldiers were being trained at the city's military academy and affluent officials of the Saigon regime were relaxing in their villas, VC cadres were doing the same thing not far away (also in villas). On 3 April 1975 Dalat fell to the North without a fight.

View overlooking Dalat
KHANG DUONG/500PX ©

Crocodile Lake (p186)

NELLA/SHUTTERSTOCK ©

Cat Tien National Park

Cat Tien comprises an amazingly biodiverse area of lowland tropical rainforest, and offers the chance to see (and hear!) one of Vietnam's rarest primates, the golden-cheeked gibbon, in the wild.

Great For...

☑ **Don't Miss**

Spotting pygmy loris in the Dao Tien Endangered Primate Species Centre (p185).

A National Treasure

The 72,000-hectare Cat Tien National Park is one of the outstanding natural reserves in Vietnam, and the hiking, mountain biking and birdwatching here are superb. However, a word of caution: visitors have to be really lucky to see any of the larger mammals like tigers and elephants.

In 2001 Unesco added Cat Tien National Park to its list of biosphere reserves. Fauna in the park includes the bison-like guar, 79 types of reptile and 41 amphibian species, plus an incredible array of insects, including 400 or so butterfly species. Of the 350-plus birds, rare species include the orange-necked partridge and Siamese fireback.

Spend at least two full days here, if possible.

❶ Need to Know

📞0251-366 9228; www.namcattien.org; adult/child 60,000/10,000d; ⏱7am-10pm ✍

✕ Take a Break

Yellow Bamboo (meals 60,000-120,000d; ⏱7am-9pm; 📶) has snacks and filling meals including hotpots.

Wild Gibbon Trek

This four-hour **trek** (www.go-east.org; per person 1,050,000d; maximum 4 people; ⏱4.30am) is perhaps the park's most popular excursion. Set off before the sun rises through the jungle to either one of two different areas that are home to gibbon families. You'll get to see and hear them in full voice as they sing their morning calls. It's a reasonably easy hike, but it's not suitable for kids under the age of 12. You'll have to spend the night before inside the park. Book ahead.

The Gibbons

Golden-cheeked gibbons are very territorial, with dominant females, and live in nuclear family groups, with the young staying with their mother for up to eight years. As with most other endangered creatures in Vietnam, they're hunted for the illegal pet trade, with parents killed and babies taken away, and also for dubious traditional medicine purposes.

The Gibbon Song

Guides string up hammocks from jungle trees at a 'listening station' so you can lounge in comfort while waiting for the melodious song of the gibbon. Once a call has been detected you'll have to hotfoot it across the jungle to find the gibbons. The gibbons only sing for around 15 minutes, but it's a magical encounter as they sing a beautiful duet across the canopy.

Dao Tien Endangered Primate Species Centre

Set on an island in the Dong Nai River, this rehabilitation **centre** (www.go-east.org; adult/child incl boat ride 300,000/150,000d; ⏱tours 8.30am & 2pm) with a stellar reputation hosts golden-cheeked gibbons, pygmy loris (both endemic to Vietnam and Cambodia), black-shanked douc and silvered langur that have been illegally trafficked. The eventual goal is to release the primates back into the forest. You can view gibbons in a semi-wild environment and hear their incredible calls.

The centre's current focus is preserving the endangered pygmy loris from extinction.

Crocodile Lake

This **lake** (Bau Sau; admission 200,000d, guide fee 550,000d, boat trip from 200,000d) is home to 200 crocs and is one of the Cat Tien National Park highlights. The lake is reachable via two different routes. The easier option involves a 9km drive or bike ride from the park headquarters and a 5km trek to the swamp; the walk takes about three hours

return. Alternatively, you can trek all the way with a guide along a tougher jungle route criss-crossed by streams. Night treks are the best option for seeing the crocodiles.

Cat Tien Bear & Wild Cat Rescue Station

Inside the Cat Tien National Park, south of the park headquarters, this rescue centre is home to a selection of sun bears and black bears, rescued from poachers and/or bear bile farms. Conditions are not ideal, though the bears space-share a large outdoor area in which they're let loose every morning. There are two tours of the facility each day, at 8.30am and 1.30pm. The centre is set to relocate a few kilometres away in the park by mid-2018.

Dong Nai River

Exploring the Park

Cat Tien National Park can be explored on foot, by mountain bike, by 4WD and also by boat along the Dong Nai River. There are 14 well-established **hiking trails** in the park, colour-coded by the level of difficulty and ranging from 2km to 26km in length. Some are flat and paved, while others are demanding, muddy slogs that require crossing streams. Only the three most difficult trails require the services of a guide, as well as transport to and from the start of the trail.

Be sure to book a guide in advance. They charge 800,000d for a day's trekking or birdwatching, regardless of group size. Take plenty of insect repellent and water. Leeches keep you company; 'leech socks' are provided by the guides. Boat trips start at 1,200,000d, plus 250,000d for a guide.

Where to Stay

The national park has **accommodation** (📞0251-366 9228; cattienvietnam@gmail.com; r 250,000-1,100,000d, camping per person 50,000d; ❄️📶) that is handy for early-morning trekking. There are also an expanding number of lodges just outside the park entrance that are considerably more comfortable; all have restaurants.

Getting There & Away

Booking a tour takes the hassle out of transport arrangements. To travel independently, all buses between Dalat and Ho Chi Minh City (every 30 minutes) pass a junction on Hwy 20 that is 24km from the park.

NELLA/SHUTTERSTOCK ©

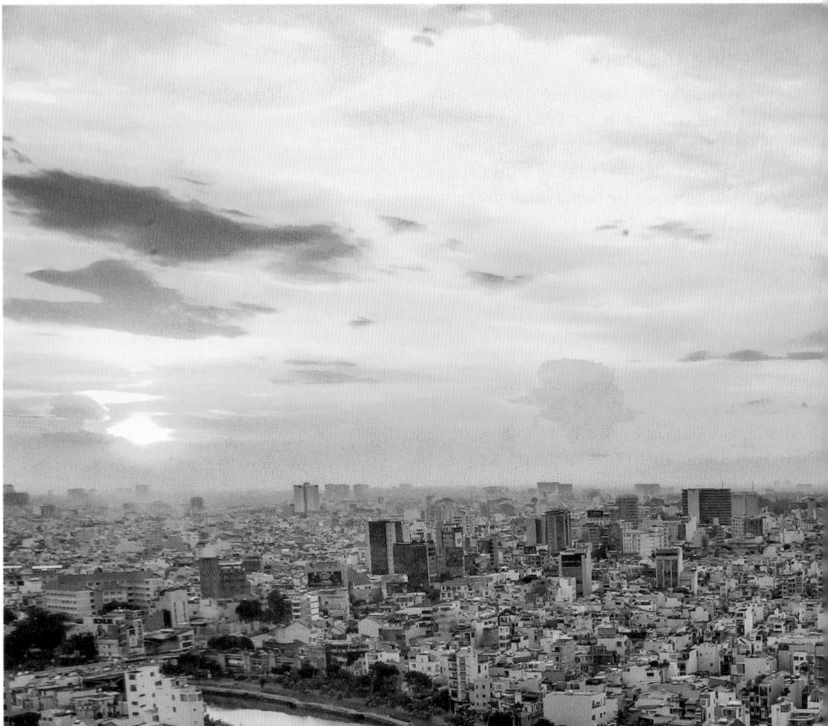

DUNG PHAM/500PX ©

HO CHI MINH CITY

Ho Chi Minh City at a Glance...

Ho Chi Minh City (HCMC) is Vietnam at its most dizzying: a high-octane city of commerce and culture that has driven the country forward with its pulsating energy. A chaotic whirl, the city breathes life and vitality into all who settle here, and visitors cannot help but be hauled along for the ride.

The ghosts of the past live on in buildings that one generation ago witnessed a city in turmoil, but now the real beauty of the former Saigon's urban collage is the seamless blending of these two worlds into one exciting mass.

A Day in Ho Chi Minh City

Check out the **War Remnants Museum** (p196) and then tour the **Reunification Palace** (p198). Lunch at **Quan Bui** (p219) then explore the buzzing area around **Ben Thanh market** (p215). Catch sky-high sunset views from **Air 360** (p225), followed by a meal at **Cuc Gach Quan** (p221) and perhaps a nightcap in **Layla** (p224).

Two Days in Ho Chi Minh City

Spend the morning in **Cholon** (p202), wandering around the market and historic temples. Catch a taxi up to District 3 for a cheap traditional lunch at **Banh Xeo 46A** (p220), then walk through Da Kao ward to the **Jade Emperor Pagoda** (p206) and **History Museum** (p201). In the evening sample a craft beer or two in **Heart of Darkness** (p223) and dine at **Hum Lounge & Restaurant** (p218).

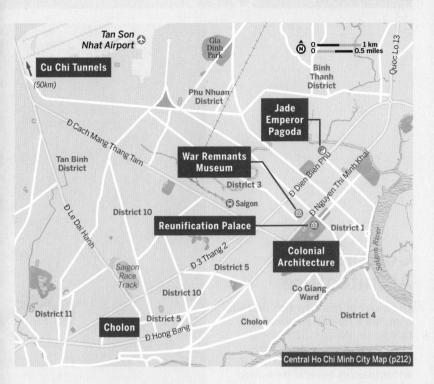

Tan Son Nhat Airport

Cu Chi Tunnels
(50km)

Gia Dinh Park

Binh Thanh District

Quoc Lo 13

0 ——— 1 km
0 ——— 0.5 miles

Đ Cach Mang Thang Tam

Phu Nhuan District

Jade Emperor Pagoda

Tan Binh District

War Remnants Museum

District 3

Đ Dien Bien Phu

Đ Nguyen Thi Minh Khai

Saigon

Đ Le Dai Hanh

District 10

Reunification Palace

District 1

Saigon River

Saigon Race Track

Đ 3 Thang 2

District 5

Colonial Architecture

Co Giang Ward

District 11

District 10

Cholon

District 5

Đ Hong Bang

Cholon

District 4

Central Ho Chi Minh City Map (p212)

Arriving in Ho Chi Minh City

Air Ho Chi Minh City's Tan Son Nhat Airport is 7km north of the central district. Taxis to central districts (around 190,000d) take about 30 minutes. There are also three air-conditioned buses: Route 152, 109 and 49 to the centre.

Train Saigon station is just west of the centre. A taxi to the central district is around 50,000d.

Where to Stay

Within District 1, the Dong Khoi area has smart hotels close to the city's best restaurants and bars, while Pham Ngu Lao scores for budget accommodation and cheap shopping. Around Ben Thanh Market has decent midrange options. See p227 for more information.

Notre Dame Cathedral (p194)

Colonial Architecture

The heart of the city, this historic area has a terrific ensemble of colonial buildings. Stretching from the august Notre Dame Cathedral to the Saigon river it encompasses several tree-lined boulevards.

Great For...

Ð Dien Bien Phu

🚉 Saigon

Notre Dam Cathedral 🔵🏛️

Central Post Office

Opera House 🔴

People's Committee Building 🔴🔴
HCMC Museum 🏛️

Saigon River

Bitexco 🔵
Financial Tower

☑ Don't Miss

A performance of ballet or opera at the Opera House (p195).

ⓘ Need to Know

Cruises of the Saigon River are wildly popular.

Notre Dame Cathedral

Built between 1877 and 1883, **Notre Dame Cathedral** (Đ Han Thuyen) enlivens the heart of Ho Chi Minh City's government quarter, facing Đ Dong Khoi. A brick, neo-Romanesque church with 40m-high square towers tipped with iron spires, the Catholic cathedral is named after the Virgin Mary. Interior walls are inlaid with devotional tablets and some stained glass survives. English-speaking staff dispense tourist information from 9am to 11am Monday to Saturday. If the front gates are locked, try the door on the side facing the Reunification Palace.

Central Post Office

Right across the way from Notre Dame Cathedral, Ho Chi Minh City's striking French

post office (2 Cong Xa Paris; ⊘7am-7pm Mon-Fri, to 6pm Sat, 8am-6pm Sun) is a period classic, designed by Marie-Alfred Foulhoux (though often credited to Gustave Eiffel) and built between 1886 and 1891. Painted on the walls of its grand concourse are fascinating historic maps of South Vietnam, Saigon and Cholon, while a mosaic of Ho Chi Minh takes pride of place at the end of its barrel-vaulted hall. Note the magnificent tiled floor of the interior and the copious green-painted wrought iron.

People's Committee Building

Ho Chi Minh City's glorious **People's Committee Building** (Hôtel de Ville; ĐL Nguyen Hue), one of the city's most prominent landmarks, is home to the Ho Chi Minh City People's Committee. Built between 1901 and 1908, the former Hôtel de Ville deco-

Municipal Theatre (Opera House)

rates the northwestern end of ĐL Nguyen Hue, but unfortunately the ornate interior is not open to the public. In 2015 the centre of ĐL Nguyen Hue was turned into a vibrant pedestrian-only mall bookended by a new statue of Ho Chi Minh to commemorate his 125th birthday.

HCMC Museum

A grand, neoclassical structure built in 1885 and once known as Gia Long Palace (and later the Revolutionary Museum), HCMC's **city museum** (Bao Tang Thanh Pho Ho Chi Minh; www.hcmc-museum.edu.vn; 65 Đ Ly Tu Trong; 30,000d; ⊗8am-5pm) is a singularly

> ✕ **Take a Break**
>
> Sample authentic street-food dishes in a garden setting at Nha Hang Ngon (p218).

LONG BAO/SHUTTERSTOCK ©

beautiful and impressive building, telling the story of the city through archaeological artefacts, ceramics, old city maps and displays on the marriage traditions of its various ethnicities. The struggle for independence is extensively covered, with most of the upper floor devoted to it.

Opera House

Gracing the intersection of Đ Dong Khoi and ĐL Le Loi, this grand colonial edifice with a sweeping staircase was built in 1897 and is one of the city's most recognisable buildings. Officially known as the Municipal Theatre, the **Opera House** (Nha Hat Thanh Pho; ☑028-3823 7419; www.hbso.org. vn; Lam Son Sq) captures the flamboyance of France's belle époque. Performances range from ballet and opera to modern dance and musicals. Check the website for English-language listings and booking information.

A popular event is the AO Show (p216), a one-hour performance combining music, dance and acrobatics.

What's Nearby?

Bitexco Financial Tower (www.ticketbox. vn/saigon-skydeck/en; 2 Đ Hai Trieu; adult/child 200,000/130,000d; ⊗9.30am-9.30pm), the 68-storey, 262m-high, Carlos Zapata–designed skyscraper, dwarfs all around it. It's reportedly shaped like a lotus bulb, but also resembles a CD rack with a tambourine shoved into it. That tambourine is the 48th-floor **Saigon Skydeck**, with a helipad on its roof. Choose a clear day and aim for sunset – or down a drink in the EON Heli Bar instead.

> ★ **Top Tip**
>
> Escape the infernal Saigon traffic on the central pedestrianised section of ĐL Nguyen Hue.

War Remnants Museum

Few museums anywhere convey the brutal effects of war on its civilian victims so powerfully. Formerly the Museum of Chinese and American War Crimes, this is an essential visit.

Many of the atrocities documented here were well-publicised, but rarely do Westerners hear the victims of US military action tell their own stories. While some displays are one-sided, many of the most disturbing photographs illustrating US atrocities are from US sources, including those of the infamous My Lai Massacre.

The War Remnants Museum is in the former US Information Service building.

Ground Floor

This floor of the museum is devoted to a collection of posters and photographs showing support for the antiwar movement internationally. This somewhat upbeat display provides a counterbalance to the horrors upstairs.

Great For...

☑ Don't Miss

The Requiem Exhibition featuring photographs by war photographer Tim Page.

ⓘ Need to Know

Bao Tang Chung Tich Chien Tranh; ☎028-3930 5587; http://warremnantsmuseum.com; 28 Đ Vo Van Tan, cnr Đ Le Quy Don; 40,000d; ⏱7.30am-noon & 1.30-5pm

✗ Take a Break

Hum Vegetarian Cafe & Restaurant (p220) is almost next door to the museum.

★ Top Tip

The museum opens at 7.30am; get here early to beat the crowds.

Casualties of War

Even those who supported the war are likely to be horrified by the photos of children affected by US bombing and napalming. You'll also have the rare chance to see some of the experimental weapons used in the war, which were at one time military secrets, such as the flechette, an artillery shell filled with thousands of tiny darts.

Requiem Exhibition

Located upstairs, this photographic collection has been curated by legendary war photographer Tim Page. It documents the work of photographers killed during the course of the conflict, on both sides, and includes works by Larry Burrows and Robert Capa.

Museum's Grounds

US armoured vehicles, artillery pieces, bombs and infantry weapons are on display outside. One corner of the grounds is devoted to the notorious French and South Vietnamese prisons on Phu Quoc and Con Son Islands. Artefacts include that most iconic of French appliances, the guillotine, and the notoriously inhumane 'tiger cages' used to house war prisoners.

What's Nearby?

One of the city's most attractive green spaces is 10-hectare **Tao Dan Park** (Đ Nguyen Thi Minh Khai), its bench-lined walks shaded with avenues of towering tropical trees, including flame trees and vast Sao Den and So Khi trees. It's fascinating to visit in the early morning and late afternoon when thousands of locals exercise. Also noteworthy is the daily flocking here of the city's bird lovers (mainly elderly gentlemen), who arrive, cages in hand, at what is universally known as the bird cafe.

Reunification Palace

Surrounded by Royal Palm trees, the dissonant 1960s architecture of this government building and its historic significance make it an essential sight.

Great For...

Need to Know

Dinh Thong Nhat; ☏028-3829 4117; www.dinhdoclap.gov.vn; Đ Nam Ky Khoi Nghia; adult/child 40,000/20,000đ; ☺7.30-11am & 1-4pm

☑ **Don't Miss**

The basement is fascinating, with its telecommunications centre, war room and warren of tunnels.

Wartime Role

The first Communist tanks to arrive in Saigon rumbled here on 30 April 1975 and it's as if time has stood still since then. The building is deeply associated with the fall of the city in 1975, yet it's the kitsch detailing and period motifs that steal the show.

After crashing through the wrought-iron gates – in a dramatic scene recorded by photojournalists and shown around the world – a soldier ran into the building and up the stairs to unfurl a VC flag from the balcony. In an ornate reception chamber, General Minh, who had become head of the South Vietnamese state only 43 hours before, waited with his improvised cabinet. 'I have been waiting since early this morning to transfer power to you', Minh said to the VC officer who entered the room. 'There is no question of your transferring power', replied the officer. 'You cannot give up what you do not have.'

Historical Background

In 1868 a residence was built on this site for the French governor-general of Cochinchina and gradually it expanded to become Norodom Palace. When the French departed, the palace became home to the South Vietnamese president Ngo Dinh Diem. So unpopular was Diem that his own air force bombed the palace in 1962 in an unsuccessful attempt to kill him. The president ordered a new residence to be built on the same site, this time with a sizeable bomb shelter in the basement. Work was completed in 1966, but Diem did not get to see his dream house as he was killed by his own troops in 1963.

Independence Palace

Independence Palace

The new building was named Independence Palace and was home to the successive South Vietnamese president, Nguyen Van Thieu, until his hasty departure in 1975. Designed by Paris-trained Vietnamese architect Ngo Viet Thu, it is an outstanding example of 1960s architecture, with an airy and open atmosphere.

Visiting the Palace

The ground floor is arranged with meeting rooms, while upstairs is a grand set of reception rooms, used for welcoming foreign and national dignitaries. In the back

> ★ **Top Tip**
>
> English- and French-speaking guides are on duty during opening hours.

ERIC VALENNE GEOSTORY/SHUTTERSTOCK ©

of the structure are the president's living quarters; check out the model boats, horse tails and severed elephants' feet. The 2nd floor contributes a shagadelic card-playing room, complete with a cheesy round leather banquette, a barrel-shaped bar, hubcap light fixtures and groovy three-legged chairs set around a flared-legged card table. There's also a cinema and a rooftop nightclub, complete with helipad: James Bond/Austin Powers – eat your heart out.

Perhaps most fascinating of all is the basement with its telecommunications centre, war room and warren of tunnels, where hulking old fans chop the air and ancient radio transmitters sit impassively. Towards the end are rooms where videos appraise the palace and its history in Vietnamese, English, French, Chinese and Japanese. The national anthem is played at the end of the tape and you are expected to stand up – it would be rude not to.

What's Nearby?

Built in 1929 by the Société des Études Indochinoises, the notable Sino-French **History Museum** (Bao Tang Lich Su; Đ Nguyen Binh Khiem; 15,000d; ☉8-11.30am & 1.30-5pm Tue-Sun) houses a rewarding collection of artefacts illustrating the evolution of the cultures of Vietnam, from the Bronze Age Dong Son civilisation (which emerged in 2000 BC) and the Funan civilisation (1st to 6th centuries AD), to the Cham, Khmer and Vietnamese. The museum is just inside the main gate to the city's botanic gardens and zoo.

> ✕ **Take a Break**
>
> Sky bar **Shri** (☎08-3827 9631; http://shri. vn; 23rd fl, Centec Tower, 72-74 Đ Nguyen Thi Minh Khai; ☉10.30am-midnight Mon-Sat, 4.30pm-midnight Sun) offers sublime vistas and fine cocktails.

Thien Hau Pagoda (p205)

Cholon

Rummage through Cholon (District 5) and lift the lid on a treasure trove of historic temples, impressive pagodas, a fine market and Chinese flavours.

Great For...

☑ **Don't Miss**

Cha Tam Church's interior is decorated with images of the stations of the cross, while holy water is dispensed from huge clam shells.

ⓘ Need to Know

A taxi from Pham Ngu Lao to Cholon costs around 110,000d or hop on bus 1 from Ben Thanh Market.

Background

Ho Chi Minh City's Chinatown is less Chinese than it once was, largely due to the 1978–79 anticapitalist and anti-Chinese campaign, when many ethnic Chinese fled the country, taking with them their money and entrepreneurial skills. A lot of those refugees have since returned (with foreign passports) to explore investment possibilities. Full-form written Chinese characters (as opposed to the simplified system used in mainland China) decorate shopfronts and temples in abundance, adding to the sensation that you have strayed into a forgotten corner of China.

Cholon means 'big market' and during the American War it was home to a thriving black market. Some traditional architecture survives and an atmospheric strip of traditional herb shops thrives between Đ Luong Nhu Hoc and Đ Trieu Quang Phuc, providing both a visual and an olfactory reminder of the old Chinese city.

Binh Tay Market

v(Cho Binh Tay; www.chobinhtay.gov.vn; 57a ĐL Thap Muoi; ☺6am-7.30pm) has a great clock tower and a central courtyard with gardens. Much of the business here is wholesale but it's popular with tour groups. The market was originally built by the French in the 1880s; Guangdong-born philanthropist Quach Dam paid for its rebuilding and was commemorated by a statue that is now in the Fine Arts Museum.

Phuoc An Hoi Quan Pagoda

Delightfully fronted by greenery and opening to an interior blaze of red, gold, green and yellow, this is one of the most beautiful-

Bin Tay Market

ly ornamented temples in town, dating from 1902. Of special interest are the elaborate brass ritual ornaments and weapons, and the fine woodcarvings on the altars, walls, columns, hanging lanterns and incense coils. From the exterior, look out for the ceramic scenes, each containing innumerable small figurines, that decorate the roof.

Thien Hau Pagoda

This gorgeous 19th-century **temple** (Ba Mieu, Pho Mieu, Chua Ba Thien Hau; 710 Ð Nguyen Trai) `FREE` is dedicated to the goddess Thien Hau, and always attracts a mix of worshippers and visitors who mingle beneath the large coils of incense suspended overhead.

> ✕ **Take a Break**
> Binh Tay Market has some terrific food stalls.

RICHIE CHAN/SHUTTERSTOCK ©

It is believed that Thien Hau can travel over the oceans on a mat and ride the clouds to save people in trouble on the high seas.

Khanh Van Nam Vien Pagoda

Built between 1939 and 1942, this **temple** (269/2 Ð Nguyen Thi Nho) is said to be the only pure Taoist temple in Vietnam and is unique for its colourful statues of Taoist disciples. Features to seek out include the unique 150cm-high statue of Laotse – the supreme philosopher of Taoism and author of the *Dao De Jing* (The Classic of the Way and its Power) – located upstairs.

Quan Am Pagoda

One of Cholon's most active and colourful temples, this **shrine** (Chua Quan Am; 12 Ð Lao Tu) `FREE` was founded in the early 19th century. It's named after the Goddess of Mercy, whose full name is Quan The Am Bo Tat, literally 'the Bodhisattva who listens to the cries of the world' (觀世音菩薩 in Chinese characters), in reflection of her compassionate mission.

Phung Son Pagoda

Built between 1802 and 1820 on the site of structures from the Funan period, dating back at least to the early centuries of Christianity, this **Buddhist temple** (Phung Son Tu, Chua Go; 1408 ÐL 3 Thang 2, District 11; ☺prayers 4-5am, 4-5pm & 6-7pm) is extremely rich in gilded, painted and beautifully fashioned bronze, wood, ceramic and beaten copper statuary. The **main dais**, with its many levels, is dominated by a large gilded A Di Da Buddha (the Buddha of Infinite Light; Amitābha). The main entrances are usually locked most of the time, but the side entrance is open during prayer times.

> ★ **Top Tip**
> For in-depth tours of Cholon, contact local expert **Tim Doling** (www.historic vietnam.com).

PHƯƠNG D. NGUYEN/SHUTTERSTOCK ©

Jade Emperor Pagoda

Built in 1909 to honour the supreme Taoist god, this is one of the most spectacularly atmospheric temples in the city, stuffed with statues of phantasmal divinities and grotesque heroes.

Great For...

☑ **Don't Miss**

A small pond in the compound seethes with turtles, some of which have shells inscribed with auspicious inscriptions.

Main Temple Structure

Inside the main building are two especially fierce and menacing Taoist figures. On the right (as you face the altar) is a 4m-high statue of the general who defeated the Green Dragon (depicted underfoot). On the left is the general who defeated the White Tiger, which is also being stepped on.

Worshippers mass before the ineffable Jade Emperor, who presides – draped in luxurious robes and shrouded in a dense fug of incense smoke – over the main sanctuary. He is flanked by his guardians, the Four Big Diamonds (Tu Dai Kim Cuong), so named because they are said to be as hard as diamonds.

The Chief of Hell

Off the Jade Emperor's chamber is another room presided over by Thanh Hoang, the

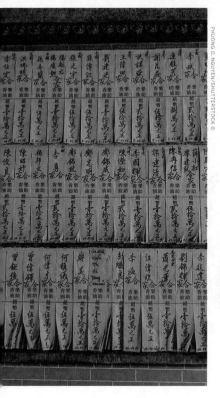

PHUONG D. NGUYEN/SHUTTERSTOCK ©

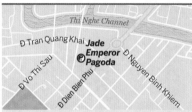

Thi Nghe Channel

Đ Tran Quang Khai **Jade Emperor Pagoda**

Đ Vo Thi Sau

Đ Nguyen Binh Khiem

Đ Dien Bien Phu

ℹ️ Need to Know

Phuoc Hai Tu, Chua Ngoc Hoang; 73 Đ Mai Thi Luu; ⏱7am-6pm daily, plus 5am-7pm 1st & 15th of lunar month FREE

✖ Take a Break

Fine dine in a historic home at Cuc Gach Quan (p221).

★ Top Tip

The temple's statues, depicting characters from Buddhist and Taoist lore are made from papier mâché.

Chief of Hell; to the left is his red horse. Other figures here represent the gods who dispense punishments for evil acts and rewards for good deeds. The room also contains the famous Hall of the Ten Hells, carved wooden panels illustrating the varied torments awaiting evil people in each of the Ten Regions of Hell. Women queue up at the seated effigy of the City God, who wears a hat inscribed with Chinese characters that announce 'At one glance, money is given'. In a mesmerising ritual, worshippers first put money into a box, then rub a piece of red paper against his hand before circling it around a candle flame.

Women's Chamber

This fascinating little room has the ceramic figures of 12 women, overrun with children and wearing colourful clothes, sitting in two rows of six. Each of the women exemplifies a human characteristic, either good or bad (as in the case of the woman drinking alcohol from a jug). Each figure represents a year in the 12-year Chinese astrological calendar. Presiding over the room is Kim Hoa Thanh Mau, the Chief of All Women. Upstairs is a hall to Quan Am, the Goddess of Mercy, opposite a portrait of Dat Ma, the bearded Indian founder of Zen Buddhism.

Day Trip: Cu Chi Tunnels

This tunnel network became legendary for its role in facilitating VC control of a large rural area during the American War. Cu Chi is justifiably the most popular day trip from HCMC.

Great For...

☑ Don't Miss

A M-41 tank and a bomb crater are near the exit of the Ben Dinh tunnels.

Extent

At its peak the tunnel system stretched from the South Vietnamese capital to the Cambodian border; in the district of Cu Chi alone more than 250km of tunnels honeycomb the ground. The network, parts of which were several storeys deep, included countless trapdoors, constructed living areas, storage facilities, weapon factories, field hospitals, command centres and kitchens.

History

The tunnels of Cu Chi were built over a period of 25 years, beginning sometime in the late 1940s. They were the improvised response of a poorly equipped peasant army to its enemy's high-tech ordnance, helicopters, artillery, bombers and chemical weapons.

Booby trap

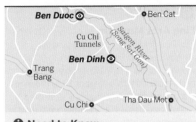

ARABEL WINGS SS/SHUTTERSTOCK ©

❶ Need to Know

adult/child 110,000/30,000d

✕ Take a Break

Snack vendors can be found around the tunnels.

★ Top Tip

Travelling here on a tour is by far the most convenient way to get to Cu Chi.

The Viet Minh built the first tunnels in the red earth of Cu Chi during the war against the French. The tunnel system later assumed enormous strategic importance when the area came under VC control.

Cu Chi Tunnels

Two sections of this remarkable tunnel network (which are enlarged and upgraded versions of the real thing) are open to the public. One is near the village of Ben Dinh and the other is 15km beyond at Ben Duoc. Most tourists visiting the tunnels end up at Ben Dinh, as it's easier for tour buses to reach. Even if you stay above ground, it's still an interesting experience learning about the region's ingenious and brave resistance activities.

Ben Dinh

The most visited of the tunnel sites, this small, renovated section is near the village of Ben Dinh, about 50km from HCMC. In one of the classrooms at the visitors centre a large map shows the extent of the network while another shows cross-section diagrams of the tunnels. The section of the tunnel system presently open to visitors is a few hundred metres south of the visitors centre. It snakes up and down through various chambers along its 50m length.

Ben Duoc

The tunnels here have been enlarged to accommodate tourists, although they're still a tight squeeze. Inside the underground chambers are bunkers, a hospital and a command centre that played a role in the 1968 Tet Offensive. The set pieces include tables, chairs, beds, lights, and dummies outfitted in guerrilla gear.

◉ SIGHTS

Fine Arts Museum Gallery

(Bao Tang My Thuat; www.baotangmythu-attphcm.com; 97a Ð Pho Duc Chinh; 10,000d; ⏱9am-5pm Tue-Sun) With its airy corridors and verandahs, this elegant 1929 colonial-era yellow-and-white building is stuffed with period details; it is exuberantly tiled throughout and home to some fine (albeit deteriorated) stained glass, as well as one of Saigon's oldest lifts. Hung from the walls is an impressive selection of art, including thoughtful pieces from the modern period. As well as contemporary art, much of it (unsurprisingly) inspired by war, the museum displays historical pieces dating back to the 4th century.

Ho Chi Minh Museum Museum

(Bao Tang Ho Chi Minh; 1 Ð Nguyen Tat Thanh, District 4; 10,000d; ⏱7.30-11.30am & 1.30-5pm Tue-Sun) Nicknamed the 'Dragon House' (Nha Rong), this former customs house was built by the French authorities in 1863. The museum houses many of Ho Chi Minh's personal effects, including some of his clothing, his sandals and spectacles.

On the waterfront, just across Ben Nghe Channel from District 1, the museum is easily reached on foot by heading south along the river on Ð Ton Duc Thang and crossing the bridge.

Mariamman Hindu Temple Hindu Temple

(Chua Ba Mariamman; 45 Ð Truong Dinh; ⏱7.30am-7.30pm) Only a small number of Hindus live in HCMC, but this colourful slice of southern India is also considered sacred by many ethnic Vietnamese and Chinese. Reputed to have miraculous powers, the temple was built at the end of the 19th century and dedicated to the Hindu goddess Mariamman.

Saigon Central Mosque Mosque

(66 Ð Dong Du) Built by South Indian Muslims in 1935 on the site of an earlier mosque, lime-green Saigon Central Mosque is an immaculately clean and well-tended island of calm in the bustling Dong Khoi area. In front of the sparkling white and blue structure, with its four decorative minarets, is a pool for the ritual ablutions required by Islamic law before prayers.

From left: Fine Arts Museum; Mariamman Temple; Saigon Central Mosque

⊕ ACTIVITIES

Les Rives   Boating
(☑0128 592 0018; www.lesrivesexperience.
com; Bach Dang jetty; sunset cruise adult/child
1,399,000/980,000d, Mekong Delta cruise
2,499,000/1,799,000d) Runs sunset boat tours
at 4pm along canals beyond the city edges,
and a Mekong Delta cruise, which departs at
7.30am and takes seven to nine hours.

Indochina Junk   Boating
(☑028-3895 7438; www.indochinajunk.com.
vn; 159/21 Đ Bach Dang) A lunch and dinner
cruise with set menus (US$15 to US$35) in
an atmospheric wooden junk on the Saigon
River, departing from the Vuon Kieng pier.
There has been discussion the departure
point may change to near the Ho Chi Minh
Museum across the river in District 4, so
check when you make your booking.

L'Apothiquaire   Spa
(La Maison de L'Apothiquaire; ☑028-3932 5181;
www.lapothiquaire.com; 64a Đ Truong Dinh, District
3; ⊗9am-9pm) Long considered the city's
most elegant spa, L'Apothiquaire is housed
in a beautiful white mansion tucked down
a quiet alley, with a pool and sauna. Guests
enjoy body wraps, massages, facials, foot
treatments and herbal baths, and L'Apothiquaire makes its own line of cosmetics.

Aveda   Spa
(☑028-3519 4679; www.facebook.com/ave-
daherbal; Villa 21, 1 Đ Xuan Thuy; ⊗9am-8pm)
Across in District 2, but worth the journey
for its intensely soothing Indian-influenced
Ayurvedic spa and massage treatments.

⊕ COURSES

Grain Cooking Classes   Cooking
(☑028-3827 4929; www.grainbyluke.com; Level
3, 71-75 ĐL Hai Ba Trung; per person from US$48;
⊗9am-noon & 2-5pm Mon-Sat) These cooking
classes are designed and coordinated
by Vietnamese-Australian celebrity chef
Luke Nguyen. Four-course menus change
regularly to reflect seasonal produce, and
Luke himself is on hand for some classes
throughout the year. See website for dates.

Central Ho Chi Minh City

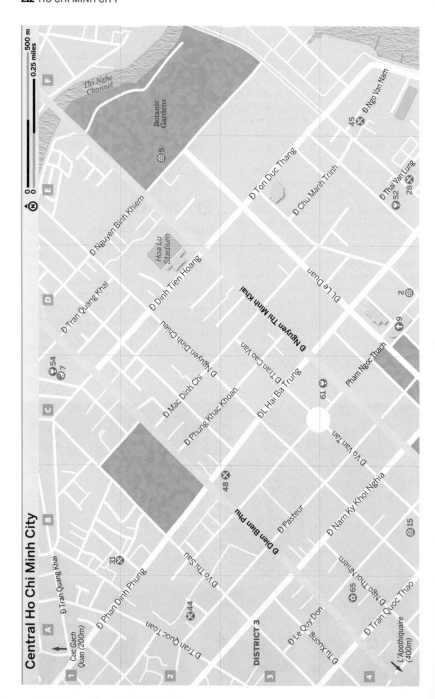

Cuc Gach Quan (200m)

Đ Tran Quang Khai

Đ Phan Dinh Phung

Đ Tran Quoc Toan

Đ Vo Thi Sau

Đ Dien Bien Phu

Đ Pasteur

Đ Nam Ky Khoi Nghia

DISTRICT 3

Đ Le Quy Don

Đ Tu Xuong

Đ Ngo Thoi Nhiem

Đ Tran Quoc Thao

L'Apothiquaire (400m)

Đ Tran Quang Khai

Đ Nguyen Binh Khiem

Hoa Lu Stadium

Đ Dinh Tien Hoang

Đ Nguyen Dinh Chieu

Đ Mac Dinh Chi

Đ Phung Khac Khoan

Đ Nguyen Thi Minh Khai

Đ Tran Cao Van

ĐL Hai Ba Trung

Đ Vo Van Tan

Thi Nghe Channel

Botanic Gardens

Đ Ton Duc Thang

Đ Chu Manh Trinh

Đ Thai Van Lung

Đ Ngo Van Nam

ĐL Le Duan

Pham Ngoc Thach

500 m

0.25 miles

Thi Nghe Channel

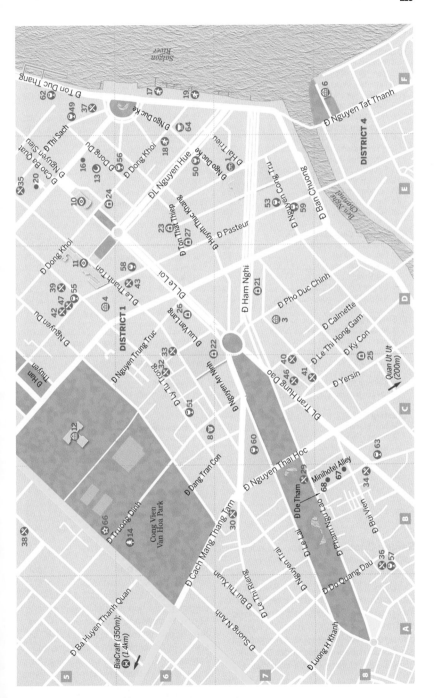

Central Ho Chi Minh City

Saigon Cooking Class   Cooking

(☏028-3825 8485; www.saigoncookingclass.
com; 74/7 ĐL Hai Ba Trung; adult/child under 12yr
US$39/25; ⊘10am & 2pm Tue-Sun) Watch and
learn from the chefs at Hoa Tuc restaurant as
they prepare three mains (including *pho bo* –
beef noodle soup – and some of their signature dishes) and one dessert. A market visit
is optional (per adult/child under 12 years
US$45/28, including a three-hour class).

TOURS

Sophie's Art Tour   Tour

(☏0933 752 402; www.sophiesarttour.com;
per person US$65; ⊘9am-1pm Tue-Sat) Highly
engaging four-hour tours from art experts
Sophie Hughes and Stu Palmer who have
their fingers on the pulse of the HCMC art
scene. Tours visit private collections and
contemporary art spaces, explaining the
influence of Vietnamese history on artistic

style and technique. Especially poignant is learning about 'combat art' crafted in the heat of battle during the Vietnam War.

Vespa Adventures   Tours

(📞0122 299 3585; www.vespaadventures. com; 169a Đ De Tham; per person from US$73) Zooming out of **Café Zoom** (www.facebook. com/cafezoomsaigon; 169a Đ De Tham; meals 65,000-150,000d; ⊙7am-2am), Vespa Adventures offers entertaining, guided city tours on vintage scooters, as well as multiday trips around southern Vietnam. Embracing food, drink and music, the Saigon After Dark tour is brilliant fun, and the new Saigon Craft Beer Tour is essential for travelling hopheads.

Saigon 2CV Tour   Driving

(📞090 978 9884; www.saigon2cvtour.com; adult/child from 1,200,000/900,000d) Explore the city in vintage open-topped Citroën vehicles. Options include an evening street food tour and a morning tour taking in HCMC's highlights.

Vietnam Photo Adventures   Tours

(📞0913 236 876; www.vietnamphotoadventures. com; per person from US$69) Get creative with your camera and produce your own photographic memories on various tours focusing on Saigon landmarks, the street life of Cholon and local neighbourhoods. Tours are conducted by an experienced photographer who is also a long-term resident of Vietnam. Longer one- and two-night trips in the Mekong Delta are also available. Check the website for occasional one-week and two-week photographic explorations of more remote areas of the country.

🛍 SHOPPING

All the following stores and markets are centrally located in the Dong Khoi area.

Antique Street Saigon   Antiques

(📞0168 481 0093; www.facebook.com/antique streetsaigon; 38 Đ Le Cong Kieu; ⊙10am-5pm Mon-Sat) The best of the arts and antiques stores along Đ Le Cong Kieu near the Fine

Arts Museum. This shop overflows with interesting discoveries and is owned by the family of the gracious Nguyen Thi Hien, one of HCMC's most respected artists. Covering many different styles and techniques, much of the artwork on display is painted by her.

Ben Thanh Market   Market

(Cho Ben Thanh; ĐL Le Loi, ĐL Ham Nghi, ĐL Tran Hung Dao & Đ Le Lai; ⊙5am-6pm) Centrally located, Ben Thanh and its surrounding streets comprise one of HCMC's liveliest areas. Everything that's commonly eaten, worn or used by the Saigonese is piled high, and souvenir items can be found in equal abundance. Vendors are determined and prices usually higher than elsewhere, so bargain vigorously and ignore any 'Fixed Price' signs.

Couleurs d'Asie – Saigon   Photography

(📞028-6889 4376; www.facebook.com/ Couleurs.dAsie.Saigon; 1st fl, 151/7 Đ Dong Khoi; ⊙8.30am-9.30pm) This recently opened gallery showcases the work of successful Hoi An–based photographer Réhahn. Especially strong are his images of Vietnam's hill tribes and minority people, and books, prints and other affordable examples of his work are all available.

Mekong Plus   Arts & Crafts

(📞028-2210 3110; https://mekong-plus.com; 1st fl, 68 ĐL Le Loi; ⊙9am-7pm) ✔ Beautiful handmade silk quilts, sewn by rural people in support of a sustainable income. It's recently had a name change to reflect other hand-crafted items it also sells – everything from bags and scarves through to very cool bamboo bikes.

Chung Cu 42 Ton That Thiep   Clothing

(42 Đ Ton That Thiep; ⊙most shops 9am-9pm) Come for the apartment building partially converted into cool boutique shops, and linger for the young, social-media-savvy fashion labels that produce stylish (but affordable) clothing. There is a sense that HCMC's hipster boom starts here. Head upstairs, and also through to the back to the second building.

Dan Sinh Market

Saigon Kitsch
Gifts & Souvenirs

(33 Đ Ton That Thiep; ⊙9am-10pm) This colourful French-run shop specialises in reproduction propaganda items, emblazoning its revolutionary motifs on coffee mugs, coasters, jigsaws and T-shirts. Also cool laptop and tablet covers fashioned from recycled Vietnamese packaging.

Dan Sinh Market
Market

(104 Đ Yersin; ⊙7am-6pm) Also known as the War Surplus Market, head here for authentic combat boots or rusty (and perhaps less authentic) dog tags among the overflowing hardware stalls. There are also rain jackets, mosquito nets, canteens, duffel bags, ponchos and boots. Check out Steven's Shop for quirky one-off and vintage discoveries. He regularly showcases the most interesting items on his Facebook page.

❂ ENTERTAINMENT

Acoustic
Live Music

(☑028-3930 2239; www.facebook.com/acousticbarpage; 6e1 Đ Ngo Thoi Nhiem; ⊙7pm-midnight; ☏) Don't be misled by

the name: most of the musicians are fully plugged in and dangerous when they take to the intimate stage of the city's leading live-music venue. And judging by the numbers that pack in, the local crowd just can't get enough. It's at the end of the alley by the upended VW Beetle; the cocktails are deceptively strong.

Observatory
Live Music

(www.facebook.com/theobservatoryhcmc; ⊙6pm-6am Wed-Sun) Following the redevelopment of its venue in late 2017, this excellent entertainment cooperative pops up at different locations around town. Check the Facebook page for where to see everything from live bands to DJs from around the globe.

AO Show
Live Performance

(www.luneproduction.com; Opera House, Lam Son Sq; from 565,000d; ⊙6pm or 8pm most days) Popular tourist-oriented showcases of Vietnamese music, dance and flying acrobats. Most hotels can book tickets and there is a box office at the Opera House.

NALIDSA/SHUTTERSTOCK ©

Golden Dragon Water Puppet Theatre
Puppetry

(📞028-3930 2196; 55b Đ Nguyen Thi Minh Khai; ticket US$7.50) Saigon's main water-puppet venue, with shows starting at 5pm, 6.30pm and 7.45pm and lasting about 50 minutes.

EATING

Ho Chi Minh City is Vietnam's culinary capital. Delicious regional fare is complemented by a well-developed choice of international restaurants, with Indian, Japanese, Thai, Italian and Asian–European fusions well represented. Unsurprisingly, given its heritage, HCMC has a fine selection of French restaurants, from the casual bistro to haute cuisine.

🍜 Dong Khoi Area

Maison Saigon Marou
Cafe $

(📞028-8730 5010; www.maisonmarou.com; 167-169 Đ Calmette; drinks & snacks from 90,000d; 🕘9am-10pm Sun-Thu, to 11pm Fri & Sat; 🛜) 🌿 This stylish and colourful cafe is home base for Marou, Vietnam's first artisan chocolate producer. Watch Marou's skilled team tempering and moulding chocolate crafted from local fair-trade cacao, and enjoy drinks and snacks also incorporating the stellar ingredients. Try the iced chocolate with cinnamon and chilli, and purchase Marou's excellent chocolate as gifts for the lucky folks back home.

Bep Me In
Vietnamese $

(📞028-6866 6128; www.facebook.com/bep mein; 136/9 Đ Le Thanh Ton; mains 55,000-115,000d; 🕘11am-11pm; 🍴) Rustic flavours from rural Vietnam come to the city at this raffish Saigon eatery concealed down an alley near Ben Thanh Market. Big shared tables welcome a mix of locals, expats and travellers, and the quirky decor includes colourful wall paintings and a vintage motorcycle rickshaw doubling as a drinks station. The upstairs dining room is more quiet and refined.

📖 HCMC History

Saigon was originally part of the kingdom of Cambodia and, until the late 17th century, was a small port town known as Prey Nokor. As Vietnamese settlers moved south it was absorbed by Vietnam and became the base for the Nguyen Lords, who were the rulers of southern Vietnam from the 16th to the 18th centuries.

During the Tay Son rebellion in the 18th century, a group of Chinese refugees established a settlement nearby, which became known by their Vietnamese neighbours as Cholon (Big Market). After seeing off the rebels, Nguyen Anh constructed a large citadel here (roughly where the American and French embassies now stand).

Both Saigon and Cholon were captured by the French in 1859 (who destroyed the citadel in the process) and Saigon became the capital of Cochin-China a few years later. It wasn't until 1931, after the neighbouring cities had sprawled into each other, that they were officially combined to form Saigon-Cholon (the name Cholon was dropped in 1956).

The city served as the capital of the Republic of Vietnam from 1956 until 1975, when it fell to advancing North Vietnamese forces and was renamed Ho Chi Minh City.

Cha Tam Church, Cholon (p202)

🍽️ Foodie Tours

Street Foodies Saigon (📞093 210 3985; www.streetfoodiessaigon.com; per person US$59) has excellent after-dark walking tours exploring the great street food scene of the alleys and byways of the less-visited Co Giang neighbourhood. Look forward to around four hours of very tasty snacking.

Take a highly entertaining three- to four-hour scooter foodie tour around the streets and backstreets of town with Barbara and her husband, Vu, from **Saigon Street Eats** (📞0908 449 408; www.saigonstreeteats.com; per person US$45-65). Select your tour according to taste: morning pho tours, lunchtime veggie or evening seafood tours, and prepare for some fun surprises.

Ben Thanh Market (p215)
ANIRUT THAILAND/SHUTTERSTOCK ©

5Ku Station — Barbecue $

(29 Đ Le Thanh Thon; meals around 150,000d; ⏱4pm-late) Hopping with evening diners, this chain of makeshift-looking alfresco barbecue restaurants is fun, boisterous, outgoing and tasty. Grab yourself a wooden box seat and a cold beer, and chow down on BBQ and hotpot alongside a mix of locals, travellers and expats.

Secret Garden — Vietnamese $

(8th fl, 158 Đ Pasteur; meals 55,000-90,000d; ⏱8am-10pm; 📷) Negotiate the stairs in this faded HCMC apartment building to arrive at Secret Garden's wonderful rooftop restaurant. Rogue chickens peck away in the herb garden, Buddhist statues add Asian ambience, and delicious homestyle dishes are served up with city views. Service can sometimes be a little *too* casual, but it's worth persevering for the great flavours.

Chi Hoa — Vietnamese $

(📞028-3827 3155; www.chihoacuisine.com; 31a Đ Le Thanh Thon; meals 55,000-155,000d; ⏱7am-10pm) Homestyle Vietnamese food served in simple but attractive surroundings. The menu ranges widely from lots of different *banh mi* sandwiches to salads and rice and noodle bowls.

Huong Lai — Vietnamese $

(📞028-3822 6814; www.huonglai2001saigon.com; 38 Đ Ly Tu Trong; meals 70,000-180,000d; ⏱noon-3pm & 6-10pm) A must for finely presented, traditional Vietnamese food, the airy and high-ceilinged loft of an old French-era shophouse is the setting for this dining experience with a difference. Staff are from disadvantaged families or are former street children and receive on-the-job training, education and a place to stay.

Hum Lounge & Restaurant — Vegetarian $$

(📞028-3823 8920; www.humvietnam.vn; 2 Đ Thi Sach; meals 80,000-190,000d; ⏱10am-10pm; 📷📷) This recent opening brings the excellent Vietnamese-inspired vegetarian cuisine of the city's long-established Hum Vegetarian Cafe & Restaurant (p220) to a central garden location. Settle into the elegant and verdant space and enjoy dishes including papaya and banana flower salads, mushrooms steamed in coconut, and the subtle combination of braised tofu with star anise and cinnamon.

Nha Hang Ngon — Vietnamese $$

(📞028-3827 7131; 160 Đ Pasteur; meals 60,000-260,000d; ⏱7am-10pm; 📷) Thronging with locals and foreigners, this is one of HCMC's most popular spots, with a large range of the very best street food in stylish surroundings across three levels. Set in a leafy garden ringed by food stalls, each cook serves up a specialised traditional dish, ensuring an authentic taste of Vietnamese, Thai, Japanese or Chinese cuisine.

Nha Hang Ngon

Quan Bui   Vietnamese $$

(☑028-3829 1545; http://quan-bui.com; 17a Đ
Ngo Van Nam; meals 69,000-169,000d; ☻8am-
11pm; ☀) Stylish Indochinese decor features
at this slick eatery in up-and-coming Đ
Ngo Van Nam. Nearby restaurants offer
Japanese flavours, but Quan Bui's focus is
on authentic Vietnamese cuisine and many
dishes feature the more hearty flavours
of northern Vietnam. Cocktails – from
the associated bar across the lane – are
among HCMC's best, and upstairs there's
an air-conditioned and smoke-free dining
room.

Nha Hang Di Mai   Vietnamese $$

(☑090 867 2388; www.nhahangdimai.com; 136-
138 Đ Le Thi Hong Gam; meals 95,000-130,000d;
☑) Here's where to go on your first or last
night in town, a colourful and quirky restaurant offering a diverse taste of flavours
from around Vietnam. Vintage decor with
a touch of Indochine style is the setting for
zingy salads, excellent noodle dishes and
good seafood. Try the refreshing juices, iced
teas and smoothies.

Old Compass Cafe   Cafe $$

(☑090 390 0841; www.facebook.com/oldcom-
passcafe; 3rd fl, 63 Đ Pasteur; meals 150,000d;
☻10.30am-10pm Sun-Thu, to 11pm Fri & Sat; 🛜)
Concealed off busy Đ Pasteur down an alley
and up narrow staircases, Old Compass is
a relaxed all-day cafe that often segues into
an interesting live music and performance
space later at night. Relax over a coffee,
wine or craft beer on the comfy sofas, or
take advantage of good-value three-course
lunch deals. Check Facebook for listings of
events.

Scott & Jeremys   American $$

(www.facebook.com/SnJ.Saigon; 40 Đ Dang Thi
Nhu; meals 130,000-190,000d; ☻11am-10pm
Tue-Sun) Part of the expanding eating and
drinking scene around Đ Dang Thi Nhu,
Scott & Jeremys offers interesting versions
of Western comfort food – look forward to
superior burgers, mac 'n' cheese and spa-
ghetti and meatballs – with the distraction
of a good wine list and craft brews from
Saigon's Đ Pasteur St. A great option when
hankering for more familiar flavours.

MAKISTOCK/SHUTTERSTOCK ©

Ben Thanh Market (p215)

Reunification Palace & Around

Banh Mi Huynh Hoa Vietnamese $

(26 Le Thi Rieng; banh mi 33,000d; ⏲2.30-11pm) This hole-in-the-wall *banh mi* joint is busy day and night with locals zipping up on motorbikes for stacks of excellent baguettes stuffed with pork, pork and more pork in tasty ways you may not have known existed. Street standing room only.

Ben Thanh Street Food Market Street Food $

(☎090 688 1707; www.facebook.com/pg/Ben-Thanhstreetfoodmarket; 26-30 Đ Thu Khoa Huan; meals from 40,000d; ⏲9am-11pm) Grab a table at the front of the market, order up some cold beers from the adjacent bar, and then go exploring to put together a mini-feast of well-priced street food. Highlights include fresh oysters from Nha Trang – optional dipping sauces include fiery wasabi – and fragrant *bun bo Hue* noodles.

Hum Vegetarian Cafe & Restaurant Vegetarian $$

(☎028-3930 3819; www.hum-vegetarian.vn; 32 Đ Vo Van Tan; meals 80,000-190,000d; ⏲10am-10pm; 🖉) Even if you're not a vegetarian, this serene and elegant restaurant requires your attention. Everything – from the charming service to the delightful Vietnamese dishes and peaceful outside tables – makes dining here an occasion to savour. There's also an equally laid-back and more central location (p218).

Da Kao & Around

Banh Xeo 46A Vietnamese $

(☎028-3824 1110; 46a Đ Dinh Cong Trang; regular/extra large 70,000/110,000d; ⏲10am-9pm; 🖉) Locals will always hit the restaurants that specialise in a single dish and this renowned spot serves some of the best *banh xeo* in town. These Vietnamese rice-flour pancakes stuffed with bean sprouts, prawns and pork (vegetarian versions available) are legendary. Other dishes include excellent *goi cuon* (fresh summer rolls with pork and prawn).

Pho Hoa
Vietnamese $

(260c Đ Pasteur; meals 60,000-75,000d; ⊗6am-midnight) This long-running establishment is more upmarket than most but is definitely the real deal – as evidenced by its popularity with regular local patrons. Tables come laden with herbs, chilli and lime, as well as *gio chao quay* (fried Chinese bread), *banh xu xe* (glutinous coconut cakes with mung-bean paste) and *cha lua* (pork-paste sausages wrapped in banana leaves).

Cuc Gach Quan
Vietnamese $$

(☑028-3848 0144; www.cucgachquan.com. vn/en; 10 Đ Dang Tat; meals 85,000-210,000d; ⊗9am-midnight) It comes as little surprise that the owner is an architect when you step into this cleverly renovated old villa. The decor is rustic and elegant at the same time, which is also true of the food. Despite its tucked-away location in the northernmost reaches of District 1, this is no secret hideaway: book ahead.

Tib
Vietnamese $$

(☑028-3829 7242; www.tibrestaurant.com.vn; 187 Đ Hai Ba Trung; mains 125,000-300,000d; ⊗11am-2pm & 5-10pm; ☎🖼) Visiting presidents and prime ministers have slunk down this lantern- and fairy-light-festooned alley and into this atmospheric old house to sample Tib's imperial Hue cuisine. Although you could probably find similar food for less money elsewhere, the courtyard setting is enchanting.

⊗ Pham Ngu Lao Area

Five Oysters
Vietnamese $

(☑09 0301 2123; www.fiveoysters.com; 234 Đ Bui Vien; meals from 45,000d; ⊗9am-11pm) With a strong seafood slant and friendly service, light and bright Five Oysters in backpackerland is frequently packed with travellers feasting on oysters (30,000d), grilled octopus, seafood soup, snail pie, *pho,* fried noodles, grilled mackerel with chilli oil and more. Bargain-priced beer also makes it a popular spot along the PNL strip.

🍴 Local Eats

Markets have a good selection of stalls whipping up tasty treats. Ben Thanh's night market is particularly good.

Banh mi – cheap filled baguettes with a French look and very Vietnamese taste – are sold by street vendors. The fresh baguettes are stuffed with something resembling pâté (don't ask), pickled vegetables and various other fillings. To really discover more of the city's great street food, a tour is an excellent option.

The largest concentration of vegetarian restaurants is around the Pham Ngu Lao area, and you'll usually find one within a chopstick's throw of Buddhist temples.

Pork banh mi
BHOFACK2/GETTY IMAGES©

Asiana Food Town
Street Food $

(☑090 377 0836; www.facebook.com/asiana foodtown; 4 Đ Pham Ngu Lao; meals 50,000-100,000d; ⊗8.30am-10pm; ❄🖼) Cooling air-con, a handy location near accommodation in Pham Ngu Lao, and a huge selection of street food from around Vietnam and the rest of Asia are the highlights of this excellent new undercover food court. There's a convenient supermarket, pharmacy and English-language bookshop as well.

Quan Ut Ut
Barbecue $$

(☑028-3914 4500; www.quanutut.com; 168 Đ Vo Van Kiet; meals 180,000-300,000d; ⊗4-

👫 HCMC for Children

At first glance, Ho Chi Minh City's hectic streets might not look that kiddie-friendly, but there's the Saigon Skydeck at **Bitexco Financial Tower** (p195), water parks, swimming pools, water puppet shows, plenty of leafy parks, family-friendly cafes and ice-cream shops. **World Games** on the basement 2 level (unit B2-18) of the **Vincom Center** (70-72 Đ Le Than Ton & 45a Đ Ly Tu Trong; ⊙9am-10pm; ☎) Tower B is a fun, centrally located amusement arcade, and **tiNiworld** on the 4th floor of the new Saigon Centre is also worth considering to keep the kids entertained. Beyond the city is **Dai Nam Theme Park** (Lac Canh Dai Nam Van Hien; ☎0274 351 2660; www.laccanhdainamvan hien.vn; adult/child 100,000/50,000đ; ⊙8am-6pm), the closest thing to Disneyland in Vietnam. Online, check out Kidz Saigon (www.kidzsaigon.com) for lots of ideas and places to keep children active and entertained in the big city.

Bitexco Financial Tower (p195)
NADEZDA MURMAKOVA/SHUTTERSTOCK ©

11.30pm) With a name roughly translating to the 'Oink Oink Eatery', this casual place with river views celebrates everything porcine with an American-style BBQ spin. Huge streetside grills prepare great ribs, spicy sausages and pork belly, and tasty sides include charred sweetcorn and grilled pineapple. Huge burgers are also good, and the owners even make their own flavour-packed craft beers.

🕸 Thao Dien (District 2)

Boat House   Bistro $$
(☎028-3744 6790; www.facebook.com/boat housevietnam; 40 Lily Rd, APSC Compound, 36 Đ Thao Dien; bar snacks 65,000-185,000đ, meals 155,000-245,000đ; ⊙8am-11pm) This versatile spot features many riverside options. Enjoy a leisurely lunch at the outside tables, sit at the bar for a few beers, or graduate to cocktails on the daybeds. Food runs from bar snacks to burgers, salads and wraps, and weekdays from 4.30pm to 6.30pm there are good happy-hour specials. Look forward to occasional live music too.

MAD House   Bistro $$
(☎028-3519 4009; www.facebook.com/mad saigon; 6/1/2 Đ Nguyen U Di; meals 150,000-300,000đ; ⊙8am-10pm; ☎☎) The MAD House is a popular option for the expat denizens of District 2. Highlights include excellent coffee, robust cocktails, and an innovative menu blending Scandinavian and Vietnamese influences – MAD House translates to Food House in Danish. Look forward to stunning tropical decor and a lovely garden area that's a perfect retreat from the bustle of the city.

Lubu   Mediterranean $$$
(☎028-6281 8371; www.luburestaurant.com; 97 B Thao Dien; meals 240,000-600,000đ; ⊙8.30am-10pm) Shared tables and a sunny whitewashed interior combine with excellent Mediterranean cuisine at this expat favourite. Spain, Morocco and Greece are the main culinary touchpoints – menu highlights include paella, souvlaki and tapas – and the city's best Bloody Mary cocktail (topped with a massive red chilli) is the perfect adjunct to a lazy weekend brunch.

Deck   Fusion $$$
(☎028-3744 6632; www.thedecksaigon.com; 33 Đ Nguyen U Di; tapas 95,000-330,000đ, meals 185,000-680,000đ; ⊙8am-midnight; ☎) Housed in an architecturally impressive pavilion set between an elegant garden and the river, you could happily linger here all afternoon, knocking off a few

bottles of wine and several dim sum plates along the way. Mains combine European cooking styles with the flavours of Asia. The three-course lunch is good value for lazy afternoon river views.

🍸 DRINKING & NIGHTLIFE

Happening HCMC is concentrated around the Dong Khoi area, with everything from dives to designer bars.

🍷 Dong Khoi Area

Heart of Darkness · Craft Beer

(📱090 301 7596; www.heartofdarknessbrewery. com; 31Đ Đ Ly Tu Trong; ◷10am-midnight) Our pick for the best of HCMC's craft breweries, with an always interesting selection of assertive and innovative beers on tap. The selection varies as Heart of Darkness brewers are always trying something, but the hoppy 7.1% Kurtz's Insane IPA is a great drop. Secure a wooden table out the front and order up excellent pizza from Pizza 4P's.

Pasteur Street Brewing Company · Craft Beer

(www.pasteurstreet.com; 144 Đ Pasteur; small/large beers from 45,000/95,000đ; ◷11am-10pm; 📶) Pasteur Street Brewing turns out a fine selection of craft beer. Brews utilise local ingredients including lemongrass, rambutan and jasmine, and up to six different beers are always available. Great bar snacks – try the spicy Nashville fried chicken – are also served in the brewery's hip space. PSBC's Imperial Chocolate Stout was judged one of the world's finest beers in 2016.

Rogue Saigon · Craft Beer

(📱090 236 5780; www.facebook.com/rogue saigon; 11 Đ Pasteur; ◷4pm-midnight Sun-Thu, to 2am Fri & Sat) Live music and Vietnamese craft beers combine on Rogue's rooftop terrace in a pleasantly rundown building on the riverside edge of District 1. Look forward to good beers like Lac Brewing's Devil's Lake IPA and music with a blues, country or rock vibe. The after-dark, shadowy views from this off-the-radar location are pretty cool too.

Cuc Gach Quan (p221)

Alley Cocktail Bar
& Kitchen   Cocktail Bar

(📞093 565 3969; www.facebook.com/thealley
saigon; 63/1 Đ Pasteur; ⏰5pm-midnight Mon-
Wed, to 1am Thu-Sat; 🛜) Good luck finding
this place off Đ Pasteur, but when you do
discover it, celebrate with a classic cocktail,
craft beer or whisky. The snacks menu
runs from antipasto and fresh spring rolls
through to burgers, and an eclectic approach to music stretches from live music
on acoustic Thursdays to the harder edge
of DJs on Friday and Saturday nights.

Heritage Republic   Lounge

(📞0906 227 576; http://fb.me/heritage
republic; 10 Đ Pasteur; ⏰24hr; 🛜) It's easy to
lose track of time in tiny Heritage. By day,
relax on a vintage sofa with a smoothie,
snuggling up to the resident bulldogs. Sud-
denly it's evening and this 24-hour lounge
transforms into one of HCMC's most
chilled bars, with a hip crowd spilling onto
the streets for beer and cocktails. Discount
days for patrons dressed in black.

L'Usine   Cafe

(📞028-6674 3565; www.lusinespace.com; 151/1
Đ Dong Khoi; ⏰7.30am-10.30pm; 🛜) Tucked
away in a colonial building with high ceilings,
marble-topped tables, photos of old Saigon
and an appetising cafe menu (sandwiches
from 100,000d). A designer homewares and
clothing store is attached; head through the
Art Arcade, turn right along the lane between
the buildings and zip upstairs.

Layla   Cocktail Bar

(📞028-3827 2279; www.facebook.com/layla
eateryandbarhcm; 2nd fl, 63 Đ Dong Du; ⏰4pm-
1am Mon-Sat, 12.30pm-1am Sun) With an
effortlessly long bar – we're talking 10m
plus here– Layla is a laid-back spot that's
perfect for the first or last cocktails of the
night. Don't be surprised if the combination
of a chic ambience, super comfy sofas
and Med-style bar snacks – think Italian
flatbreads and Spanish tortilla – sees you
staying longer than planned.

Workshop   Coffee

(www.facebook.com/the.workshop.coffee; 10 Đ
Ngo Duc Ke; coffee from 45,000d; ⏰8am-9pm;
🛜) Coffee-geek culture comes to HCMC
at this spacious upstairs warehouse space
that's also perfect if you need to do some
writing or other work. Single-origin fair-
trade roasts from Dalat feature, and there's
a great display of B&W photos of old Saigon
to peruse while you're waiting for your
Chemex or cold brew.

Vesper   Bar

(www.facebook.com/vespersaigon; ground fl,
Landmark Bldg, 5b Đ Ton Duc Thang; ⏰10am-1am
Mon-Sat; 🛜) From the sinuous curve of the
hardwood bar to the smoothly arranged
bottles on the shelves, soft chill-out rhythms,
funky caramel leather furniture and fine tapas menu, Vesper is a cool spot by the river.

La Fenetre Soleil   Bar

(📞028-3824 5994; www.facebook.com/la
fenetre.soleil.3; 1st fl, 44 Đ Ly Tu Trong; coffee
from 40,000d; ⏰10am-midnight Mon & Tue,
to 1am Sun, Wed & Thu, to 2am Fri & Sat; 🛜)
Making the most of the bones of a French
colonial building, this shabby-chic upstairs
hang-out has exposed brickwork and
beams, chandeliers, frilly mirrors, overhead
fans chopping a breeze and an Indonesian
menu. Live music – blues, Latin, reggae and
funk – draws crowds in the evening, and
lazy Sunday afternoon sessions slow the
weekend down from 1pm to 5pm.

Apocalypse Now   Club

(📞028-3824 1463; www.facebook.com/apo
calypsenowsaigon; 2c Đ Thi Sach; ⏰7pm-4am)
'Apo' has been around since 1991 and
remains one of the must-visit clubs. A
sprawling place with a big dance floor and
an outdoor courtyard, the bar's eclectic
cast combines travellers, expats and Vietnamese movers and shakers. The music is
thumping and it's apocalyptically rowdy.

Broma: Not a Bar   Bar

(📞0126 387 2603; www.facebook.com/broma
bar; 41 ĐL Nguyen Hue; ⏰5pm-2am Sun-Thu,
to 4am Fri & Sat) Compact and bohemian

rooftop bar overlooking the busy pedestrian mall of Đ Nguyen Hue. Look forward to a good selection of international beers, live gigs, and DJs with a funk, hip-hop and electronica edge.

🔵 Reunification Palace & Around

BiaCraft   Craft Beer
(📞028-3933 0903; www.biacraft.com; 11 Đ Le Ngo Cat; ⏰11am-11pm) With almost 40 taps, BiaCraft is an essential destination for beer fans. Complementing its own brews are beers and ciders from craft breweries in Saigon and Hanoi; it's possible to take out freshly sealed cans of all available beers. Combine a tasting paddle with probably the city's best bar food. The barramundi ceviche and grilled Nha Trang oysters are excellent.

There is also a (less impressive) BiaCraft **branch** (www.biacraft.com; 90 Đ Xuan Thuy, Thao Dien; ⏰11am-midnight) in the District 2 area.

East West Brewing   Craft Beer
(📞0913 060 728; www.eastwestbrewing.vn; 181-185 Đ Ly Tu Trong; ⏰11am-midnight) Prepare to be wowed by East West's spectacular District 1 set-up, and remain equally impressed by the carefully crafted beers on offer. All brewed on site, standout beers include the Far East IPA with American and New Zealand hops; seasonal brews could include interesting ingredients like yuzu, lychee or lemongrass. The food's also decent with good burgers, salads and seafood.

Saigon Soul
Pool Party   Bar
(📞0122 734 8128; www.facebook.com/saigon soul; New World Saigon Hotel, 76 Đ Le Lai; admission 150,000d; ⏰10am-10pm) Cool beats, cold beers and a fun crowd of locals, expats and visitors all combine at the New World Saigon Hotel on Saturday afternoons from late November to early June. With around 500 pool-going guests, what could possibly go wrong?

Air 360   Bar
(www.facebook.com/air360skylounge; Ben Thanh Tower, 21st fl, 136-138 Đ Le Thi Hong Gam; ⏰5.30pm-2am) Happy hour runs from 5.30pm to 8pm at this modern sky bar – perfect to make the most of sunset and secure a good discount on the pricey drinks menu. Pâtés, terrines and charcuterie selections underpin the food menu. It's just a short walk from the heaving backpacker bars on Pham Ngu Lao.

🍷 Pham Ngu Lao

Ong Cao   Bar
(📞091 199 6160; www.facebook.com/ongcao saigon; 240 Đ Bui Vien; ⏰5-11pm Tue-Sun; 📶) A hoppy cut above the backpacker bars lining Bui Vien, Ong Cao is your best bet for craft brews in Pham Ngu Lao. Bar snacks, including cheese and charcuterie plates, partner well with 16 taps serving mainly local HCMC beers. Yes, it is more expensive than that 10,000d Bia Saigon along the road, but it's worth it.

Whiskey & Wares   Bar
(📞0163 279 4179; www.facebook.com/Whis-keyandWares; 196 Đ De Tham; ⏰4.30pm-2am Tue-Sun; 📶) 🍴 Just a short stroll from Đ Bui Vien, Whiskey & Wares' blend of fine whisky, good cocktails and local craft beer is a more sophisticated but still relaxed alternative to Pham Ngu Lao's backpacker bars. It's also a top spot to purchase local artisanal goods, and products for sale include hip T-shirts, fragrant soaps and cool prints and postcards.

LGBT friendly but welcoming to all.

🔵 Other Areas

Saigon Outcast   Bar
(www.saigonoutcast.com; 188 Đ Nguyen Van Huong; ⏰10am-11.45pm) Head across to District 2 for this venue's diverse combo of live music, DJs, cinema nights and good times amid funky street art. Cocktails, craft beer and local ciders are available in the raffish garden bar, and there's a cool outdoor market occasionally on Sunday mornings.

Check the website for what's on. From District 1, it's around 200,000d in a taxi.

Indika Saigon Bar

(☎0122 399 4260; www.facebook.com/indika saigon; 43 Đ Nguyen Van Giai; ☉9am-midnight) Tucked down a narrow laneway, the off-the-radar Indika Saigon is definitely worth venturing to. Negotiate past the hipster barbecue joint and beer bar at the front to Indika's raffish multiroom labyrinth that's used for concerts, open-mic sessions, movie nights and DJs. Check out the Facebook page for listings, and be surprised at the emerging energy of the new Saigon.

❶ INFORMATION

DANGERS & ANNOYANCES

Be careful at all times but especially in the Dong Khoi area, around Pham Ngu Lao and the Ben Thanh Market, and along the Saigon riverfront. Motorbike 'cowboys' specialise in bag- and phone-snatching.

TRAVEL AGENCIES

Go Go Vietnam (☎0903 119 200; www. gogo-vietnam.com; 40/7 Đ Bui Vien) Well-run tour company and travel agency with excellent credentials in visa extensions and renewals, and good-value day trips.

Sinh Tourist (☎028-3838 9593; www.thesinh tourist.vn; 246 Đ De Tham; ☉6.30am-10.30pm) Popular budget travel agency.

❶ GETTING THERE & AWAY

HCMC is served by Tan Son Nhat Airport, 7km from the centre of town. Domestic airlines include Vietnam Airlines, VietJet Air, Jetstar Pacific Airlines and Vietnam Air Service Company (VASCO; for the Con Dao Islands).

Trains from **Saigon train station** (Ga Sai Gon; ☎028-3823 0105; 1 Đ Nguyen Thong, District 3; ☉ticket office 7.15-11am & 1-3pm) head north to destinations including Danang. Purchase tickets from travel agents or www.baolau.com for a small booking fee.

Destinations including Mui Ne are best reached by bus, try Sinh Tourist.

❶ GETTING AROUND

Metered taxis cruise the streets and are very affordable. Expect to pay around 28,000d (US$1.30) from Dong Khoi to Pham Ngu Lao.

Mai Linh Taxi (☎028-3838 3838) and **Vinasun Taxi** (☎028-3827 2727) can be trusted. Uber is also popular.

A metro is under construction but will not be operational until 2020 at the earliest.

Where to Stay

District 1 is the obvious lodging choice in HCMC given its proximity to almost everything of interest, relative closeness to the airport and tempting array of establishments across all price ranges.

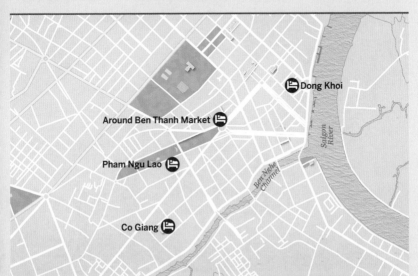

Neighbourhood	Atmosphere
Dong Khoi Area	Well-heeled area with grand thoroughfares and French colonial elegance; home to the city's top-notch hotels and sprinkled with attractive midrange options; good foodie neighbourhood.
Pham Ngu Lao Area	The budget and backpacker zone; more than 100 accommodation choices, including countless family-run guesthouses and minihotels, and even a few dorms; midrange travellers can also find excellent deals here; good-value eateries and cheap shopping.
Around Ben Thanh Market	Has decent midrange options; one of Saigon's liveliest areas, with market shopping and food stalls.
Co Giang	For a quieter and slightly cheaper alternative to Pham Ngu Lao, there's a string of guesthouses in a quiet alley connecting Đ Co Giang and Đ Co Bac; you'll need to book well ahead; further from major sights.

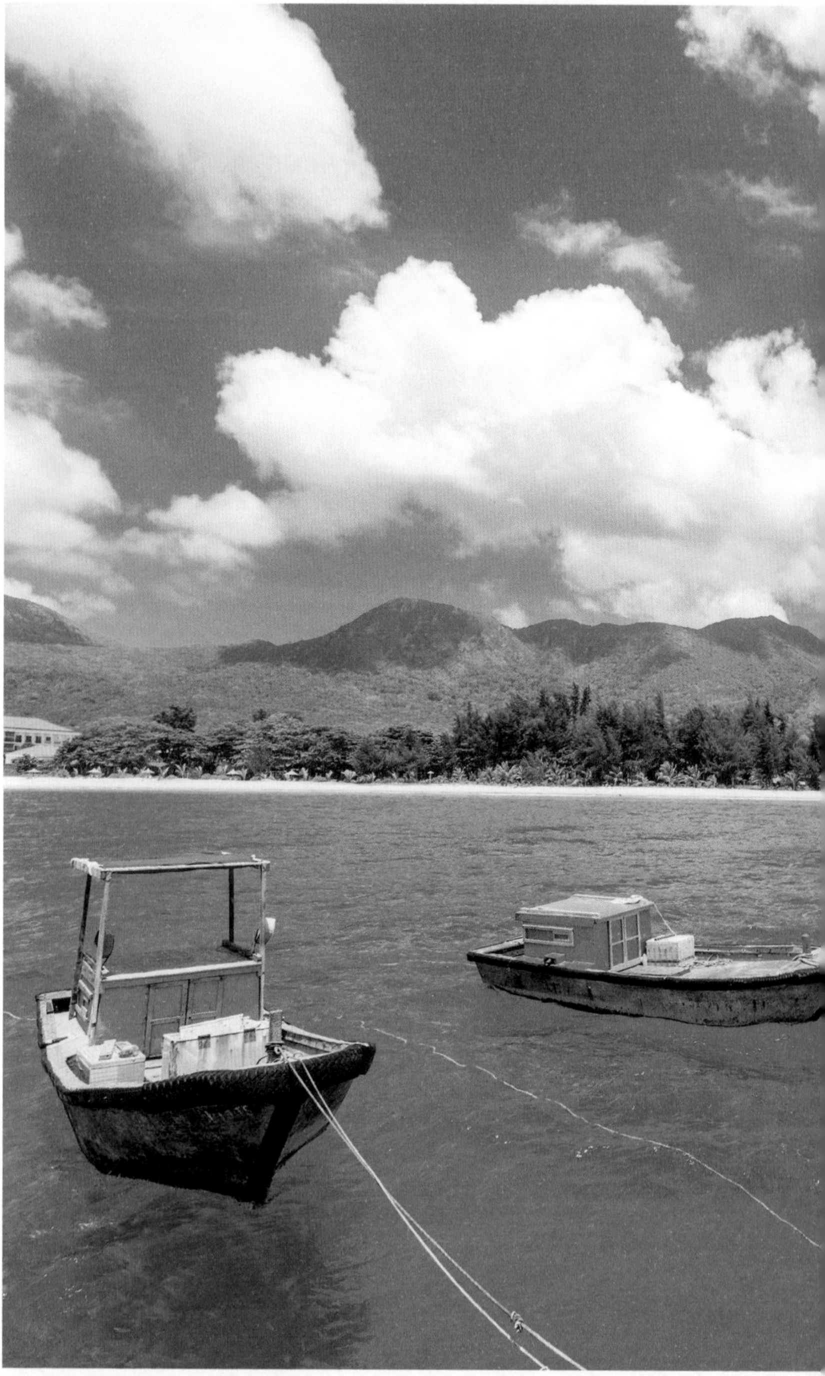

STUDIOLOCO/SHUTTERSTOCK ©

CON DAO ISLANDS

Con Dao Islands at a Glance...

Isolated from the mainland, the Con Dao Islands are one of Vietnam's star attractions. Long the Devil's Island of Indochina, the preserve of political prisoners and undesirables, they are now turning heads thanks to their striking natural beauty and tranquillity.

Con Son, the largest of the 15 islands and islets, is ringed with lovely beaches, coral reefs and scenic bays, and remains partially covered in rainforest. In addition to hiking, diving and exploring deserted coastal roads and beaches, there are excellent wildlife-watching opportunities. Tranquil Con Son Town makes a delightful historic base for exploration.

A Day in Con Dao

Head straight to the beautiful beach of **Bai Dat Doc** (p232) for a morning swim, then into **Con Son Town** for lunch at **Villa Maison Con Dao Restaurant** (p235). Spend the rest of the afternoon acquainting yourself with Con Dao's sombre history, starting with the **Bao Tang Con Dao Museum** (p235), followed by the **Tiger Cages** (p234).

Two Days in Con Dao

Rise early to catch the local **market** (p235) at its busiest then visit the hilltop **Van Son Temple** (p235). Tour the rest of the island's historic sites, including **Phu Hai Prison** (p234) and peaceful **Hang Duong Cemetery** (p234). Then take a trek through the dense rainforest of Con Son Island's interior, or join a diving or snorkelling trip out to the island reefs.

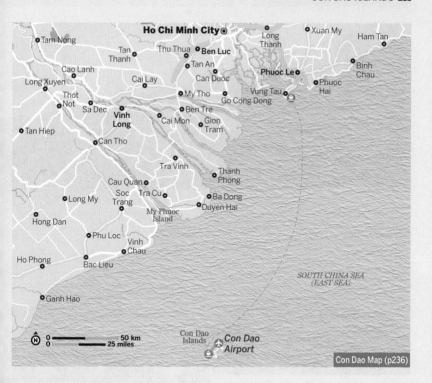

Con Dao Map (p236)

Arriving in Con Dao

Con Son Airport The tiny airport is about 15km from the town centre. There are seven daily flights between Con Son and Ho Chi Minh City.

Ben Dam Port Superdong (p237) schedules two daily ferries (310,000d, 2½ hours) from Tran De, Soc Trang province in the Mekong Delta. This service began in July 2017 and its reliability is untested.

Where to Stay

Accommodation options have greatly improved in Con Dao over the last few years and there are now about 30 guesthouses and minihotels in Con Son Town. However, expect to pay about double the rate for the equivalent place on the mainland.

Bai Dram Trau

OLDCATPHOTO/GETTY IMAGES ©

Beaches & Islands

Blessed with stunning beaches and loaded with natural allure, Con Dao is the ultimate castaway experience in Vietnam.

Great For...

☑ **Don't Miss**

The grave of Vo Thi Sau in Con Son's cemetery, a place of pilgrimage.

Bai Dat Doc

This simply beautiful cove on Con Son Island consists of a kilometre-long crescent of pale sand, fringed by wooded hills. The beach's profile is gently shelving and there's no pollution, so it's ideal for swimming. It's backed by the luxury bungalows of the Six Senses hotel. Though it's not a private beach, access is quite tricky; you can scramble down at points around the edge of the hotel grounds.

Bai Dram Trau

Reached via a dirt track 1km before the airport on Con Son Island, Bai Dram Trau is a sublime but remote 700m half-moon crescent of soft sand, fringed by casuarina trees and bookended by forest-topped rocky promontories. It's best visited at low tide.

ⓘ Need to Know

The driest season is November to February, though seas are calmest from March to July.

✕ Take a Break

Bar200 Con Dao (p237) has a welcoming vibe and good coffee.

★ Top Tip

The wonderful beach **Bai Dram Trau** looks private but is open to the public.

There's some snorkelling on reefs offshore and three very simple seafood shacks (all open noon till dusk only).

Bai Loi Voi

On the north side of Con Son Town, Bai Loi Voi is a broad sand-and-shingle beach with lots of seashells and shade-providing coastal trees. At low tide swimming is not possible, but you can walk for miles across the sand here.

Bai An Hai

On the south side of Con Son Town, this appealing beach has a green mountain backdrop, but there are a good number of fishing boats moored nearby.

Other Islands

Bay Canh Island

Perhaps the best all-round island to visit is Bay Canh, to the east of Con Son Island, which has lovely beaches, old-growth forest, mangroves, coral reefs and sea turtles (seasonal). There is a fantastic two-hour walk to a functioning French-era lighthouse on Bay Canh's eastern tip, although it involves a steep climb of 325m. Once at the summit, the panoramic views are breathtaking.

Tre Lon Island

This islet, west of Con Son Island, has a couple of tiny, pristine, empty cove beaches. Talk to boat captains in Con Dao about setting up a trip here.

⊙ SIGHTS

There's nowhere quite like Con Son Town in all Vietnam. This delightful pocket-sized island capital has litter-free streets, well-kept municipal buildings and an air of calm and prosperity.

Of course, the town's genteel appearance and character is tempered considerably by the presence of several prisons, cemeteries and reminders of the islands' historic role as a penal colony. There are ghosts everywhere in Con Son.

Phu Hai Prison   Historic Building
(off Đ Ton Duc Thang; joint ticket 20,000d; ☺7-11.30am & 1-5pm) The largest of the 11 jails on the island, this prison dates from 1862. Thousands of prisoners were held here, with up to 200 prisoners crammed into each detention building. During the French era, all prisoners were kept naked, chained together in rows, with one small box serving as a toilet for hundreds. One can only imagine the squalor and stench. Today, emaciated mannequins that are all too lifelike recreate the era. One ticket gives you entry here, the Tiger Cages and Bao Tang Con Dao Museum.

Tiger Cages   Historic Building
(joint ticket 20,000d; ☺7-11.30am & 1-5pm) The notorious cells dubbed 'tiger cages' were built in 1940 by the French to incarcerate nearly 2000 political prisoners. There are 120 chambers with ceiling bars, where guards could poke at prisoners like tigers in a Victorian zoo. Prisoners were beaten with sticks from above, and sprinkled with quick lime and water (which burnt their skin and caused blindness).

Hang Duong Cemetery   Cemetery
Some 20,000 Vietnamese prisoners died on Con Son and 1994 of their graves can be seen at the peaceful Hang Duong Cemetery, located at the northeastern edge of town. Sadly, only 700 of these graves bear the name of the victim.

> ❝ *...guards could poke at prisoners like tigers in a Victorian zoo.* ❞

Bao Tang Con Dao Museum

TONKINPHOTOGRAPHY/SHUTTERSTOCK ©

Vietnam's most famous heroine, Vo Thi Sau (1933–52), was buried here. She was the first woman executed by a firing squad in Con Dao, on 23 January 1952.

Bao Tang Con Dao Museum
Museum

(Đ Nguyen Hue; joint ticket 20,000d; ⊙7-11am & 1.30-5pm) An impressive museum with more than 2000 exhibits, including many rare documents, dioramas and excellent photographs, which comprehensively record the islands' history, including the French colonial era and of course the 'prison period'. Modern displays including audio-visuals are used.

Van Son Temple
Buddhist Pagoda

(1km southwest of centre; ⊙6am-8pm) **FREE**
This large hilltop temple complex enjoys fine views over Con Son Town and islands offshore to an ocean-filled horizon. A steep staircase (of over 100 steps) leads up to the traditionally designed pagoda structures, each supported by thick wooden columns and topped with an elaborate tiled roof.

🟢 ACTIVITIES

There are lots of **treks** around Con Son Island, as much of the interior remains heavily forested. Many hikes require a permit from the **National Park** (📞0254-383 0669; www.condaopark.com.vn; 29 Đ Vo Thi Sau; ⊙7-11.30am & 1.30-5pm) office, which can also advise about boat trips.

It's a steep uphill hike to the old fruit plantations of **So Ray**, following a slippery but well-marked trail through dense rainforest. The plantation is home to a sociable troop of long-tailed macaques, with sweeping views. The return hike takes about 90 minutes. There's another trail to rocky **Ong Dung Bay**, where there's a good coral reef offshore.

Con Dao is the most pristine marine environment in the country, perfect for **scuba diving** and **snorkelling**. There's abundant healthy coral and marine life including turtles, rays, triggerfish and parrotfish.

Con Dao Climate

The driest time to visit Con Dao is from November to February, although the seas are at their calmest from March to July.

The rainy season lasts from June to September, but there are also northeast and southwest monsoons from September to November that can bring heavy winds.

September and October are the hottest months, though even then the cool island breezes make Con Dao relatively comfortable.

Con Son Bay
TONKINPHOTOGRAPHY/SHUTTERSTOCK ©

Con Dao Dive Center
Diving

(📞0903 700 8483; http://divecondao.com; Bar200, Đ Vo Thi Sau; ⊙7.30am-10pm) An established PADI dive resort, offering instruction and courses (Open Water is US$550), fun dives (two-dive trips US$160), snorkelling and freediving trips. Owner Rhys is happy to chat about diving options and things to do on Con Dao. It's based at Bar200 (p237).

🍴 EATING & DRINKING

All these places are in Con Son Town.

Con Son Market
Vietnamese $

(Đ Vo Thi Sau; meals 15,000-25,000d; ⊙6am-5pm) A good spot for breakfast, with delicious noodle dishes and pancakes churned out at wallet-friendly rates. You can stock up on fruit and snacks here, too.

Con Dao

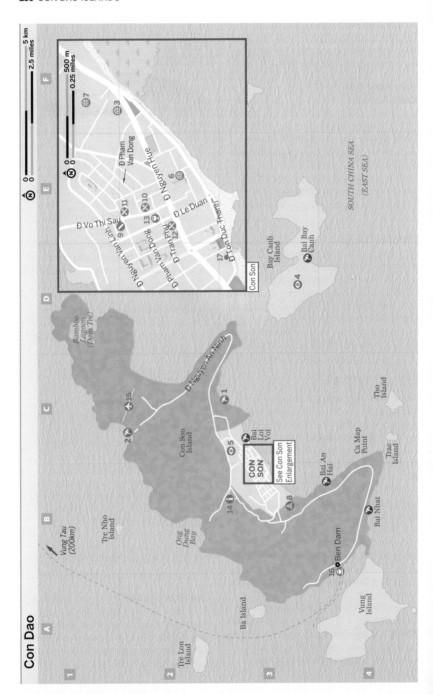

5 km

2.5 miles

500 m

0.25 miles

Vung Tau
(200km)

Bamboo
Lagoon
(Đam Tre)

Đ Nguyen An Ninh

Con Son
Island

Tre Nho
Island

Tre Lon
Island

Ong
Dung
Bay

Ba Island

Ben Dam

Vung Island

Bai Nhat

Ca Map
Point

Bai An
Hai

CON
SON

See Con Son
Enlargement

Bai
Loi
Voi

Trac
Island

Tho
Island

Bay Canh
Island

Bai Bay
Canh

SOUTH CHINA SEA
(EAST SEA)

Con Son (Enlargement)

Đ Pham Van Dong

Đ Nguyen Hue

Đ Nguyen Van Linh

Đ Vo Thi Sau

Đ Le Duan

Đ Pham Van Dong

Đ Tran Phu

Đ Tran Duc Thanh

Con Son

Con Dao

Villa Maison Con Dao Restaurant
International $$

(☏0254-383 0969; www.villamaisoncondaoboutiquehotel.com; 46 Đ Nguyen Hue; mains 140,000-270,000d; ⊙10.30am-10pm; ☎) A supremely relaxing and elegant setting for a meal, this fine hotel restaurant features Asian dishes like panfried fish with lemongrass and chili and great Vietnamese curry. There's a comprehensive wine list, including options by the glass, as well as superb cocktails and mocktails.

Thu Ba
Vietnamese, Seafood $$

(☏0254-383 0255; Đ Vo Thi Sau; meals 80,000-230,000d) Thu Ba is renowned for seafood (consult what's on offer from the tanks by the entrance) and hotpots. The gregarious owner speaks great English and is happy to make suggestions based upon what's seasonal and fresh.

Bar200 Con Dao
Cafe $$

(http://divecondao.com; Đ Vo Thi Sau; meals 120,000-220,000d; ⊙10am-2pm & 5-10pm; ☎) With an attractive terrace and cosy interior, this popular cafe is great for coffee (including espresso and cappuccino) or smoothies (from 80,000d), plus Western comfort grub including filling breakfasts, burgers, pizza and sandwiches. After dark the beers and cocktails start flowing. It's run by a friendly team who are clued-up on island info and can help plan days out.

La Casa Con Dao
Cocktail Bar

(10 Đ Tran Phu; ⊙noon-midnight; ☎) Perhaps surprisingly, Con Son Town has one of the best bars in southern Vietnam, featuring perfectly mixed classic cocktails and expertly prepared homespun creations too. The ambience is relaxed and loungy, with mellow music and a convivial vibe – this is the perfect spot to unwind. The owners plan to introduce a tapas menu too.

ⓘ GETTING THERE & AROUND

There are seven daily flights between Con Son and HCMC jointly operated by Vasco and Vietnam Airlines.

The tiny airport is about 15km from the town centre. All of the big hotels on the island provide free transport both to and from the airport. Con Son Island has several taxis; hotels rent motorbikes and bicycles.

Con Son is also connected by **Superdong** (☏029 9384 3888; http://superdong.com.vn; Ben Dam port) ferries to Tran De in the Mekong Delta.

MEKONG DELTA

Mekong Delta at a Glance...

The 'rice bowl' of Vietnam, the delta is carpeted in a dizzying variety of greens. It's a water world that moves to the rhythms of the mighty Mekong, where boats, houses and markets float upon the innumerable rivers, canals and streams that criss-cross the landscape like arteries.

The bustling commerce of its towns contrasts sharply with the languid, almost soporific pace of life in the countryside. Mangrove forests teem with a wealth of bird life and bristle with the remains of Viet Cong bunkers, ornate Khmer pagodas and Buddhist temples reaching for the sky.

Two Days in the Mekong Delta

Join the throngs amid the bustling floating markets on a boat trip from **Can Tho** (p246), explore the city's temples, museums and pagodas, and then dine with a river view at **Spices Restaurant** (p249). The following day, head to nearby **Vinh Long** (p249) for a homestay experience with a local family.

Four Days in the Mekong Delta

Head to **Chau Doc** (p249) close to the border with Cambodia, a likeable town with significant Chinese, Cham and Khmer communities, and explore its cultural sights and market. Eat at **Memory Delicatessen** (p251). The next day head to sacred **Sam Mountain**, then enjoy a sundowner in **Tan Chau Salon Bar** (p251) and a memorable meal at **Bassac Restaurant** (p251).

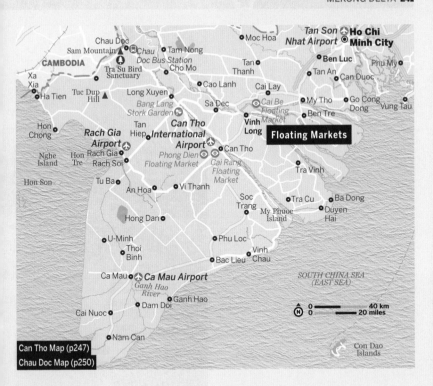

Moc Hoa •   Tan Son Ho Chi
  Nhat Airport Minh City

Chau Doc •
Sam Mountain ▲ • Chau • Tam Nong   Ben Luc •   Phu My •
CAMBODIA   Doc Bus Station   Tan •   Tan An •
Xa   Tra Su Bird • Cho Mo   Thanh   Can Duoc •
Xia   Sanctuary   • Cao Lanh   Cai Lay •
• Ha Tien   Tuc Dup ▲   Long Xuyen •   Cai Be • My Tho   • Go Cong
  Hill   Bang Lang   Sa Dec   Floating   • Ben Tre   Dong   Vung Tau
Hon •   Stork Garden   Vinh   Market
Chong   Tan   *Rach Gia* • *Can Tho*   Long   **Floating Markets**
  Hiep   *Airport*   *International*
Nghe   Hon   • Rach Gia   *Airport* • Can Tho
Island   Tre   Rach Soi •   *Phong Dien* •   *Cai Rang*
Hon Son   *Floating Market*   *Floating* • Tra Vinh
  Tu Ba •   • Vi Thanh   *Market*
  An Hoa •   Soc •   • Tra Cu   • Ba Dong
  Trang   My Phuoc   • Duyen
  Hong Dan •   Island   Hai
  • U-Minh   • Phu Loc
  • Thoi   Vinh
  Binh   • Bac Lieu • Chau   *SOUTH CHINA SEA*
  Ca Mau •   *Ca Mau Airport*   *(EAST SEA)*
  Ganh Hao
  River • Ganh Hao
  Cai Nuoc •   • Dam Doi   0   40 km
  Ⓝ 0   20 miles
  • Nam Can   Con Dao
  Islands

Can Tho Map (p247)
Chau Doc Map (p250)

Arriving in the Mekong Delta

The cities of Can Tho, Ben Tre, My Tho
and Vinh Long are all very accessible by
bus (or on tours) from Ho Chi Minh City.

Can Tho also has a busy **airport**, with
flights to HCMC, Dalat, Danang, Hanoi
and Phu Quoc.

Where to Stay

The towns and cities all have a decent
selection of good-value budget and midrange (and some luxury) hotels, but also
consider a stay in a **homestay** (p249)
to get to know rural life in the Mekong:
Vinh Long has a good selection.

Cai Rang Floating Market (p244)

Floating Markets

For many visitors, experiencing a Mekong Delta floating market is a highlight of their trip. There are many in the region, but those around Can Tho are the most famous.

Great For...

ⓘ Need to Know

Visit floating markets as early as possible in the morning for the best experience.

★ **Top Tip**
Taking a well-organised tour like Hieu's Tour (p247) will save a lot of hassle.

Can Tho has two huge floating markets, but Chau Doc and Vinh Long are two other possibilities.

Cai Rang Floating Market

Just 6km from Can Tho, Cai Rang is the biggest **floating market** (◷5am-noon) **FREE** in the Mekong Delta. There is a bridge here that serves as a great vantage point for photography. The market is best around 6am to 7am, and it's well worth getting here early to beat boatloads of tourists. This is a wholesale market, so look at what's tied to the long pole above the boat to figure out what they're selling to smaller traders.

Cai Rang can be seen from the road, but getting here is far more interesting by boat (US$10 to US$15). From the market area in Can Tho it takes about 45 minutes by river, or you can drive to the Cau Dau Sau boat landing (by the Dau Sau Bridge), from where it takes only about 10 minutes to reach the market.

Phong Dien Floating Market

The Mekong Delta's most intimate and best **floating market** (◷5am-noon) **FREE**, Phong Dien has fewer motorised craft and more stand-up rowing boats, with local vendors shopping and exchanging gossip. Less crowded than Cai Rang, there are also far fewer tourists. It's at its bustling best between 5am and 7am. The market is 20km southwest of Can Tho; you can get there by road but many operators now offer a six-hour combined Cai Rang–Phong Dien tour, returning to Can Tho through quieter backwaters.

Phong Dien Floating Market

Cai Be Floating Market

This **river market** (⊙5am-noon) is still the principal attraction on a boat tour from Vinh Long, though it has shrunk considerably due to the building of bridges in the delta and the subsequent transportation of goods by road rather than river. The market is at its best around 6am. Wholesalers on big boats moor here, each specialising in different types of fruit or vegetable, hanging samples of their goods from tall wooden poles. It's an hour by boat from Vinh Long.

A notable sight is the huge and photogenic Catholic cathedral on the riverside.

✖ Take a Break

Mekong (☏0292-369 9179; 38 Đ Hai Ba Trung; meals from 60,000d; ⊙7am-8pm; ☏) caters for all tastes and wallets.

Most people make detours on the way there or back to see the canals or visit orchards. For those travelling on an organised tour of the delta, it is customary to board a boat here, explore the islands and moor in Vinh Long before continuing to Can Tho.

To Market, To Market

Can Tho is the only place in the Delta where you may experience hassle from would-be guides. Some may accost you as soon as you get off the bus and even turn up at your lodgings after asking your *xe om* driver where you're headed. To choose who you go with, consider the following:

❍ What does the tour include? Is it a 40-minute dash to Cai Rang, returning to Can Tho straight away, or a half-day tour taking in smaller waterways?

❍ How big is the boat? Larger boats come equipped with life jackets, have roofs and get to the markets faster, but you'll be in a large group. Smaller boats make for a more intimate experience, but not all carry life jackets and may have flimsy roofs (or none at all), so you may end up doing a wet rat impression in a downpour.

❍ When does the tour depart? If you start out after 6.30am, you've missed the best of the action.

❍ Does the guide speak good English? Small boats along the riverside near the giant statue of Ho Chi Minh offer the cheapest deals, but you won't get a commentary on riverside life.

❍ Costs range from around 120,000d per hour (depending on your negotiating skills) for a small boat with the operator speaking a few words of English to around US$30 per person for a seven-hour tour taking in both markets, with a fluent English-speaking guide.

☑ Don't Miss

The Bang Lang (p246) bird sanctuary between Can Tho and Vinh Long.

Can Tho

The epicentre of the Mekong Delta, Can Tho is the largest city in the region. As the political, economic, cultural and transportation centre of the delta, it's a buzzing town with a lively waterfront lined with sculpted gardens, an appealing blend of narrow backstreets and wide boulevards. It is also the perfect base for nearby floating markets, the major draw for tourists who come here to boat along the many canals and rivers leading out of town.

◎ SIGHTS

Ong Temple   Temple

(32 Đ Hai Ba Trung; ⏱6am-8pm) FREE In a fantastic location facing the Can Tho River and decorated with huge, constantly burning incense coils, this Chinese temple is set inside the **Guangzhou Assembly Hall**, and

> *...astonishing views of thousands of resident storks and snowy egrets.*

wandering through its fragrant-smoke-filled interior is very enjoyable. It was originally built in the late 19th century to worship Kuang Kung, a deity symbolising loyalty, justice, reason, intelligence, honour and courage, among other merits. If you wait long enough, you'll witness how the incense coils are lit and hung up on long poles.

Pitu Kohsa
Rangsay Pagoda   Buddhist Pagoda

(Chua Pitu Khosa Rangsay; Map p231; http://coi phat.net; 27/2 Truong Dinh; ⏱dawn-dusk) FREE Trying to hide down a quiet backstreet, but gloriously gold, this three-level Theravada Buddhist pagoda from 1948 contrasts sharply against the grey adjacent buildings. Carved detailed wall patterns, painted columns, a huge Buddha statue and city views from the balcony are all impressive. Its charitable pursuits include helping disadvantaged youths to study.

Bang Lang
Stork Garden   Bird Sanctuary

(Vuon Co Bang Lang; Map p231; 8000đ; ⏱5am-6pm) On the road between Can

Ong Temple

SALAJEAN/SHUTTERSTOCK ©

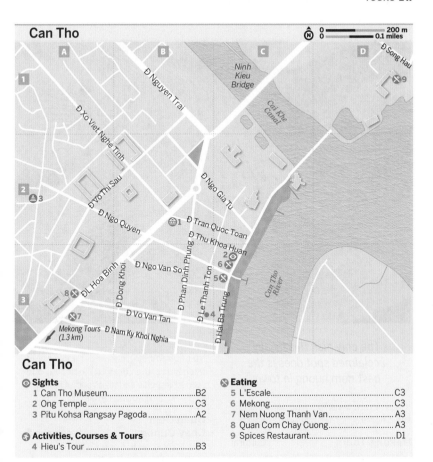

Can Tho

Tho and Long Xuyen, this is a magnificent 1.3-hectare bird sanctuary with astonishing views of thousands of resident storks and snowy egrets. There is a tall viewing platform to see the birds filling the branches; the best times to view this incredible sight are around dawn and dusk.

Can Tho Museum   Museum
(Bao Tang Can Tho; ☎0292-382 0955; 1 ĐL Hoa Binh; ⊗8-11am & 2-5pm Tue-Thu, 8-11am & 6.30-9pm Sat & Sun) FREE This large, well-presented museum brings local history to life. Displays (with ample English translations) focus on the Khmer and Chinese

communities, plant and fish specimens, rice production and, inevitably, various wars.

⊕ TOURS

Hieu's Tour   Cultural
(☎0939 666 156; www.hieutour.com; 27a Đ Le Thanh Ton) Young, enthusiastic, English-speaking guide Hieu and his team offer excellent, unique tours around Can Tho, from early-morning jaunts to the floating markets (US$25 to Cai Rang, US$29 to both markets per person) to cycling tours, food tours and even visits to **Pirate Island** (Quan Dao Ha Tien; Hai Tac) further afield. Hieu

Elephant-ear fish

ANN MOORE/SHUTTERSTOCK ©

The only dish this locally acclaimed spot does is the best nem nuong in town.

is keen to show visitors true delta culture and a floating homestay is in the works.

Mekong Tours Cultural

(📞090 785 2927; www.mekongtours.info; 93 Đ Mau Than) Based at Xoai Hotel, this operator offers highly recommended tours of the floating markets (Cai Rang US$25 to US$42 per boat for three people), as well as an entertaining nightly street food tour that departs the hotel at 6.30pm.

🍴 EATING

Nem Nuong
Thanh Van Vietnamese $

(📞0292-0382 7255; cnr Nam Ky Khoi Nghia & 30 Thang 4; meals 45,000d; ☺8am-9pm) The only dish this locally acclaimed spot does is the best *nem nuong* in town. Roll your own rice rolls using the ingredients provided: pork sausage, rice paper, green banana, star

fruit (carambola), cucumber and a riot of fresh herbs, then dip into the peanut-and-something-else sauce, its secret jealously guarded. Simple and fantastic!

Quan Com
Chay Cuong Vegetarian $

(9 Đ De Tham; meals from 15,000d; ☺11am-10pm; 🖉) On a street with plenty of eating options, this is one of the better and larger *com chay* (vegetarian) eateries in the city. The vegetable, rice and mock-meat dishes (including mock-chicken hotpot) are nicely prepared and the service is friendly. Order from the English menu or point at what you like at the buffet.

L'Escale International $$

(📞0292-381 9139; http://nambocantho.com; Nam Bo Boutique Hotel, 1 Đ Ngo Quyen; meals 180,000-500,000d; ☺6am-10.30pm; 🖉) With tantalising river views from the top of the Nam Bo Hotel and subdued romantic lighting, this is the place to canoodle with your sweetie over glasses of wine and beautifully executed dishes such as clay-pot fish with pineapple, sautéed garlic shrimp with spinach and smoked-duck salad.

Spices
Restaurant International $$$

(☎0292-0381 0111; Victoria Can Tho Resort, Cai Khe, Ninh Kieu; meals 200,000-680,000d; ⊙6am-10pm; ☎☑) Go for a table overlooking the river at this fine restaurant, refined without being stuffy, and opt for the beautifully presented trio of salads (green papaya, banana flower, green mango) or the assortment starter for two, and follow up with deep-fried elephant fish or pork-stuffed squid. Lamb shanks and seared duck cater to homesick palates and the desserts are magnificent.

GETTING THERE & AWAY

Can Tho International Airport (www.cantho airport.com; Đ Le Hong Phong), 10km northwest of the city centre, has flights to Dalat, Danang, Hanoi and Phu Quoc.

Long-distance buses depart from the main bus station, 2.5km northwest of the centre, to Can Tho and HCMC very regularly.

Chau Doc

Draped along the banks of the Hau Giang River (Bassac River), Chau Doc sees plenty of travellers washing through on the river route between Cambodia and Vietnam. Chau Doc's cultural diversity – apparent in the mosques, temples, churches and nearby pilgrimage sites – makes it fascinating to explore. It's also a good base for trips to Sam Mountain.

SIGHTS

Floating Houses House

(Đ Tran Hung Dao) These rusty houses, whose floats consist of empty metal drums, are both a place to live and a livelihood for their residents. Under each house, fish are raised in suspended metal nets. The fish flourish in their natural river habitat; the family can feed them whatever scraps are handy. You

 Vinh Long 'Homestays'

For many travellers, the chance to experience river life and get to know a local family is a highlight of a Mekong visit. Perhaps 'homestay' is the wrong word: in most cases you will actually be staying in specially constructed rustic hostels and guesthouses.

Some homestays have large communal rooms with bunks, while others offer basic bungalows with shared facilities and some even have rooms with en suites. Breakfast is usually included; in some places you'll share a meal with the family, while in bigger places there are simple restaurants. The only constant is a verdant, rustic setting and a taste of rural life.

Although many tourists book through group tours in Ho Chi Minh City, you can just take the ferry from Vinh Long and then a *xe om* to your preferred choice. Some hosts don't speak much English, but welcome foreign guests just the same.

Can Tho homestay

can get a close-up look by hiring a tourist boat (p247).

Chau Doc
Floating Market Market

(⊙5am-noon) You need to get up at the crack of dawn to see the best of this floating market. The action is busiest around 5am to 6am, when locals gather to buy fresh produce wholesale. Less colourful and much calmer than other floating markets.

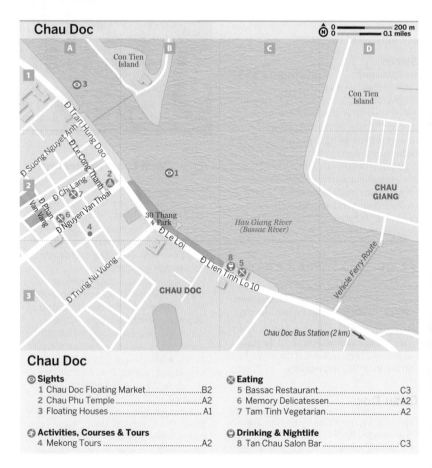

Chau Doc

Chau Phu Temple
Buddhist Temple

(Dinh Than Nguyen Huu Canh; cnr Đ Nguyen Van Thoai & Đ Gia Long; ☺dawn-dusk) FREE In 1926 this temple was built to worship the Nguyen dynasty official Thoai Ngoc Hau, buried at Sam Mountain. The grubby yellow structure is decorated with both Vietnamese and Chinese motifs; inside are funeral tablets bearing the names of the deceased as well as biographical information about them. There's also a shrine to Ho Chi Minh.

⊙ TOURS

Mekong Tours
Cultural

(☏098 308 6355; 41 Đ Quang Trung) Local travel agency for booking boat or bus transport to Phnom Penh, boat trips on the Mekong, cars with drivers and day tours. One of the few ways to join a Tra Su Bird Sanctuary group tour (US$12), in comfortable small buses, with pick-up from your hotel. Staff speak good English.

🍴 EATING & DRINKING

Tam Tinh Vegetarian
Vegetarian $

(Com Chay Tam Tinh; 🖉0296-386 5064; Quang Trung near Chi Lang; meals 25,000d; 🖉) There's vegetarian and then there's exceptional smoky mock chicken, lemongrass tofu and garlic morning glory all on a plate with rice, plus a sweet and sour soup, for a bargain price. Point and choose from the display out front.

Memory Delicatessen
International $$

(57 Đ Nguyen Huu Canh; meals 60,000-179,000d; ☺6am-10pm; ❄🛜🖉) This glossy cafe-restaurant that attracts local trendies is memorable for its wonderful melange of international dishes, from the excellent pizzas topped with imported ingredients to the fragrant vegetable curry with coconut milk and lemongrass, accompanied by an array of fresh juices and imaginative shakes. Skip dessert, though, unless it's the homemade ice cream.

Bassac Restaurant
French, Vietnamese $$$

(🖉0296-386 5010; 32 Đ Le Loi; meals 170,000-450,000d; ☺6am-10pm; 🖉) Chau Doc's most sophisticated dining experience is at the Victoria Chau Doc Hotel where the menu veers between wonderful interna-tional dishes (roast rack of lamb, seared duck breast), dishes with a French accent (provençale tart, gratin dauphinoise) and beautifully presented Vietnamese dishes, such as grilled squid with green pepper-corns. The apple pie with cinnamon ice cream makes for a sublime ending.

Tan Chau Salon Bar
Bar

(www.victoriahotels.asia; Victoria Chau Doc Hotel, 32 Đ Le Loi; ☺6am-11pm) Sip a cocktail amid elegant Indochine surroundings.

 Tra Su Bird Sanctuary

This immense 800,000-hectare **forest** (Rung Tram Tra Su; admission 120,000d, boat rides per person 75,000d; ☺7am-4pm) is home to an astounding number of wading birds. Much of the wetland is off-limits to visitors so that the birds' breeding grounds are not disturbed, but visits include a short speedboat ride and a tranquil 20-minute paddle along narrow channels through the gnarled and green sunken forest. Even if you only spot a few birds, it's a beautiful, if short, green trip. The sanctuary is 23km west of town.

The best time to visit is December to January, when the babies hatch. Motorbike tours from Chau Doc cost around US$20 per person. Group tours organised by Mekong Tours cost US$12 per person, with pick-up in comfortable small buses, admission and rides in-cluded. While there's a greater likelihood of sharing rowboats, with three passen-gers per boat it's hardly a problem.

Cruising the Mekong River
ANDREAS ROSE/SHUTTERSTOCK ©

ℹ️ GETTING THERE & AWAY

Comfortable long-distance buses to Can Tho and HCMC are operated by Phuong Trang, departing from the main bus station, around 2km out of the centre.

Sao Beach (p259)

PHU QUOC

Phu Quoc at a Glance...

Fringed with white-sand beaches and with large tracts still cloaked in dense, tropical jungle, Phu Quoc has rapidly morphed from a sleepy island backwater to a must-visit beach escape.

Beyond the resorts lining Long Beach and development beginning on the east coast, there's still ample room for exploration and escaping. Dive the reefs, kayak in the bays, eat up the back-road miles on a motorbike, or just lounge on the beach, indulge in a massage and dine on fresh seafood.

Two Days on Phu Quoc

Savour the tropical life by enjoying a day relaxing on **Long Beach** (p260), strolling along the powdery white sand, swimming and perhaps indulging in a massage. Dine at **Saigonese** (p263). The next day book a tour of the gorgeous **An Thoi Islands** (p260), which are perfect for snorkelling.

Four Days on Phu Quoc

Investigate Duong Dong town, and take in the (infamous) **Fish Sauce Factory** (p260) and **Dinh Cau Temple** (p261). In the afternoon head to beautiful **Sao Beach** (p259). On day four explore the island, visiting remote coves such as **Cua Can Beach** (p258) and the spectacular **Ho Quoc Pagoda** (p260). Finish off with a seafood feast at **Phu Quoc Night Market** (p262).

CAMBODIA
Hon Ban
VIETNAM

0 — 10 km
0 — 5 miles

Thom Beach

Ganh Dau

Phu Quoc
National Park

Hon Doi Moi
(Turtle Island)

Dai
Beach

Cua Can River

Vung Bau
Beach

Cua Can
Beach

Khu
Tuong

Bai Bung

Ong Thay

Ong Lang
Beach

Gulf of
Thailand

**Duong
Dong**

Suoi
Tranh

Suoi Da Ban

Ham Ninh

Coi Nguon
Museum

Phu Quoc
International Airport

Long
Beach

Vong Beach

Ho Quoc Pagoda

Dam Beach

Cau Sau Hamlet
Phu Quoc Prison
Sao Beach

Tau Ru
Bay
An Thoi

Khem Beach

Duong Dong Map (p262)

Arriving on Phu Quoc

Air Phu Quoc airport has excellent connections to Ho Chi Minh City, Can Tho and Hanoi plus international connections including Singapore and Bangkok.

Boat There are fast boats to Phu Quoc from the mainland towns of Ha Tien and Rach Gia, and also car ferries.

Where to Stay

Long Beach has an excellent selection of accommodation, while coves such as Ong Lang and Sao Beach also offer a great beach base.

Sao Beach (p259)

Beach Hopping on Phu Quoc

Phu Quoc is developing fast, but still liberally sprinkled with picture-perfect white-sand beaches and lovely coves. As most locals dislike sunbathing, beaches are rarely packed in the heat of the day.

Great For...

☑ **Don't Miss**

The Suoi Tranh (p261) waterfall is perfect for a cooling dip after a hot day on the road.

ℹ Need to Know

The island is 48km long and hilly in the north; set off early if you want to do the entire loop described here.

Beyond the resorts lining Long Beach, development beginning on the east coast and mega resorts in sight of Sao Beach, there's still room for exploration and escaping the sometimes littered waters. Explore the island on a scooter, or join an island tour.

From Duong Dong head north along the coastal road and you'll pass a succession of lovely sandy bays perfect for chilling. If you've time, you can also take in a ride through the national park and some of the scenery on the remote east coast too before returning via a waterfall to Duong Dong.

Cua Can Beach

The most accessible of the northern beaches, **Cua Can** (Bai Cua Can) is about 11km from Duong Dong. It remains mercifully quiet during the week, but can get busy at weekends. A ride through the villages around Cua Can is interesting, with the road crossing the river several times on rickety wooden bridges.

Vung Bau Beach

Appealing northern **beach** (Bai Vung Bau) reachable via the coastal road. The waves are rough and it's a little neglected (with some rubbish evident), but this means that you can have the beach without the crowds. The few resorts here have nothing around them but beach, and even electricity is currently switched off at night.

Dai Beach

A relatively isolated northern **beach** (Bai Dai) that retains its remote tropical charm.

Phu Quoc National Park

Phu Quoc National Park

About 90% of Phu Quoc is forested and the trees and adjoining marine environment enjoy official protection. This is the last large stand of forest in the south, and in 2010 the park was declared a Unesco Biosphere Reserve. The forest is densest in northern Phu Quoc, in the **Khu Rung Nguyen Sinh** forest reserve; you'll need a motorbike or mountain bike to tackle the bumpy dirt roads that cut through it. There are no real hiking trails.

Thom Beach

The road from Dai Beach to **Thom Beach** (Bai Thom) via Ganh Dau is very beautiful, passing through dense forest with tantalising glimpses of the coast below.

Sao Beach

With picture-perfect white sand, the delightful curve of beautiful **Sao Beach** (Bai Sao) bends out alongside a sea of mineral-water clarity just a few kilometres from An Thoi, the main shipping port at the southern tip of the island. There are a couple of beachfront restaurants, where you can settle into a deckchair or partake in water sports.

> ✕ **Take a Break**
> The deck at Mango Bay Restaurant (p263) makes the perfect setting for a languid lunch.

O. SHUMILOVA/SHUTTERSTOCK ©

> ★ **Top Tip**
> Pack a mask and snorkel in your daypack.

⊙ SIGHTS

Long Beach   Beach

(Bai Truong) Long Beach is draped invitingly along the west coast from Duong Dong almost to An Thoi port. Development concentrates in the north near Duong Dong, where the recliners and rattan umbrellas of the various resorts rule; these are the only stretches that are kept garbage-free. With its west-facing aspect, sunsets can be stupendous.

Although not the prettiest, Long Beach is a good budget choice for accommodation and socialising, and from its north end, Duong Dong and its night market are in walking distance.

An Thoi Islands   Island

(Quan Dao An Thoi) Just off the southern tip of Phu Quoc, these 15 islands and islets are a paradise of white sand and blue waters. They can be visited by chartered boat for a fine day of sightseeing, fishing, swimming and snorkelling. Hon Thom (Pineapple Island) is about 3km in length and is the largest island in the group.

Most boats depart from An Thoi on Phu Quoc, but you can make arrangements through hotels on Long Beach, as well as dive operators.

Ho Quoc Pagoda   Buddhist Temple

(Chua Truc Lam Ho Quoc; Thien Vien Truc Lam Ho Quoc; P) FREE On a remote stretch of coastal road 10km north of Sao Beach, climb the stairs for one of the best views from any temple in Vietnam – blue sky and the water off Bai Dam Beach frame the temple-gate eaves. Behind you, green hills. Ho Quoc was only built in 2012 and features a Quan Am statue and a giant bell. Admirers of Ho Quoc venture here for sunrise and full moon evenings.

Fish Sauce Factory   Factory

(www.hungthanhfishsauce.com.vn; Duong Dong; ⊙8-11am & 1-5pm) FREE The distillery of Nuoc Mam Hung Thanh is the largest of Phu Quoc's fish-sauce makers, a short walk

> *...climb the stairs for one of the best views from any temple in Vietnam...*

Ho Quoc Pagoda

TONKINPHOTOGRAPHY/SHUTTERSTOCK ©

from the market in Duong Dong. At first glance, the giant wooden vats may make you think you've arrived for a wine tasting, but one sniff of the festering *nuoc mam* essence jolts you back to reality. Take a guide along unless you speak Vietnamese.

Phu Quoc Prison   Museum
(Nha Tu Phu Quoc; Coconut Prison; http://
phuquocprison.org; Nguyen Van Cu; ⊗8-11.30am
& 1.30-5pm) **FREE** Not far from Sao Beach in the south of the island, Phu Quoc's notorious old prison, built by the French in the late 1940s, contains a small museum that narrates (in English) the gruesome history of the jail. Much of the site comprises mannequins of Vietnamese soldiers in chilling reenactments, such as being forced to stand and starve in exposed outdoor barbed wire cages. A war memorial stands south of the prison on the far side of the road.

Coi Nguon Museum   Museum
(149 Tran Hung Dao; 20,000d; ⊗8am-5pm) With displays on Vietnamese medicines, Stone Age tools, a boatful of barnacle-encrusted ceramics, oddly compelling shell-covered furniture and a small room devoted to the island prison, this dusty private museum is an oddball introduction to Phu Quoc history and culture. But did the marine fauna section really require the untimely demise of 14 hawksbill turtles?

Dinh Cau Temple   Taoist Temple
(Cau Castle; Đ Bach Dang, Duong Dong) **FREE**
This combination temple and lighthouse was built in 1937 to honour Thien Hau, the Goddess of the Sea, who provides protection for sailors and fishers. Sometimes called a 'castle', or 'rock temple' for the rocky outcrop it clings to, Dinh Cau gives you a good view of the harbour entrance. The promenade is popular with locals taking a stroll at sunset.

🏃 ACTIVITIES
Flipper Diving Club   Diving
(☏0297-399 4924; www.flipperdiving.com; 60 Đ
Tran Hung Dao; ⊗7am-7pm) Centrally located,

 Waterfalls

Compared with the waterlogged Mekong Delta, Phu Quoc has very little surface moisture, but there are several springs originating in the hills and a couple of waterfalls.

The most accessible of these is 4m high **Suoi Tranh** (☏0297-384 9863; 5000d; ⊗7am-9pm); look for the entrance sign and concrete tree from the Duong Dong–Vong Beach road. From the ticket counter it's a 10-minute walk through the forest to the falls.

Suoi Da Ban (admission 5000d, motorbike 1000d) is a white-water creek tumbling across some attractive large granite boulders. There are deep pools and it's nice enough for a dip. Bring plenty of mosquito repellent. For the falls, the best months to visit are between May and September – by the end of the dry season there's little more than a trickle.

Suoi Tranh
FRANK FISCHBACH/SHUTTERSTOCK ©

multilingual PADI dive centre for everything from novice dive trips to full instructor courses. Very professional, with plenty of diving experience worldwide, and with instructors who put you at ease if you're a newbie.

🌀 TOURS
Jerry's Jungle Tours   Boat Tour, Hiking
(☏0938 226 021; www.jerrystours.wixsite.com/
jerrystours; 106 Đ Tran Hung Dao; day trips from
US$30) Archipelago explorations by boat,

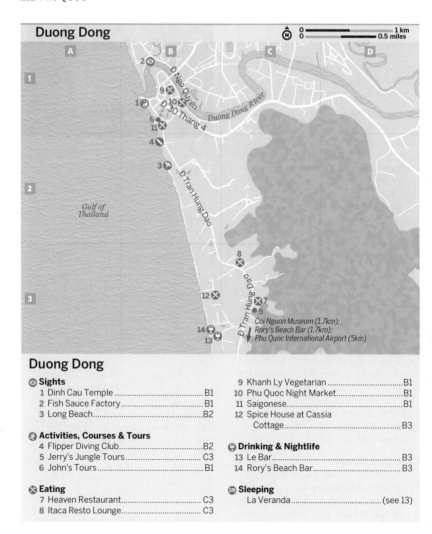

Duong Dong

with snorkelling, fishing, one-day and multiday trips to islands, motorbike tours, bouldering, birdwatching, hiking and cultural tours around Phu Quoc.

⊗ EATING

Phu Quoc Night Market   Seafood $
(Cho Dem Phu Quoc; Đ Bach Dang; meals from 50,000d; ⊙4.30pm-3am;) The most atmospheric and best-value place to dine on

the island, Duong Dong's busy night market has stalls of snacks, coconut ice cream and a parade of outdoor restaurants serving a delicious range of Vietnamese seafood, grills and vegetarian options. Quality can be a mixed bag, so follow the discerning local crowd. Riverside tables can be a bit whiffy.

Khanh Ly Vegetarian   Vegan $
(☏0297-281 0180; 35 Đ Nguyen Trai; meals 20,000-45,000d; ⊙8am-8pm;) Pick and

choose from a buffet of Vietnamese vegan-vegetarian dishes, such as mock shrimp on sugarcane, to accompany green veg and rice for an excellent value, delicious plate. Staff are friendly, and there are also hearty noodle soups to tempt carnivores.

Heaven Restaurant   Vietnamese $

(☑0975 542 769; 141 Đ Tran Hung Dao; meals 40,000-90,000d; ◷8am-11pm; 🖋) You may not expect heaven to have basic wooden tables opening onto a road, but it does at this good-value family joint. Expect fresh, generous servings of Vietnamese dishes such as lemongrass chicken, and a very long list of vegetarian options.

Spice House at Cassia Cottage   Vietnamese $$

(www.cassiacottage.com; 100c Đ Tran Hung Dao; meals 190,000-300,000d; ◷7-10am & 11am-10pm) Nab a seaview table, order a papaya salad, grilled garlic prawns, *banh xeo* (Vietnamese pancake), cinnamon-infused okra, a delectable Khmer fish curry or grilled beef skewers wrapped in betel leaves and time dinner to catch the sunset at this excellent restaurant. There's even a single romantic cabana table right on the sand. It's the best resort option, attracting plenty of non-resort guests.

Saigonese   Fusion $$

(☑0938 059 650; 14 Đ Tran Hung Dao; meals 150,000-220,000d; ◷9am-1pm & 5-11pm Wed-Mon) The hippest, casual dining on Phu Quoc delights with fusion dishes lifted from designer cookbooks. The appetizers excel in *bao* (steamed buns filled with pulled beef and beetroot), and squid with avocado cream. Try the caramelised shrimp claypot and for dessert, popcorn banana cake. Manager Thao's experiences abroad show in the chic ambience; the biggest surprise is the reasonable bill for on-trend eats.

Mango Bay Restaurant   International $$

(☑0297-398 1693; http://mangobayphuquoc. com; Mango Bay Resort, Ong Lang Beach; meals 135,000-410,000d; ◷7am-9pm; 🖋) One of the best eating experiences around is to sit on the deck at Mango Bay, dining on tamarind blue-swimmer crab and peering out to sea. There are Australian beef steaks, honey duck breast and lots of Thai flavours too. The calm atmosphere and bar with a good drinks list add to the pleasure.

Itaca Resto Lounge   Fusion $$$

(www.itacalounge.com; 119 Đ Tran Hung Dao; tapas 90,000-195,000d, meals 170,000-550,000d; ◷6pm-11.45pm Thu-Tue; 🖥🖋) This much-applauded restaurant has a winning Mediterranean-Asian fusion menu (with tapas), a much-enjoyed alfresco arrangement and friendly, welcoming hosts. Don't expect sea views, but do expect wagyu beef burgers, seared tuna with passion fruit, wild-mushroom risotto and a charming ambience.

🍷 DRINKING & NIGHTLIFE

Rory's Beach Bar   Bar

(☑0919 333 950; 118/10 Đ Tran Hung Dao; ◷9am-1am) Phu Quoc's liveliest and most fun beach bar draws a steady torrent of travellers and island residents down the path to its seaside perch. Expect bonfires on the beach, great happy hour specials and staff happy to chat.

Le Bar   Bar

(118/9 Đ Tran Hung Dao; ◷8am-11pm; 🖥) With its gorgeous tiled floor, art deco furniture and colonial charms, this highly elegant and well-poised upstairs lounge-bar at **La Veranda** (☑0297-398 2988; www.laveranda resort.com; r US$225-340, villas US$400-570; 🏵◉🖥🏊) is a superb spot for a terrace sundowner.

ℹ GETTING THERE & AROUND

Phu Quoc International Airport (www.phuquo-cairport.com) is 10km southeast of Duong Dong. Motorbikes and bicycles can be hired from most hotels. **Mai Linh** (☑0297-397 9797) is a reliable taxi operator.

Trieu Chau Assembly Hall, Hoi An (p134)

In Focus

Hanoi (p34)

QUANG VU/500PX ©

Vietnam Today

For most Vietnamese, the past 20 years have been
something of a golden era. The conflicts of the past
century are not forgotten but long over, the standard of
living has risen remarkably and the nation's economy
is thriving. Yet Vietnam remains resolutely a one-party
state, its leaders very sensitive to protest and dissent.

Online Activism

In May 2016 the hashtag #*toichonca* ('I choose fish') became Vietnam's most used social media slogan. This somewhat unlikely phrase went viral in response to an industrial toxic spill by Formosa, a Taiwanese company. An investigation confirmed the company had contaminated a 200km stretch of central Vietnamese coastline resulting in millions of dead fish and thousands of idle fishermen. Formosa's initial response was to suggest people choose either to catch fish or have industry, sparking nationwide protests. But the company later acknowledged responsibility and agreed to pay US$500 million in compensation.

Environmental disasters are not uncommon in Vietnam but the post-Formosa protests were unusual in a country where the internet is tightly controlled and dissent is not tolerated. Nguyen Ngoc Nhu Quynh, who uses the moniker 'Mother Mushroom', is a blogger

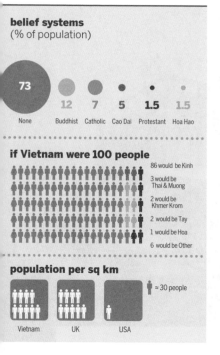

belief systems
(% of population)

73 None
12 Buddhist
7 Catholic
5 Cao Dai
1.5 Protestant
1.5 Hoa Hao

if Vietnam were 100 people

86 would be Kinh
3 would be Thai & Muong
2 would be Khmer Krom
2 would be Tay
1 would be Hoa
6 would be Other

population per sq km

≈ 30 people

Vietnam
UK
USA

who campaigns on environmental, social and political issues (such as bauxite mining and police brutality) and was a very vocal protester against Formosa. She's currently in jail: a 10-year prison term was issued to her for conducting 'propaganda against the state'. Human Rights Watch, which has campaigned for the release of other activists in Vietnam, has called for her immediate release, claiming the government is using her as an example to intimidate others. The government's position is that she was prosecuted in accordance with Vietnamese law regarding anti-state activity.

Asian Tiger

Vietnam has enjoyed over two decades of consistent growth, matching China as one of the world's fastest-growing economies. Per-capita income has risen from just US$98 in 1993 to US$2290 in 2017, as Vietnam has joined the ranks of East Asian 'tiger' nations. Record numbers of Vietnamese (6.5 million in 2016) are travelling abroad. The country is a leading agricultural exporter – the second-largest coffee producer in the world – and has a strong industrial and manufacturing base. This period has not been without growing pains, but with record levels of foreign investment continuing, Vietnam's future looks bright.

Walk This Way

Crossing the road in Vietnamese cities can feel like dodging bullets in a firing range, such are the numbers of motorbikes on the road. In a nation addicted to two-wheeled travel, where over 80% of the population owns a motorcycle, traffic-free zones have been somewhat slow to get off the ground. But pedestrianisation schemes have now been established in Hoi An, Hue, HCMC and Hanoi (albeit only for limited hours). Negotiating Vietnamese sidewalks is another formidable challenge, as access is routinely blocked by an intimidating combo of missing paving slabs, food stalls, the odd open sewer, and yes, lots of parked motorbikes.

In February 2017, a worthy (if optimistic) initiative to reclaim the sidewalks was launched in HCMC by the city authorities seeking to encourage citizens to take up walking instead. And for Doan Ngoc Hai, nicknamed 'Captain Sidewalk' – the official tasked with keeping pavements clear and orderly – that has meant death threats.

Getting the Saigonese off their scooters will be a tough task; *Tuoi Tre* (Youth) newspaper reported that many of the city's office workers walk only 600 steps a day. Initiatives are certainly urgently needed to tackle urban air pollution in Vietnam, which verges on toxic: Hanoi ranked as the second-most polluted city in the world in October 2016 and tens of thousands of premature deaths are caused by high levels of particulate matter.

Ho Chi Minh's Mausoleum (p44)

History

The Vietnamese trace their roots back to the Red River Delta where farmers first cultivated rice. Millennia of struggle against the Chinese then followed. Vietnam only became a united state in the 19th century, but quickly faced the ignominy of French colonialism and then the devastation of the American intervention. The Vietnamese nation has survived tempestuous, troubled times, but its strength of character has served it well.

2789 BC
The Van Lang kingdom, considered the first independent Vietnamese state, is founded by the Hung Vuong kings.

2000 BC
The Bronze Age Dong Son culture emerges in the Red River Delta around Hanoi, renowned for rice cultivation and bronzeware.

111 BC
The Han emperors of China annex the Red River Delta region of Vietnam, heralding 1000 years of Chinese rule.

Tomb of Khai Dinh (p119)

STEVE LOVEGROVE/SHUTTERSTOCK ©

The Early Days

Humans first inhabited northern Vietnam about 500,000 years ago, though it took until 7000 BC for these hunter gatherers to practise rudimentary agriculture. The sophisticated Dong Son culture, famous for its bronze moko drums, emerged sometime around the 3rd century BC. The Dong Son period also saw huge advances in rice cultivation and the emergence of the Red River Delta as a major agricultural centre.

From the 1st to 6th centuries AD, southern Vietnam was part of the Indianised Cambodian kingdom of Funan – famous for its refined art and architecture. Funan's principal port city was Oc-Eo in the Mekong Delta, and archaeological excavations here suggest there was contact with China, Indonesia, Persia and even Mediterranean countries.

The Hindu kingdom of Champa emerged around present-day Danang in the late 2nd century AD. Like Funan, it adopted Sanskrit as a sacred language and borrowed heavily from Indian art and culture. By the 8th century, Champa had expanded southward to include what is now Nha Trang and Phan Rang. The Cham were a feisty bunch who

AD 40	602	1010
The Trung Sisters vanquish the Chinese and proclaim themselves queens of an independent Vietnam.	Rebellions by leaders including Ly Bon and Trieu Quang Phuc against Chinese rule ultimately fail.	Thang Long (City of the Soaring Dragon), known today as Hanoi, is founded and becomes the new capital of Vietnam.

War Remnants Museum (p196)

★ **The War in Numbers**

3689 US fixed-wing aircraft lost

4857 US helicopters downed

15 million tonnes of US ammunition expended

58,183 Americans killed or MIA

Four million Vietnamese dead or injured

conducted raids along the entire coast of Indochina, and thus found themselves in a perpetual state of war with the Vietnamese to the north and the Khmers to the south. Ultimately this cost them their kingdom, as they found themselves squeezed between these two great powers.

One Thousand Years of Chinese Domination

The Chinese conquered the Red River Delta in the 2nd century BC. Over the following centuries, large numbers of Chinese settlers, officials and scholars moved south, seeking to impress a centralised state system on the Vietnamese.

In the most famous act of resistance, in AD 40, the Trung Sisters (Hai Ba Trung) rallied the people, raised an army and led a revolt against the Chinese. The Chinese counterattacked, but, rather than surrender, the Trung Sisters threw themselves into the Hat Giang River.

The early Vietnamese learned much from the Chinese, including the advancement of dykes and irrigation works – reinforcing the role of rice as the 'staff of life'. As food became more plentiful the population expanded, forcing the Vietnamese to seek new lands south along the coast.

During this era, Vietnam was a key port of call on the sea route between China and India. The Chinese introduced Confucianism, Taoism and Mahayana Buddhism to Vietnam, while the Indian influence brought Theravada Buddhism and Hinduism.

Liberation from China

In the early 10th century, the Tang dynasty collapsed, provoking the Vietnamese to launch a revolt against Chinese rule. In AD 938, popular patriot Ngo Quyen defeated Chinese forces by luring the Chinese fleet up the Bach Dang River in a feigned retreat, only to counterattack and impale their ships on sharpened stakes hidden beneath the waters.

1427	16th century	1516
Le Loi triumphs over the Chinese, declaring himself emperor, the first in the long line of the Le dynasty.	HCMC begins life as humble Prey Nokor, a backwater Khmer village in what was then the eastern edge of Cambodia.	Portuguese traders land at Danang, sparking the start of European interest in Vietnam.

From the 11th to 13th centuries, Vietnamese independence was consolidated under the emperors of the Ly dynasty, founded by Ly Thai To. This was a period of progress that saw the introduction of an elaborate dyke system for flood control and cultivation, and the establishment of the country's first university. During the Ly dynasty, the Chinese, the Khmer and the Cham launched attacks on Vietnam, but all were repelled.

The Chinese took control of Vietnam again in the early 15th century, taking the national archives and some of the country's intellectuals back to Nanjing – a loss that was to have a lasting impact on Vietnamese civilisation. Heavy taxation and slave labour were also typical of the era.

But in 1418, wealthy philanthropist Le Loi sparked the Lam Son Uprising by refusing to serve as an official for the Chinese Ming dynasty. By 1425, local rebellions had erupted in several regions and Le Loi travelled the countryside to rally the people, and eventually defeat the Chinese.

Le Loi and his successors launched a campaign to take over Cham lands to the south, which culminated in the occupation of its capital Vijaya, near present-day Quy Nhon in 1471.

> ### Street Names
>
> All Vietnamese street names are controlled by an intensely patriotic Communist Party. These reflect important dates, battles, heroes and heroines.
>
> **30 Thang 4** The date (30th April) Communist forces captured Saigon.
>
> **Hai Bai Trung** Two sisters who lead a revolt against Chinese rule in AD 40.
>
> **Le Loi** Robin Hood–style rebel leader; vanquished the Chinese in 1427.
>
> **Nguyen Thai Hoc** Lead the Yen Bai revolt against the French.
>
> **Quang Trung** Ruthless 18th-century military leader, emperor and reformer.
>
> **Tran Hunh Dao** Defeated Kublai Khan and invading Mongol forces.

Division & Unity

Vietnam found itself divided in two throughout much of the 17th and 18th centuries. The powerful Trinh Lords ruled the North. To the South were the Nguyen Lords. By this time, several European nations were interested in Vietnam's potential and were jockeying for influence, while China again contested control of the North.

In 1802, Nguyen Anh proclaimed himself Emperor Gia Long, thus beginning the Nguyen dynasty. When he captured Hanoi, his work was complete and, for the first time in two centuries, Vietnam was united, with Hue as its new capital city.

1802	**1883**	**1941**
Emperor Gia Long takes the throne and the Nguyen dynasty is born, ruling over Vietnam until 1945.	The French impose the Treaty of Protectorate on the Vietnamese, marking the start of 70 years of colonial control.	Ho Chi Minh forms the Viet Minh, a liberation movement seeking independence from France and fighting the Japanese occupation.

The French Takeover

France's military activity in Vietnam began in 1847, when the French Navy attacked Danang harbour. Saigon was seized in early 1859 and, in 1862, Emperor Tu Duc signed a treaty that gave the French the three eastern provinces of Cochinchina.

In 1872 Jean Dupuis, a merchant seeking to supply salt and weapons via the Red River, seized the Hanoi Citadel. A French conquest of the North followed, and in 1883 they attacked Hue and the Treaty of Protectorate was imposed on the imperial court.

The French colonial authorities carried out ambitious public works, such as the construction of the Saigon–Hanoi railway and draining of the Mekong Delta swamps. These projects were funded by heavy government taxes, which had a devastating impact on the rural economy.

Fight for Independence

Throughout the colonial period, the desire of many Vietnamese for independence simmered below the surface. Nationalist aspirations often erupted into open defiance of the French.

Leading patriots soon realised that modernisation was the key to an independent Vietnam. Vietnamese intellectuals favoured the education of the masses, the modernisation of the economy and working with the French towards independence.

The most successful of the anti-colonialists were the communists who were able to tune into the frustrations and aspirations of the population – especially the peasants. In 1941 Ho Chi Minh formed the Viet Minh, which resisted the Vichy French government, as well as Japanese forces, and carried out extensive political activities during WWII. As well as being a communist, Ho appeared pragmatic, patriotic and populist and understood the need for national unity.

For a time, Vietnam was spared the ravages of Japanese occupation. However, as WWII drew to a close, Japanese rice requisitions, combined with floods and breaches in the dykes, caused a horrific famine in which perhaps two million North Vietnamese people starved to death.

By the spring of 1945 the Viet Minh controlled large swathes of the country, particularly in the north. In mid-August, Ho Chi Minh called for a general uprising, later known as the August Revolution, then, on 2 September 1945 he declared independence. Throughout this period, he wrote eight letters to the US asking for aid, but received no replies.

With near anarchy in the South and the Chinese occupying the North, Ho decided to accept a temporary return of the French deeming them less of a long-term threat than the Chinese. But the détente quickly began to unravel as fighting broke out in Hanoi, and Ho Chi Minh and his forces fled to the mountains to regroup, where they would remain for the next eight years.

1945	1954	1955
Ho Chi Minh proclaims Vietnamese independence on 2 September in Ba Dinh Square in central Hanoi.	French forces surrender to Viet Minh fighters as the siege of Dien Bien Phu comes to a dramatic close on 7 May.	Vietnam is 'temporarily' divided into North Vietnam and South Vietnam and people are given 300 days to relocate.

Conflict between the French and Viet Minh rumbled on for years. But on 7 May 1954, after a 57-day siege, more than 10,000 starving French troops surrendered to the Viet Minh at Dien Bien Phu. This defeat brought an end to the French colonial adventure in Indochina.

Resolutions included the 'temporary' division of Vietnam into two zones at the Ben Hai River (near the 17th Parallel) until nationwide elections could be held. The South was ruled by a government led by Ngo Dinh Diem, a fiercely anti-communist Catholic. Nationwide elections were never held, as the Americans rightly feared that Ho Chi Minh would win with a massive majority.

As time went on Diem became increasingly tyrannical, closing Buddhist monasteries, imprisoning monks and banning opposition parties and doling out power to family members. The US began to see Diem as a liability and threw its support behind a military coup, launched by a group of young generals in November 1963.

'We Were Wrong'

Commentators and historians have since observed that if Washington had allowed Vietnam's long history of successfully repelling invaders to deter it, the extensive tragedy of the American War might have been averted, and likewise the resulting social disruption in America, as people sought to come to terms with what had happened in Vietnam. An entire generation of Americans had to assess its conduct. Years later, one of the architects of the war, former Defense Secretary Robert NcNamara, stated in his memoir, 'We were wrong, terribly wrong. We owe it to future generations to explain why'.

War with the Americans

The communists' campaign to liberate the South began in 1959. The Ho Chi Minh Trail reopened for business, universal military conscription was implemented and the National Liberation Front (NLF), later known as the Viet Cong (VC), was formed.

As the NLF launched its campaign, the Diem government quickly lost control of the countryside. By early 1965 the Saigon government was on its last legs. The army was getting ready to evacuate Hue and Danang, and the central highlands seemed about to fall.

The Americans saw France's war in Indochina as an important element in the worldwide struggle against communist expansion. Vietnam was the next domino and could not topple.

A decisive turning point in US strategy came with the August 1964 Gulf of Tonkin incident. Two US destroyers claimed to have come under unprovoked attack off the North Vietnamese coast. On US president Lyndon Johnson's orders, 64 sorties unleashed bombs on the North – the first of thousands of such missions that would hit every single road and rail bridge in the country, as well as 4000 of North Vietnam's 5788 villages.

1960	**1963**	**1965**
The National Liberation Front launch a guerrilla war against the Diem government, sparking the 'American War'.	South Vietnam's president Ngo Dinh Diem is overthrown and killed in a coup backed by the USA.	To prevent collapse of the Saigon regime, the US bombs North Vietnam and dispatches combat troops to the South.

As the military situation of the Saigon government reached a new nadir, the first US combat troops splashed ashore at Danang in March 1965. By December 1965, there were 184,300 US military personnel in Vietnam and 636 Americans had died. By December 1967, the figures had risen to 485,600 US soldiers in the country and 16,021 dead. There were 1.3 million soldiers fighting for the Saigon government, including the South Vietnamese and other allies.

By 1966 the buzz words in Washington were 'pacification', 'search and destroy' and 'free-fire zones'. Pacification involved developing a pro-government civilian infrastructure in each village. To protect the villages from VC raids, mobile search-and-destroy units of soldiers moved around the country hunting VC guerrillas. In some cases, villagers were evacuated so the Americans could use heavy weaponry such as napalm and tanks in areas that were declared free-fire zones.

These strategies were only partially successful: US forces could control the countryside by day, while the VC usually controlled it by night. Even without heavy weapons, VC guerrillas continued to inflict heavy casualties in ambushes and through extensive use of mines and booby traps.

Tet Offensive

In January 1968 North Vietnamese troops launched a major attack on the US base at Khe Sanh in the Demilitarised Zone (DMZ). This battle, the single largest of the war, was in part a massive diversion from the Tet Offensive.

The Tet Offensive marked a decisive turning point in the war. On the evening of 31 January, as the country celebrated the Lunar New Year, the VC broke an unofficial holiday ceasefire with a series of coordinated strikes in more than 100 cities and towns. As the TV cameras rolled, a VC commando team took over the courtyard of the US embassy in central Saigon. However, the communists miscalculated the mood of the population, as the popular uprising they had hoped to provoke never materialised.

Although the US were utterly surprised – a major failure of military intelligence – they immediately counter-attacked with massive firepower, bombing and shelling heavily populated cities. The counter-attack devastated the VC, but also traumatised the civilian population.

The VC may have lost the battle, but were on the road to winning the war. Watching the killing and chaos in Saigon beamed into their living rooms, public tolerance of the war and its casualties reached breaking point.

Simultaneously, stories began leaking out of Vietnam about atrocities and massacres carried out against unarmed Vietnamese civilians, including the infamous My Lai Massacre.

1968
The Viet Cong launches the Tet Offensive. Hundreds of Vietnamese civilians are killed in the My Lai Massacre.

1969
After a revolutionary life, Ho Chi Minh dies in Hanoi of heart failure. He's succeeded by a 'collective leadership', led by Le Duan.

1972
The North Vietnamese cross the Demilitarised Zone (DMZ) at the 17th parallel to attack South Vietnam and US forces.

Peace Talks & Accords: Beginning of the End

The first half of 1969 saw the conflict escalate further as the number of US soldiers in Vietnam reached an all-time high of 543,400. Australia, New Zealand, South Korea, the Philippines and Thailand also sent military personnel to South Vietnam as part of what the Americans called the 'Free World Military Forces', whose purpose was to help internationalise the American war effort in order to give it more legitimacy.

While the fighting raged, Nixon's chief negotiator, Henry Kissinger, pursued peace talks in Paris with his North Vietnamese counterpart Le Duc Tho.

In 1969, the Americans began secretly bombing Cambodia in an attempt to flush out Vietnamese communist sanctuaries. This new escalation provoked violent anti-war protests in the US and elsewhere. A peace demonstration at Kent State University in Ohio resulted in four protesters being shot dead. It was clear that the war was tearing America apart.

In the spring of 1972, the North Vietnamese launched an offensive across the 17th Parallel; the USA responded with increased bombing of the North. Eventually, the Paris Peace Accords were signed by the USA, North Vietnam, South Vietnam and the VC on 27 January 1973, which provided for a ceasefire, the total withdrawal of US combat forces and the release of 590 American POWs.

Victory & Reunification

Most US military personnel departed Vietnam in 1973, leaving behind a small contingent of technicians, advisors and CIA agents. Still the war rumbled on, only now the South Vietnamese were fighting alone.

In January 1975, the North Vietnamese launched a massive ground attack across the 17th Parallel. The invasion provoked panic in the South Vietnamese army as whole brigades fled southward, joining hundreds of thousands of civilians clogging Hwy 1. City after city – Hue, Danang, Quy Nhon, Nha Trang – were simply abandoned with hardly a shot fired.

The North Vietnamese pushed on to Saigon and on the morning of 30 April 1975, their tanks smashed through the gates of Saigon's Independence Palace (now called Reunification Palace). General Duong Van Minh, president for just two days, formally surrendered, marking the end of the war.

Just a few hours before the surrender, the last Americans were evacuated by helicopter from the US embassy roof. Harrowing images of US Marines booting Vietnamese people off their helicopters were beamed around the world. And so more than a quarter of a century of American military involvement came to a close. Throughout the entire conflict, the USA never actually declared war on North Vietnam.

The Americans weren't the only ones who left. Hundreds of thousands of Vietnamese fled the country as 'boat people', refugees risking everything to undertake perilous journeys on the South China Sea.

1975	1978	1986
On 30 April 1975, Saigon falls to the North Vietnamese. Saigon is re-named Ho Chi Minh City.	Vietnamese forces invade Cambodia on Christmas Day 1978, sweeping through the shattered country.	*Doi moi* is launched with a rash of economic reforms.

China & the Khmer Rouge

Relations with China to the north and the Khmer Rouge were rapidly deteriorating. War-weary Vietnam felt encircled by enemies. An anti-capitalist campaign was launched in March 1978, seizing private property and businesses. Most of the victims were ethnic Chinese – hundreds of thousands of whom fled as 'boat people' – and relations with China soured further.

After repeated attacks on Vietnamese border villages by the Khmer Rouge, Vietnamese forces entered Cambodia on Christmas Day 1978. They succeeded in driving the Khmer Rouge from power on 7 January 1979 and set up a pro-Hanoi regime in Phnom Penh. China viewed the attack on the Khmer Rouge as a serious provocation. In February 1979 Chinese forces invaded Vietnam and fought a brief, 17-day war before withdrawing.

Liberation of Cambodia from the Khmer Rouge soon turned to occupation and a long civil war, which exacted a heavy toll on Vietnam economically.

Embracing Change

In 1985, President Mikhail Gorbachev came to power in the Soviet Union. *Glasnost* (openness) and *perestroika* (restructuring) were in, radical revolutionaries were out. Vietnam followed suit in 1986 by choosing *doi moi* (economic reform). The Vietnamese decided to unilaterally withdraw from Cambodia in September 1989, as they could no longer afford the occupation. The party in Vietnam was on its own and needed to reform to survive.

Dramatic changes in Eastern Europe in 1989 and the collapse of the Soviet Union in 1991 forced the pace of change. Economically the Vietnamese decided to embrace the market. Capitalism has since taken root, and Vietnam joined the Association of Southeast Asian Nations (ASEAN) in 1995.

Relations with Vietnam's old nemesis, the USA, have also vastly improved. In early 1994, the USA lifted its economic embargo. Full diplomatic relations were restored and presidents Bill Clinton, George W Bush, Barack Obama and Donald Trump have subsequently visited Vietnam.

1994
The US trade embargo on Vietnam, in place in the North since 1964 and extended to the reunified nation since 1975, is revoked.

2009
Pro-democracy activists are jailed for 'spreading propaganda against the government'.

2017
Danang hosts APEC (Asia-Pacific Economic Co-operation) summit attended by President Trump and many other heads of state.

Hmong woman

SUTPRATTANA STUDIO/SHUTTERSTOCK ©

People & Culture

Industrious, proud, stubborn and yet mischievous, quick to laugh and fond of a joke, the Vietnamese are complex. For Westerners, the national character can be difficult to fathom: direct questions are frequently met with evasive answers. A Vietnamese person would never tell a stranger their life story or profound personal thoughts. Their deep respect for tradition, family and the state reflects core Confucian principles.

The National Psyche

Historically the national mentality has been to work as a team, in harmony rather than in conflict; but times are changing. If you're on the highway or doing business, it's everyone for themselves. It's these attitudes (towards traffic and commerce) that many outsiders, not just Westerners, find most alien. 'Face' is vital, and Vietnamese people hate giving way, often employing elaborate tactics of bluster and bluff (and cunning) to ensure they get where they want to go.

Floating market, Mekong River

BANANA REPUBLIC IMAGES/SHUTTERSTOCK ©

My Generation

In many ways Vietnam is still a traditional, conservative society, particularly for the older generation, who remember the long, hard years and every inch of the territory for which they fought. Brought up on restraint and moderation, many remain unmoved by 21st-century consumer culture. For the new generation, Vietnam is very different: a place to succeed and to ignore the staid structures set by the Communists. And yes, to show off that gleaming new motorbike, sharp haircut or iPhone.

North–South Divide

The north–south divide lingers on. It's said that Southerners think, then do, while Northerners think, then think some more. Southerners typically reckon Northerners have 'hard faces', that they take themselves too seriously and don't know how to have fun. Northerners are just as likely to think of Southerners as superficial, frivolous and business-obsessed. Stereotypes these may be, but they shed light on the real differences between north and south that reach beyond the (very different) regional dialects.

Climate plays its part too. Life is easier in the south, where the fertile Mekong Delta allows three rice harvests a year. The north endures a long winter of grey skies, drizzle, mist and cool winds. Think of the differences between northern and southern Europe (or Maine and Alabama) and you have a snapshot of how one people can become two. Don't forget that the north has also lived with communism for more than half a century, while the south had more than two decades of free-wheelin' free-for-all with the Americans.

Face

Face is all important in Asia, and in Vietnam it is above all. Having 'big face' is synonymous with prestige, and prestige is particularly important. All families, even poor ones, are expected to have elaborate wedding parties and throw their money around like it's water in order to gain face. This is often ruinously expensive, but far less distressing than 'losing face'.

Foreigners should never lose their tempers with the Vietnamese; this will bring unacceptable 'loss of face' to the individual involved and end any chance of a sensible solution to the dispute. Similarly, it's also not culturally acceptable for Vietnamese traders to shout at, tug or pressure tourists when trying to do a deal. Hustlers can adopt these tactics during a hard sell. Walk on.

Lifestyle

Traditionally, Vietnamese life has revolved around family, fields and faith, with the rhythm of rural existence continuing for centuries at the same pace. All this has been disrupted by war, the impact of communism and globalisation. While it's true that several generations may still share the same roof, the same rice and the same religion, lifestyles have changed immeasurably.

Vietnam is experiencing its very own '60s swing, which is creating feisty friction as sons and daughters dress as they like, date who they want and hit the town until all hours. But few live on their own and they still come home to Mum and Dad at the end of the day, where arguments might arise, particularly when it comes to marriage and settling down.

Some things never change. Most Vietnamese despise idleness and are early risers. You'll see parks full of t'ai chi devotees as dawn breaks, and offices are fully staffed by 7am. Indeed the whole nation seems supercharged with energy and vitality, no matter how hot and humid it is.

Main Minority Groups

Tay (population 1.6 million) Live at low elevations between Hanoi and the Chinese border.

Thai (population 1.5 million) Northern tribe usually categorised by colour: Red, Black and White Thai.

Muong (population 1.4 million) Known for their folk literature, poems and music.

Hmong (population over 500,000) Spread across the far northern mountains; most are animists. Each Hmong group – Black, White, Red, Green and Flower – has its own dress code.

Nung (population 800,000) This tribe lives in small villages in the far northeastern provinces.

Jarai (population 350,000) These people still practise animistic rituals, paying respect to their ancestors and nature.

Family

In Vietnam the status of your family is more important than your salary. A family's reputation commands respect and opens doors.

Extended family is important to the Vietnamese and that includes second or third cousins, the sort of family that many Westerners may not even realise they have. The extended family comes together during times of trouble and times of joy, celebrating festivals and successes, mourning deaths or disappointments. This is a source of strength for many of the older generation.

Women in Vietnam

As in many parts of Asia, Vietnamese women take a lot of pain for little gain, with plenty of hard work to do but little authority at the decision-making level. Vietnamese women were highly successful as guerrillas in the American War. After the war, their contributions were given much fanfare, and indeed women went on to prop up a country that had lost three million men, but most of the government posts were given to men. Today female parliamentary delegates still make up less than 20%. In the countryside, you'll see women doing backbreaking jobs, such as crushing rocks at construction sites and carrying heavy baskets.

Religion

Many Vietnamese are not very religious and some surveys indicate that only 20% of the population consider themselves to have a faith. That said, over the centuries, Confucianism, Taoism and Buddhism have fused with popular Chinese beliefs and ancient Vietnamese animism to create the Tam Giao (Triple Religion) that many Vietnamese identify with.

Christianity, present in Vietnam for 500 years, and Cao Daism (unique to the region) are other important religions.

Education is changing the divide, and today more women are delaying marriage to get an education. Although only just over 17% of company directors in Vietnam are women, this is high for Asia's average of just under 8%.

The People of Vietnam

Vietnamese culture and civilisation have been profoundly influenced by the Chinese, who occupied the country for 1000 years and whose culture deeply permeates Vietnamese society.

History has, of course, influenced the mix of Vietnamese minorities. The steady expansion southwards in search of cultivable lands absorbed first the Kingdom of Champa and later the eastern extent of the Khmer Empire; both the Chams and the Khmers are sizeable minorities today.

Traffic was not only one-way. Many of the 50 or more minority groups that live in the far northwest only migrated to these areas from Yunnan (China) and Tibet in the past few centuries. They moved into the mountains that the lowland Vietnamese considered uncultivable, and help make up the most colourful part of the ethnic mosaic that is Vietnam today.

The largest minority group in Vietnam has always been the ethnic-Chinese community, which makes up much of the commercial class in the cities. The government has traditionally viewed them with suspicion, and many left the country as 'boat people' in the 1970s. Today, however, they play a major part in economic development.

Temple of Literature (p56)

VIETNAM STOCK IMAGES/SHUTTERSTOCK ©

Arts & Architecture

Vietnam has a fascinating artistic and architectural heritage. Historically, the nation has absorbed influences from China, India and the Khmer kingdoms and fused them with indigenous traditions. Then the French, Americans and Soviet Union left their mark.

Arts

Contemporary Music

Vietnam's contemporary music scene is diverse and influenced by trends in the West and east Asia. As all artists are monitored by the government, subjects that could be deemed subversive are largely avoided (or heavily coded).

Hot bands include indie-ish The Children; metal merchants Black Infinity, Little Wings and Unlimited; punk band Giao Chi and also alt-roots outfit 6789.

Viet-American Trace is an emerging artist whose moody, indie-tronic album *Low* received rave reviews upon its release in 2017.

Trinh Cong Son, who died in 2001, was a prolific writer-composer of antiwar and reconciliation songs.

Hip Hop & Electronica

There's a small but growing hip-hop scene, with HCMC-born Suboi acknowledged as Vietnam's leading female artist.

Vietnam's electronic scene is dominated by commercial DJs playing EDM. However, HCMC's Heart Beat (www.heartbeatsaigon.com) promotes excellent underground dance events around the city while Bass Republic nights feature beats DJs. In the north, the Quest Festival (www.questfestival. net) pioneers electronic music, as well as indie and acoustic acts.

Traditional Music

Vietnam's traditional music uses the five-note (pentatonic) scale of Chinese origin. Folk tunes are usually sung without any instrumental accompaniment (and have been adapted by the Communist Party for many a patriotic marching song).

Indigenous instruments include the *dan bau,* a single-stringed zither that generates an astounding array of tones, and the *trung,* a large bamboo xylophone. Vietnam's minorities use distinctive instruments: reed flutes, gongs and stringed instruments made from gourds.

Dance

Traditionally reserved for ceremonies and festivals, Vietnamese folk dance is again mainstream thanks to tourism. The Conical Hat Dance is visually stunning: women wearing *ao dai* (the national dress of Vietnam) spin around, whirling their classic conical hats.

Theatre

Vietnamese theatre fuses music, singing, recitation, dance and mime into an artistic whole. Classical theatre is very formal, employing fixed gestures and scenery and has an accompanying orchestra and a limited cast of characters. Popular theatre *(hat cheo)* expresses social protest through satire.

Puppetry

Conventional puppetry *(roi can)* and the uniquely Vietnamese art form of water puppetry *(roi nuoc)* draw their plots from the same legendary and historical sources as other forms of traditional theatre. Water puppetry was first developed by farmers in northern Vietnam, who manipulated wooden puppets and used rice paddies as a stage. There are water-puppet theatres in both Hanoi and HCMC.

Painting

Much modern work has political rather than aesthetic or artistic motives – some of this propaganda art is now highly collectable. Some young artists have gone back to the traditional-style silk or lacquer paintings, while others experiment with contemporary subjects.

Literature

Contemporary writers include Nguyen Huy Thiep, who articulates the experiences of Vietnamese people in *The General Retires and Other Stories.* Both Duong Van Mai Elliot's memoir, *The Sacred Willow: Four Generations in the Life of a Vietnamese Family* and Viet Thanh Nguyen's *The Sympathizer* have been nominated for Pulitzer prizes.

Leading Viet Kieu (Overseas Vietnamese) writers include Andrew Lam, Nam Le, Le Ly Hayslip, Monique Truong, Andrew X. Pham, Amy Quan Barry and Lan Cao.

Cinema

In Nguyen Khac's *The Retired General* (1988), the central character copes with adjusting from his life as a soldier to that of a civilian family man.

Dang Nhat Minh is perhaps Vietnam's most prolific film-maker. In *The Return* (1993), he hones in on the complexities of modern relationships, while *The Girl on the River* (1987) tells the stirring tale of a female journalist.

Overseas-Vietnamese films include Tran Anh Hung's touching *The Scent of Green Papaya* (1992) and *Cyclo* (1995), his visually stunning masterpiece. Vietnamese-American Tony Bui's exquisite feature debut *Three Seasons* (1999) was set in HCMC while Nguyen Vo Nghiem Minh's *Buffalo Boy* (2004) and *2030* (2014) have both won prestigeous international film awards.

City of Bridges

The dynamic city of Danang must have one of Asia's best collections of contemporary bridges over its Han River. These include the aptly named Dragon Bridge (p132), which spews fire and water on weekends at 9pm.

Architecture

Traditional Vietnamese architecture is unusual, as most important buildings are single-storey structures with heavy tiled roofs based on a substantial wooden framework.

Quirky Vietnamese styles include the narrow tube houses of Hanoi's Old Quarter. The Nung minority people's homes are also unusual, sometimes built with mud walls and with only one part elevated on stilts.

Colonial Buildings

Vietnam's French legacy is pronounced in the nation's architecture. Stately neoclassical buildings reinforced notions of European hegemony in the colonial era, and many still line grand city boulevards.

After the 1950s, most of these were left to rot as they symbolised an era many Vietnamese wished to forget. However recent renovation programs have led to structures such as the former Hôtel de Ville (People's Committee Building) in HCMC and the Sofitel Metropole Hotel in Hanoi being restored to their former glory.

Colonial churches were built in a range of architectural styles: in Hanoi, the sombre neo-Gothic form of St Joseph Cathedral is enhanced by dark grey stone.

Art deco curiosities built under French rule include Dalat's wonderful train station, with its multicoloured windows, and the sleek La Residence Hotel in Hue.

Pagodas & Temples

Vietnamese religious structures do not follow a specific national prototype. Pagoda styles echo the unique religious make-up of the nation, with strong Chinese content, while southern Cham temples reflect influences from India, Hindu culture and the Khmer empire.

Pagodas *(chua)* incorporate Chinese ornamentation and motifs, with buildings grouped around garden courtyards and adorned with statues and stelae. Most have single or double roofs with elevated hip rafters, though there are some with multitiered towers *(thap)* like Hue's Thien Mu Pagoda.

Vietnamese pagodas are designed according to feng shui (locally called *dia ly*). They're primarily Buddhist places of worship, even though they may be dedicated to a local deity. Most are single-storey structures, with three wooden doors at the front. Inside are a number of chambers, usually filled with statues of Buddhas, bodhisattvas and assorted heroes and deities (Thien Hau, Goddess of the Sea, is popular in coastal towns). Flashing fairy lights, giant smoking incense spirals, gongs and huge bells add to the atmosphere.

Check out Hanoi's Temple of Literature for a superb example of a traditional Vietnamese temple or the wonderful pagodas in Hue.

Banh xeo

Food & Drink

Prepare to be amazed by Vietnam's cuisine. From traditional street stalls to contemporary big-city temples of upscale dining, the country serves up an endless banquet of exquisite eating. Over the centuries locals have adapted Chinese, Indian, French and Japanese techniques and specialities to create one of the world's greatest cuisines.

Flavours

Vietnamese palates vary from north to south, but no matter where they are, local cooks work to balance hot, sour, salty and sweet flavours in each dish.

Salty & Sweet

Vietnamese food's saltiness comes from salt but also from the fermented seafood sauces, the most common of which is *nuoc mam* (fish sauce). Cooks also use sugar to sweeten dipping sauces, and flavour dishes such as *kho*, a sweet-savoury dish of fish or meat simmered in a clay pot.

Hot & Sour

Vietnamese cooking uses less hot chilli than Thai cuisine, though it's a key ingredient in central Vietnamese meals. Vietnam is a huge peppercorn exporter, and ground black and white peppercorns season everything from *chao* (rice porridge) to beef stew. Sour flavours are derived from lime and *kalamansi* (a small, green-skinned, orange-fleshed citrus fruit) as well as tamarind and vinegar (in the north).

Herbs

Vietnamese food is often described as 'fresh' and 'light' owing to the plates heaped with gorgeous fresh herbs that seem to accompany every meal: coriander, mint, Thai basil, *perilla* leaves, peppery *rau ram* leaves and *rau om* (a rice-paddy herb), which has a hint of lemon and cumin.

Vegetarians & Vegans

The Vietnamese are voracious omnivores. While they dearly love veggies, they also adore much of what crawls on the ground, swims in the sea or flies in the air.

However, there are vegetarian *(com chay)* establishments in most towns, usually near Buddhist temples. Often these are local, simple places popular with observant Buddhists. Many use 'mock meat', tofu and gluten, to create meat-like dishes that can be quite delicious.

Otherwise, be wary. Any dish of vegetables may well have been cooked with fish sauce or shrimp paste.

Staples

Rice

Rice *(com)* is the very bedrock of Vietnamese cuisine: if a local says '*an com*' (literally 'let's eat rice'), it's an invitation to lunch or dinner. It's eaten in a soupy state as *chao* (rice porridge) and stir-fried with egg, vegetables and other ingredients as *com rang*. Sticky rice (white, red and black) is eaten as a filling breakfast treat or mixed with sugar and coconut milk as a sweet treat.

Rice flour is also a base for everything from noodles and sweets to crackers and rice paper rolls.

Meat, Fish & Fowl

Chicken and pork are widely eaten, while you'll also find goat (eaten in hotpots with a curried broth) and frog.

Seafood is a major source of protein. From the ocean comes fish such as tuna, pomfret, red snapper and sea bass, as well as prawns, crabs and shellfish. Seafood restaurants always keep their catch live in tanks or bowls, so you can be assured it's ocean fresh. Freshwater eats include *ca loc* (snakehead fish), catfish and clams.

Fruit

Depending on when you're travelling, you'll be able to gorge on mangoes, crispy and sour green or soft, and tartly floral pink guavas, juicy lychees and longans, and exotic mangosteen, passion fruit and dragon fruit.

Vietnamese Coffee Culture

Vietnamese coffee can be prepared in myriad ways. Popular options include the following:

Caphe sua da Iced coffee with condensed milk

Caphe da Iced coffee without milk

Caphe den Black coffee

Caphe sua chua Iced coffee with yoghurt

Caphe trung da Coffee topped with a beaten egg white

Drinks

Alcoholic Drinks

Memorise the words *bia hoi*, which means 'draught beer'. Probably the cheapest beer in the world, *bia hoi* starts at around 5000d a glass, so anyone can afford a round. Foreign labels brewed in Vietnam include Tiger, Carlsberg and Heineken. National and regional brands include Halida and Hanoi in the north, Huda and La Rue in the centre, and 333 (ba ba ba) in the south.

A new craft beer scene is sweeping the nation, but is strongest in Ho Chi Minh City and Hanoi, where you'll find many specialist pubs and bars perfect for quaffing an IPA, dark ale or wheat beer.

Wine and spirits are available, and you may be offered *ruou* (distilled sticky-rice wine) often flavoured with herbs, spices, fruits and even animals.

Non-alcoholic Drinks

Vietnam is also a major coffee producer, and whiling away a morning or an afternoon over endless glasses of iced coffee is something of a ritual for Vietnam's male population. Espresso-based coffee is also common in the main towns. Tea (black leaf and green) is also popular, particularly in the north.

You'll find fizzy drinks, fruit juices and smoothies are widely available. Look out for *mia da,* a sugar-cane juice that's especially refreshing served over ice with a squeeze of *kala-mansi*. *Sinh to* are fresh-fruit smoothies blended to order.

Regional Specialities

Travelling north to south is a Vietnamese journey that, geographically and gastronomically, begins in China and ends in Southeast Asia. Differences in history, culture and geography combine for many techniques, ingredients and tastes, all linked by the Vietnamese love for vibrant flavours, fresh herbs, noodles and seafood.

Northern Vietnam

Northern Vietnamese food bears the imprint of centuries of Chinese occupation. Comforting noodle dishes, generally mild flavours and rustic elegance are all hallmarks. Soy sauce is used as frequently as fish sauce.

Pho Bo A northern culinary classic is *pho bo* (beef noodle soup). A good pho hinges on the broth, which is made from beef bones boiled for hours with shallot, ginger, fish sauce, black cardamom, star anise and cassia.

Banh Cuon These rolls are made from rice-flour batter that's poured onto a piece of muslin cloth stretched over a steamer; once firm, the noodle sheet is scattered with chopped pork, mushrooms and dried shrimp, then rolled up, sprinkled with crispy shallots, and served alongside a tangle of bean sprouts, slivered cucumber and chopped fresh herbs, with a saucer of *nuoc cham* (dipping sauce) for drizzling.

Bun Cha This street favourite features barbecued sliced pork or pork patties served with thin rice vermicelli, fresh herbs and green vegetables, and a bowl of lightly-sweetened *nuoc mam* with floating slices of pickled vegetables.

Central Vietnam

Positioned between culinary extremes, the food of central Vietnam combines moderation and balance – except where it concerns the locals' love of chilli. Expect gutsy and spicy flavours, including briny shrimp sauce and lemongrass.

Banh Khoai These hearty, dessert-plate-sized crêpes are made with rice-flour batter and cooked with oil. With a spare filling of shrimp, pork, egg and bean sprouts, they are encased with fresh herbs in lettuce, and then dunked in a sauce based on earthy fermented soybeans.

Bun Bo Hue This punchy rice-noodle soup with beef and pork is tinged yellow-orange by chillies and annatto; the broth is laden with lemongrass notes and anchored by savoury shrimp sauce *(mam tom)*. It's accompanied by herbs and leafy greens.

Com Hen Rice is served with the flesh of tiny clams, their cooking broth, and garnishes including roasted rice crackers, crisp pork crackling, peanuts, sesame seeds, fresh herbs and vegetables.

Southern Vietnam

Southern cuisine tends to be on the sweet side and coconut milk infuses mild curries. The southern love of fresh herbs, fruit and vegetables comes to the fore in refreshing *goi* (salads) of green papaya, grapefruit-like pomelo, or lotus stems.

Canh Chua Ca This soup is the Mekong Delta in a bowl: plentiful snakehead or catfish; fruits like tomato and pineapple; and vegetables including bean sprouts, okra and *bac ha* (taro stem), all in a broth that's tart with tamarind and salty with *nuoc mam*, and finally topped with vivid green herbs and golden fried garlic.

Banh Mi This baguette sandwich is a legacy of French and Chinese colonialism, but it's 100% Vietnamese. The filling might be a smearing of pâté or a few slices of silky sausage. Mayonnaise moistens the bread and a sprinkling of soy sauce imparts *umami* (savoury) goodness.

Banh Xeo This giant crispy, chewy rice crêpe is crammed with pork, shrimp, mung beans and bean sprouts. Take a portion and encase it in lettuce or mustard leaf, add some fresh herbs, then dunk it in *nuoc cham*.

Cai Be (p245), Mekong Delta

Environment

Vietnam is one of the most diverse countries on earth, with tropical lowlands, intensely cultivated rice-growing regions, a remarkable coastline and karst mountains. But due to population pressure, poverty and a lack of environmental protection, many regions, and the nation's wildlife, are under threat.

The Landscape

As the Vietnamese are quick to point out, their nation resembles a *don ganh,* the ubiquitous bamboo pole with a basket of rice slung from each end. The baskets represent the main rice-growing regions of the Red River Delta in the north and the Mekong Delta in the south. The country bulges in the north and south and has a very slim waistline – at one point it's only 50km wide. Mountain ranges define most of Vietnam's western and northern borders.

Coast & Islands

Vietnam's extraordinary 3451km-long coastline is one of the nation's biggest draws and it doesn't disappoint, with sweeping sandy beaches, towering cliffs, undulating dunes and countless offshore islands. The largest of these islands is Phu Quoc in the Gulf of Thailand; others include Cat Ba, the 2000 or so islets of Halong Bay and the fabled Con Dao Islands way out in the South China Sea.

River Deltas

The Red River and Mekong River deltas are both pancake-flat and prone to flooding. Silt carried by the Red River and its tributaries, confined to their paths by 3000km of dykes, has raised the level of the river beds above the surrounding plains. The Mekong Delta has no such protection, so when *cuu long* ('the nine dragons', ie the nine channels of the Mekong in the delta) burst their banks, it creates havoc for communities and crops.

Highlands

Three-quarters of the country consists of rolling hills (mostly in the south) and mighty mountains (mainly in the north), the highest of which is 3143m Fansipan, close to Sapa. The Truong Son Mountains, which form the southwest highlands, run almost the full length of Vietnam along its borders with Laos and Cambodia. The coastal ranges near Nha Trang and those at Hai Van Pass (Danang) are composed of granite. However, northern Vietnam's incredible karst formations are probably the nation's most iconic physical features.

Responsible Travel

o Consider shunning elephant rides. Working elephants are still illegally trapped and conservation groups have grave concerns about their living conditions.

o When snorkelling or diving be careful not to touch coral as this hinders its growth.

o Avoid touching limestone formations as it affects their development and turns the limestone black.

o Most 'exotic' meats such as porcupine and squirrel have been illegally poached from national parks.

o Many civets are kept in appalling conditions to produce 'poo coffee'.

o Before downing snake wine or snake blood consider that the reptiles (sometimes endangered species) are killed without anaesthesia and can carry salmonella.

Wildlife

We'll start with the good news. Despite some disastrous bouts of deforestation, Vietnam's flora and fauna is still incredibly exotic and varied. Intensive surveys by the World Wildlife Fund along the Mekong River place this area in the top-five biodiversity hot spots in the world.

The other side of the story is that despite this outstanding diversity, the threat to Vietnam's remaining wildlife has never been greater due to poaching, hunting and habitat loss. Three of the nation's iconic animals – the elephant, saola and tiger – are on the brink. It's virtually certain that the last wild Vietnamese rhino was killed inside Cat Tien National Park in 2010.

And for every trophy animal there are hundreds of other less 'headline' species that are being cleared from forests and reserves for the sake of profit (or hunger).

Paradise Cave (p103)

DUDAREV MIKHAIL/SHUTTERSTOCK ©

Animals

Vietnam has plenty to offer those who are wild about wildlife, but in reality many animals live in remote forested areas and encountering them is extremely unlikely.

With a wide range of habitats – from equatorial lowlands to high, temperate plateaus and even alpine peaks – the wildlife of Vietnam is enormously diverse. One recent tally listed 275 species of mammals, more than 800 birds, 180 reptiles, 80 amphibians, hundreds of fish and tens of thousands of invertebrates.

Rare and little-known birds previously thought to be extinct have been spotted and no doubt there are more in the extensive forests along the Laos border including Edwards's pheasant.

Even casual visitors will spot a few bird species: swallows and swifts flying over fields and along watercourses; flocks of finches at roadsides and in paddies; and bulbuls and mynas in gardens and patches of forest.

Environmental Issues

Vietnam's environment is under threat across the entire nation. While the government signed up to key conservation treaties and hosted an Illegal Wildlife Trade conference in 2016, the state's main priorities are job creation and economic growth. There's minimal monitoring of pollution and dirty industries, while many loggers and animal traffickers escape trouble through bribery and official inaction.

Key issues include the following:

Deforestation While 44% of the nation was forested in 1943, by 1983 only 24% of forest cover was left and by 1995 it was down to 20%.

Wildlife Poaching This has decimated forests of animals; snares capture and kill indiscriminately, whether animals are common or critically endangered.

Urban and Industrial Pollution Hanoi is the most contaminated city in Southeast Asia while water pollution affects many regions. A massive toxic leak from a Formosa Plastics plant in 2016 decimated sealife in the South China Sea.

Global Warming A sea-level rise of only a metre would flood more than 6% of the country and affect up to 10 million people.

Survival Guide

Directory A–Z

Accommodation

Accommodation in Vietnam is superb value for money. Big cities and the main tourism centres have everything from hostel dorm beds to luxe hotels. In the countryside and visiting provincial towns you'll usually be deciding between guesthouses and midrange hotels.

Cleanliness standards are generally good but communication can often be an issue (particularly off the beaten track, where few staff speak English).

Prices are quoted in dong or US dollars. Most rooms fall into a budget price category and dorm bed prices are given individually. Dis-counts are often available at quiet times of year. Some hotels (particularly those on the coast) raise their prices in the main tourist season (July and August) and for public holidays.

Hostels, Guesthouses & Hotels

Hotels are called *khach san* and guesthouses *nha khach* or *nha nghi*. Many hotels have a wide variety of rooms (a spread of between US$20 and US$70 is not unusual). Often the cheapest rooms are at the end of several flights of stairs or lack a window.

Budget places Hostels with dorms (typically US$6 to US$10 per bunk) are quite popular in the main tourism centres, but rare elsewhere. Guesthouses (usually family-run) vary enormously; often the newest places are in the best condition. Most rooms are very well equipped, with US$12 to US$18 often bagging you in-room wi-fi, air-con, hot water and a TV. Some places even throw in a free breakfast, too. Towards the upper end of this category, minihotels – small, smart private hotels – usually represent excellent value for money.

Midrange hotels At the lower end of this bracket, many of the hotels are similar to budget hotels but with bigger rooms or balconies. Flash a bit more cash and the luxury factor rises exponentially, with contemporary design touches and a swimming pool and massage or spa facilities becoming the norm.

Top-end hotels Expect everything from faceless business hotels, colonial places resonating with history and chic boutique hotels in this bracket. Resort hotels are dotted along the coastline. Villa-hotels and ecolodges are also increasing.

Taxes

Most hotels at the top end levy a tax of 10% and a service charge of 5%, displayed as ++ (plus plus) on the bill. Some midrange hotels (and even the odd budget place) also try to levy a 10% tax.

Electricity

The usual voltage is 220V, 50 cycles, but you'll (very rarely) encounter 110V, also at 50 cycles, just to confuse things.

127V/220V/50Hz

Book Your Stay Online

For more accommodation reviews by Lonely Planet authors, check out http://hotels.lonelyplanet.com/vietnam. You'll find independent reviews, as well as recommendations on the best places to stay. Best of all, you can book online.

Climate

Vietnam has very complicated weather patterns. Broadly there are two completely different climate zones.

Anywhere south of Nha Trang is hot and dry between November and March and the rainy season is roughly late April to October. Conversely central and northern Vietnam's rainy, cool season is October to March, and summers (April to September) are hot and steamy.

Central Vietnam is most affected by typhoons; August to November are the most stormy months.

Health

Health issues (and the quality of medical facilities) vary enormously depending on where you are in Vietnam. The major cities are generally not high risk and have good facilities, though rural areas are another matter.

Travellers tend to worry about contracting infectious diseases in Vietnam, but serious illnesses are rare. Accidental injury (especially traffic accidents) account for most life-threatening problems.

Before You Go

Don't travel without health insurance – accidents do happen. If your health insurance doesn't cover you for medical expenses abroad, get extra insurance – check our website (www.

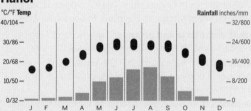

Hanoi

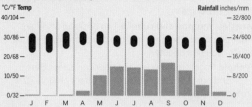

Ho Chi Minh City

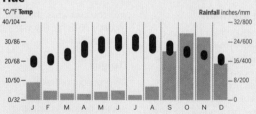

Hue

lonelyplanet.com) for more information. Emergency evacuation is expensive – bills of US$100,000 are not unknown – so make sure your policy covers this.

Vaccinations

The only vaccination required is yellow fever, which is required if you have visited a country in the yellow-fever zone within six days of entering Vietnam. You should also consider vaccinations for adult diphtheria and tetanus; hepatitis A and B; measles, mumps and rubella; typhoid and varicella.

Sleeping Price Ranges

The following price ranges refer to a double room with bathroom in high season. Unless otherwise stated, tax is included, but breakfast isn't.

$ less than US$25 (560,000d)

$$ US$25 to US$75 (1,700,000d)

$$$ more than US$75

Recommended Vaccinations

The World Health Organization (WHO) recommends the following vaccinations for travellers to Southeast Asia:

Adult diphtheria and tetanus Single booster recommended if you've had none in the previous 10 years.

Hepatitis A Provides almost 100% protection for up to a year; a booster after 12 months provides at least another 20 years' protection.

Hepatitis B Now considered routine for most travellers. A rapid schedule is also available, as is a combined vaccination with Hepatitis A. Lifetime protection occurs in 95% of people.

Measles, mumps and rubella Two doses of MMR are required unless you have had the diseases. Many young adults require a booster.

Typhoid Recommended unless your trip is less than a week and only to cities. The vaccine offers around 70% protection and lasts for two or three years.

In Vietnam

The significant improvement in Vietnam's economy has brought with it some major advances in public health. However, in remote parts, local clinics will only have basic supplies – if you become seriously ill in rural Vietnam, get to a private clinic in Ho Chi Minh City, Danang or Hanoi as quickly as you can. Most Vietnamese state hospitals are overcrowded and basic. For surgery or other extensive treatment, don't hesitate to fly to Bangkok, Singapore or Hong Kong.

Infectious Diseases

Other diseases present in the region include bird flu, Japanese B encephalitis, rabies, schistosomiasis, tuberculosis (TB), typhoid and typhus. There have also been people infected with the Zika virus, though by early 2018 the risk was considered low.

Dengue

This mosquito-borne disease is quite common: several hundred thousand people are hospitalised in Vietnam every year, but the fatality rate is less than 0.3%. As there is no vaccine available, it can only be prevented by avoiding mosquito bites.

Symptoms include a high fever, a severe headache and body aches. There is no specific treatment, just rest and paracetamol – do not take aspirin as it increases the likelihood of haemorrhaging. See a doctor to be diagnosed and monitored.

Hepatitis A

This food- and water-borne virus infects the liver, causing jaundice (yellow skin and eyes), nausea and lethargy. There is no specific treatment for hepatitis A – you just need to allow time for the liver to heal. All travellers to Vietnam should be vaccinated against hepatitis A.

Hepatitis B

The only serious sexually transmitted disease that can be prevented by vaccination, hepatitis B is spread by body fluids, including sexual contact.

Malaria

Get expert advice as to whether your trip actually puts you at risk. Most parts of Vietnam, particularly city and resort areas, have minimal to no risk of malaria including virtually the whole coastline, Danang, Hanoi, HCMC and Nha Trang. In rural areas there's more of a risk.

Malaria is caused by a parasite transmitted by the bite of an infected mosquito. Fever is a symptom, but headaches, diarrhoea, cough or chills may also occur. Diagnosis can only be made by taking a blood sample.

Two strategies should be combined to prevent malaria – mosquito avoidance and antimalarial medications.

Travellers' Diarrhoea

Travellers' diarrhoea is by far the most common problem affecting travellers. In over 80% of cases, travellers' diarrhoea is caused by a bacteria, and responds promptly to treatment with antibiotics. It can also be provoked by a change of diet, and your stomach may settle down again after a few days.

Treatment consists of staying hydrated, or you could take rehydration solutions.

Loperamide is just a 'stopper' and doesn't get to the cause of the problem.

Environmental Hazards

Food

Eating in restaurants is the biggest risk factor for contracting travellers' diarrhoea. Help avoid it by eating only freshly cooked food, and peel all fruit.

Heat

Many parts of Vietnam are hot and humid throughout the year. Take it easy when you first arrive. Avoid dehydration and excessive activity in the heat. Drink rehydration solution and eat salty food.

Bites & Stings

Both poisonous and harmless snakes are common in Vietnam, though very few travellers are ever bothered by them.

Jellyfish are present in Vietnamese waters but most are not dangerous, just irritating. Pour vinegar (or urine) onto the affected area.

Internet Access

Internet and wi-fi is very widely available. Something like 98% of hotels and guesthouses have wi-fi; only in very remote places (such as national parks) is it not standard. It's almost always free of charge.

Many cafes and restaurants also have wi-fi. Connection speeds in towns and cities are normally good. Cybercafes are also plentiful, usually costing 3000d to 8000d per hour.

Most travellers also surf the net using 3G or 4G mobile phone connections.

Legal Matters

Drugs

The country has a very serious problem with heroin and methamphetamine use, and the authorities clamp down hard. Marijuana and, in the northwest, opium are readily available.

Note that there are many plain-clothes police in Vietnam and if you're arrested, the result might be a large fine, a long prison term or both.

Police

Few foreigners experience much hassle from police and demands for bribes are very rare. If something does go wrong, or if something is stolen, the police can't do much more than prepare an insurance report for a negotiable fee – take an English-speaking Vietnamese with you to translate.

LGBT Travellers

Vietnam is a relatively hassle-free place for gay, lesbian and trans travellers. There are no official laws prohibiting same-sex relationships, or same-sex sexual acts in Vietnam, nor is there much in the way of individual harassment.

VietPride (www.facebook.com/vietpride.vn) marches have been held in Hanoi and HCMC since 2012. Hanoi and HCMC both have gay scenes, but gay venues still keep a low profile.

Tipping

Hotels Not expected. Leave a small gratuity for cleaning staff if you like.

Restaurants Not expected; 5% to 10% in smart restaurants or if you're very satisfied. Locals don't tip.

Guides A few dollars on day trips is sufficient, more for longer trips if the service is good.

Taxis Not necessary, but a little extra is appreciated, especially at night.

Bars Never expected.

Money

ATMs

ATMs are widespread in Vietnam and present in virtually every town in the country. Watch out for stiff withdrawal fees, however (typically 25,000d to 50,000d), and withdrawal limits – most are around 2,000,000d.

Cash

The US dollar remains king of foreign currencies and can be exchanged widely. Other major currencies can be exchanged at banks, including Vietcombank and HSBC.

Credit Cards

Visa and MasterCard are accepted in major cities and many tourist centres, but don't expect noodle bars to take plastic. Commission charges (around 3%) sometimes apply.

Currency

The Vietnamese currency is the dong (abbreviated to 'd').

Opening Hours

Typical year-round opening hours are as follows:

Banks 8am to 3pm weekdays, to 11.30am Saturday

Museums 7am or 8am to 5pm or 6pm; generally closed Monday and some take a lunch break

Offices 7am or 8am to 5pm or 6pm

Restaurants 11.30am to 9pm

Shops 8am to 6pm

Temples & Pagodas 5am to 9pm

Public Holidays

If a public holiday falls on a weekend, it is observed on the Monday.

New Year's Day (Tet Duong Lich) 1 January

Vietnamese New Year (Tet) January or February; a three-day national holiday

Founding of the Vietnamese Communist Party (Thanh Lap Dang CSVN) 3 February

Hung Kings Commemorations (Hung Vuong) 10th day of the 3rd lunar month (March or April)

Liberation Day (Saigon Giai Phong) 30 April

International Workers' Day (Quoc Te Lao Dong) 1 May

Ho Chi Minh's Birthday (Sinh Nhat Bac Ho) 19 May

Buddha's Birthday (Phat Dan) Eighth day of the fourth moon (usually June)

National Day (Quoc Khanh) 2 September; commemorates the Declaration of Independence

Safe Travel

All in all, Vietnam is an extremely safe country to travel in: reports about muggings, robberies or sexual assaults are very rare. There are scams and hassles in some cities, particularly in Hanoi, HCMC and Nha Trang (and to a lesser degree in Hoi An).

Be extra careful if you're travelling on two wheels on Vietnam's anarchic roads – traffic accident rates are

Exchange Rates

Australia	A$1	17,925d
Canada	C$1	18,222d
Euro	€1	26,845d
Japan	¥100	20,345d
New Zealand	NZ$1	16,297d
UK	£1	30,170d
US	US$1	22,709d

For current exchange rates, see www.xe.com.

woeful and driving stand-
ards are pretty appalling.

Telephone

A mobile phone with a local
SIM card and a Skype/Viber
(or similar) account will
allow you to keep in touch
economically with anyone in
the world.

Mobile Phones

If you have an unlocked
phone, it's virtually essential
to get a local SIM card for
longer visits in Vietnam. Its
3G and 4G data packages
are some of the cheapest
in the world at around
150,000d for 3GB and will
enable you to use the net if
wi-fi is weak; some packages include call time too.

Get the shop owner (or
someone at your hotel) to
set up your phone in English
or your native language. The
three main mobile-phone
companies are Viettel, Vina-
phone and Mobifone.

International Calls

It's usually easiest to use wi-
fi and a calling app such as
Skype/Viber. Mobile phone
rates for international
phone calls can be less than
US$0.10 a minute.

Domestic Calls

Domestic calls are very inexpensive using a Vietnamese
SIM.

Phone numbers in Hanoi,
HCMC and Haiphong have
eight digits. Elsewhere

around the country phone
numbers have seven digits.
Telephone area codes are
assigned according to the
province.

Phone Codes

Most regional phone codes
(59 of Vietnam's 63 prov-
inces) changed in 2017. Inevitably, many publications
and web pages have yet to
update numbers using new
codes.

Time

Vietnam is seven hours
ahead of Greenwich Mean
Time/Universal Time
Coordinated (GMT/UTC).
Vietnam does not have
daylight-saving or summer
time.

Tourist
Information

Tourist offices in Vietnam
are really travel agencies
whose primary interests are
booking tours and turning
a profit. Don't expect inde-

Ordnance

Since 1975 more than 40,000 Vietnamese have been
maimed or killed by war ordnance. The central provinces are particularly badly affected. While cities, cultivated
areas and well-travelled rural roads and paths are safe
for travel, straying from these areas could land you in
danger. Never touch any rockets, artillery shells, mor-
tars, mines or other relics of war you may come across.

pendent travel information.
Vietnam Tourism (www.
vietnamtourism.com), the
main state organisation,
and Saigon Tourist (www.
saigon-tourist.com) are
examples of this genre.

Travel agents, backpack-
er cafes and your fellow
travellers are a much better
source of information.

Visas

Some nationalities need a
visa in advance for all visits,
some don't.

Types of Visa

The (very complicated)
visa situation has recently
changed for many nation-
alities, and is fluid – always
check the latest regulations.

Firstly, if you are staying
more than 15 days and from
a Western country, you'll
still need a visa (or approval
letter from an agent) in
advance. If your visit is less
than 15 days, some nationalities are now visa-exempt
(for a single visit not
multiple-entry trips).

Tourist visas are valid for
either 30 days or 90 days.

A single-entry 30-day visa costs US$20, a three-month multiple-entry visa is US$70. Only US nationals are able to arrange one-year visas.

Until recently there have been two methods of applying for a visa: a Visa on Arrival (VOA) via online visa agents, or via a Vietnamese embassy or consulate. That is changing as e-visas have been rolled out (for a limited number of nationalities).

Visa on Arrival (VOA)

Visa on Arrival (VOA) is the preferred method for most travellers arriving by air, since it's cheaper, faster and you don't have to part with your passport by posting it to an embassy. Online visa agencies email the VOA to you directly.

It can only be used if you are flying into any of Vietnam's six international airports, not at land crossings. The process is straightforward: you fill out an online application form and pay the agency fee (around US$20). You'll then receive by email a VOA approval letter signed by Vietnamese immigration, which you print out and show on arrival, where you pay your visa stamping fee in US dollars, cash only. The single-entry stamping fee is US$25; a multiple-entry stamping fee is US$50.

There are many visa agents, but there are some inefficient, even dodgy, cut-priced operators out there. Stick to well-established companies; the following two are professional and efficient:

Vietnam Visa Choice (www. vietnamvisachoice.com) Online support from English-speakers and this agency guarantees your visa will be issued within the time specified.

Vietnam Visa Center (www. vietnamvisacenter.org) Competent all-rounder with helpful staff well-briefed on the latest visa situation. Offers a two-hour express service for last-minute trips.

Visa via an Embassy or Consulate

You can also obtain visas through Vietnamese embassies and consulates around the world but fees are normally higher than using a visa agent, the process can be slow, and you have to relinquish your passport for a period of time.

E-visas

A pilot e-visa program introduced in early 2017 allows visitors to apply for visas online. Citizens of 40 countries are eligible, including those from the UK and the USA.

E-visas are single-entry only, valid for 30 days (nonextendable), and cost US$25. Processing takes three to five days.

However, this e-visa system has not exactly been efficiently implemented. The official website is glitch-prone and often fails to load. We've also heard of several cases where applications have gone AWOL and photos rejected for not being picture-perfect.

There have been reports of visitors being deported due to incorrect details (such as wrong date of birth or mispelt names) on the online application form. If you do apply for an e-visa, double-check all your information provided is 100% accurate.

Visa-Exempted Nationalities

At this time, citizens of the following countries do not need to apply in advance for a Vietnamese visa (when arriving by either air or land) for certain lengths of stay. Always double-check visa requirements before you travel as policies change regularly.

Country	Days
Brunei, Myanmar	14
Belarus, Denmark, Finland, France, Germany, Italy, Japan, Norway, Russia, south Korea, Spain, Sweden, UK	15
Philippines	21
Cambodia, Indonesia, Laos, Malaysia, Singapore, Thailand	30
Chile	90

E-visas can be applied for online at www.immigration.gov.vn.

Women Travellers

Vietnam is relatively free of serious hassles for Western women. There are issues to consider, of course, but thousands of women travel alone through the country each year and love the experience. In Vietnam the sexes mix freely and society does not expect women to behave in a subordinate manner.

Transport

Most travellers enter Vietnam by plane or bus, but there are also train links from China and boat connections from Cambodia via the Mekong River. Flights, tours and rail tickets can be booked online at www.lonelyplanet.com/bookings.

Getting There & Away

Air

There are six main international airports in Vietnam.

Cam Ranh International Airport (http://camranhairport.vn) Located 36km south of Nha Trang, with expanding range of flights including Hong Kong and Seoul.

Danang Airport (www.danangairport.vn/en) International flights to China, South Korea, Japan, Hong Kong, Thailand, Cambodia and Singapore.

Noi Bai Airport (www.hanoiairportonline.com) Serves the capital Hanoi.

Phu Quoc International Airport (www.phuquocairport.com) International flights including Singapore, Bangkok and some charters to Europe.

Tan Son Nhat International Airport (www.tsnairport.hochiminhcity.gov.vn/vn) For Ho Chi Minh City.

Cat Bi International Airport Near Haiphong, 60km west of Halong City, with flights to China and South Korea.

Land

Vietnam shares land borders with Cambodia, China and Laos, and there are plenty of border crossings open to foreigners. Standard times that foreigners are allowed to cross are usually 7am to 5pm daily. Buses connect Vietnam with Cambodia, Laos and China, and a daily train links Hanoi with Nanning.

River

There's a river border crossing between Cambodia and Vietnam on the banks of the Mekong; regular fast boats ply the route between Phnom Penh in Cambodia and Chau Doc in Vietnam.

Getting Around

Air

Vietnam has excellent domestic flight connections, with new routes opening up all the time, and very affordable prices (if you

Climate Change & Travel

Every form of transport that relies on carbon-based fuel generates CO_2, the main cause of human-induced climate change. Modern travel is dependent on aeroplanes, which might use less fuel per kilometre per person than most cars but travel much greater distances. The altitude at which aircraft emit gases (including CO_2) and particles also contributes to their climate change impact. Many websites offer 'carbon calculators' that allow people to estimate the carbon emissions generated by their journey and, for those who wish to do so, to offset the impact of the greenhouse gases emitted with contributions to portfolios of climate-friendly initiatives throughout the world. Lonely Planet offsets the carbon footprint of all staff and author travel.

book early). Airlines accept bookings on international credit and debit cards. Note, however, that cancellations are quite common.

Vietnam Airlines (www.viet namairlines.com.vn)
Jetstar Airways (www.jetstar. com)
Vietjet Air (www.vietjetair.com)
Vasco (www.vasco.com.vn)

Bicycle

Bikes are a great way to get around Vietnam, particularly when you get off the main highways. Safety, however, is a considerable concern.

Hotels and some travel agencies rent bicycles for US$1 to US$3 per day; better-quality models cost from US$6.

Boat

The Mekong Delta region has numerous possible river rides. Scenic day trips are also possible on rivers in Hoi An, Danang, Hue and HCMC.

Cruising the islands of Halong Bay is a must for visitors to northern Vietnam and trips to the Cham Islands and around Con Dao and Phu Quoc are good days out.

Bus

Vietnam has an extensive network of bus routes. Modern buses, operated by myriad companies, run on all the main highways. However, most travellers never visit a Vietnamese bus station at all, preferring to stick to the convenient, tourist-friendly open-tour bus network.

Deluxe Buses

Mai Linh Express (www. mailinhexpress.vn) is a reliable, punctual company that operates clean, comfortable deluxe buses across Vietnam.

The Sinh Tourist (www. thesinhtourist.com) is an efficient company that has nationwide bus services, including sleepers. Book ahead online.

Open-Tour Buses

These air-con buses use convenient, centrally located departure points and allow you to hop on, hop off at any major city along the main north to south route. Prices are reasonable. An open-tour ticket from

HCMC to Hanoi costs between US$30 and US$70.

Travellers' cafes, tour agencies and budget hotels sell tickets. The Sinh Tourist has a good reputation, with computerised seat reservations.

Local Buses

Slow and stop frequently. Conductors also tend to routinely overcharge foreigners.

Car & Motorcycle

Having your own set of wheels gives you maximum flexibility to visit remote regions.

Car hire always includes a driver and costs from US$60 to US$120 per day.
Motorbikes (from US$4 per day) can be rented from virtually anywhere, including cafes, hotels and travel agencies. Local drivers will act as a chauffeur and guide for US$20 to US$30 per day. It's compulsory to wear a helmet.

Cyclo

These are bicycle rickshaws. Bargaining is imperative; settle on a fare before starting out. A short ride should be 12,000d to 30,000d.

Taxi

Taxis with meters, found in all cities, are very cheap by international standards and a safe way to travel around at night. Average tariffs are about 12,000d to 15,000d per kilometre.

However, as dodgy taxis with go-fast meters do roam

Metro Progress

Metro lines are under construction in both HCMC and Hanoi; services should start in the next few years. The line in HCMC is a Japanese-Vietnamese partnership; eventually, the plan is for there to be three monorails and six underground lines.

China is the financial muscle behind the Hanoi metro, which has been beset by construction troubles. Two lines are currently being built; the first is due to open in 2018.

the streets, stick to these recommended companies: Mai Linh (www.mailinh.vn) and Vinasun (www.vinasun taxi.com).

Tours

The quality of bottom-end budget tours being peddled in HCMC and Hanoi is often terrible. You tend to get what you pay for.

Buffalo Tours (☏024-3828 0702; www.buffalotours.com; Level 10, 70-72 Ba Trieu, Hanoi) Diverse and customised trips, including superb Halong Bay tours.

Handspan Travel Indochina (☏04-3926 2828; www. handspan.com; Hanoi) Expert locally-owned company that offers a wide range of innovative, interesting tours to seldom-visited regions.

Ocean Tours (☏04-3926 0463; www.oceantours.com.vn; 82 Ma May, Hanoi) Professional tour operator based in Hanoi with excellent trips around the north.

Train

Operated by national carrier Vietnam Railways (www. vr.com.vn), the Vietnamese railway system is an ageing but pretty dependable service, and offers a relaxing way to get around the nation.

Routes

Aside from the main HCMC–Hanoi run, a spur runs to Lao Cai (for Sapa and trains on to Kunming, China). 'Fast' trains between Hanoi and HCMC take between 32 and 36 hours.

Private Train Carriages

Comfortable, even luxurious, private carriages tagged onto the back of trains offer a classy way of travelling between Lao Cai and Hanoi: those offered by Orient Express Trains (www.orientexpresstrainsapa.com) and Victoria Hotels are renowned and very pricey, but there are many other options including Livitrans (www. livitrans.com).

Livitrans, Violette (http://en.violetexpresstrain.com) and other companies offer luxury carriages between Hanoi and Hue (US$75 to US$85) and Danang (US$85 to US$95), as do several other companies.

Classes & Costs

Trains classified as SE are the smartest and fastest. There are four main ticket classes: hard seat, soft seat, hard sleeper and soft sleeper. These classes are further split according to whether they have air-conditioning. Presently, air-con is only available on the faster express trains. Ticket prices vary depending on the train; the fastest trains are the most expensive.

Reservations

You can book online using the travel agency Bao Lau (www.baolau.vn), which has an efficient website, details seat and sleeper berth availability, and accepts international cards.

E-tickets are emailed to you; there's a small commission per ticket. For sleeping berths, reserve well in advance. Many travel agencies, hotels and cafes will also buy you train tickets for a small commission.

Schedules

Train schedules change frequently, so check departure times on the Vietnam Railways website, Bao Lau's website or www.seat61. com, the international train website.

A bare-bones train schedule operates during the Tet festival, when most trains are suspended for nine days.

Xe Om

The *xe om* (zay-ohm) is a motorbike taxi. Fares are comparable with those for a cyclo, but negotiate the price beforehand.

Language

Vietnamese pronunciation is not as hard as it may seem at first as most Vietnamese sounds also exist in English. Note that the vowel a is pronounced as in 'at', aa as in 'father', aw as in 'law', er as in 'her', oh as in 'doh!', ow as in 'cow', u as in 'book', uh as in 'but' and uhr as in 'fur' (without the 'r'). Vowel sounds can also be combined in various ways within a word – we've used dots (eg dee·úhng) to separate the different vowel sounds to keep pronunciation straightforward. As for the consonants, note that the ng sound, which is also found in English (eg in 'sing') can also appear at the start of a word in Vietnamese. Also note that d is pronounced as in 'stop', đ as in 'dog' and ğ as in 'skill'.

There are six tones in Vietnamese, indicated in the written language by accent marks above or below the vowel: mid (ma), low falling (mà), low rising (mả), high broken (mã), high rising (má) and low broken (mạ). Note that the mid tone is flat. In the south, the low rising and the high broken tones are both pronounced as the low rising tone. The vocabulary variation between the north and the south is indicated here by (N) and (S).

To enhance your trip with a phrasebook, visit **lonelyplanet.com**. Lonely Planet iPhone phrasebooks are available through the Apple App store.

Basics

Hello.
Xin chào.   sin jòw
Goodbye.
Tạm biệt.   daạm bee·ụht
Yes.
Vâng. (N)   vuhng
Dạ. (S)   yạ
No.
Không.   kawm
Please.
Làm ơn.   laàm ern
Thank you
Cảm ơn.   ğaảm ern

You're welcome.
Không có chi.   kawm ğó jee
Excuse me/Sorry.
Xin lỗi.   sin lõy

Eating & Drinking

Do you have a menu in English?
Bạn có thực   baạn káw tụhrk
đơn bằng tiếng   đern bùhng díng
Anh không?   aang kawm
Not too spicy, please.
Xin đừng cho cay quá.   sin đừrng jo ğay gwaá
I'm a vegetarian.
Tôi ăn chay.   doy uhn jay
I'm allergic to (peanuts).
Tôi bị dị ứng   doy beẹ zeẹ úhrng
với (hạt lạc).   ver·eé (haạt laạk)
Can I have a (beer), please?
Xin cho tôi (chai bia)?   sin jo doy (jai bee·uh)
Cheers!
Chúc sức khoẻ!   júp súhrk kwả
Thank you, that was delicious.
Cám ơn, ngon lắm.   ğaám ern ngon lúhm
The bill, please.
Xin tính tiền.   sin díng dee·ùhn

Emergencies

Help!
Cứu tôi!   ğuhr·oó doy
I'm lost.
Tôi bị lạc đường.   doi beẹ laạk đuhr·èrng
Where is the toilet?
Nhà vệ sinh ở đâu?   nyaà vẹ sing ẻr đoh
Please call the police.
Làm ơn gọi công an.   laàm ern gọy ğawm aan
Please call a doctor.
Làm ơn gọi bác sĩ.   laàm ern gọy baák seẽ
I'm sick.
Tôi bị đau.   doy beẹ đoh

Transport & Directions

Where is ...?
... ở đâu ?   ... ẻr đoh
What is the address?
Địa chỉ là gì?   đee·ụh cheẻ laà zeè

Behind the Scenes

Writer Thanks

Iain Stewart

Many thanks to my co-authors, destination editor Laura Crawford and Lonely Planet's product editors. On the ground I was aided by Caroline and Neil in Hoi An, Mark in Ho Chi Minh City and many others up and down the coast.

Brett Atkinson

It's always a thrill and pleasure to return to one of my favourite countries, and my thanks go to Mark Zazula in Ho Chi Minh City, Ben, Bich, Seamus and the gang in Phong Nha, and the Hoi An crew of Neil, Caroline, Mark and Leanne. Cheers also to Tam in Dong Ha and Sy in Dong Hoi, and it was great for my wife Carol to finally meet my good friend Kien and his family in Hanoi.

Austin Bush

I'm grateful for all the wonderful people on the ground in northern Vietnam, but my trip was made especially easier and more enjoyable by Mr Tung at Cat Ba Ventures, James and Mr Minh at Vision Travel, and the villagers of Na Hu, as well as my helpful destination editor, Laura Crawford.

David Eimer

Special thanks to Curtis, Thuy, Le and Thuan for the nights out in Dalat and their sound local advice. Thanks also to Laura Crawford, Iain Stewart and all the Lonely Planet crew. As ever, much gratitude to everyone I met on the road who passed on tips, whether knowingly or unwittingly.

Phillip Tang

Many thanks to the Vietnamese people and friends, especially Pham Hoang Manh in Hanoi, Nam, Tri and Liam Le in Saigon, Mr The for Ha Tien, and Hon Chong, Nghiêm Nguyen and Anthony in Can Tho, Phuc Anh for the adventure to Tra Vinh. Thank you Laura Crawford for having me on board again. Thanks to Daniel Belfield for dressing gowns, bao, cocktails and *xe om* teaming.

Acknowledgements

Climate map data adapted from Peel MC, Finlayson BL & McMahon TA (2007) 'Updated World Map of the Köppen-Geiger Climate Classification', Hydrology and Earth System Sciences, 11, 1633-44.

Illustration pp116-17 by Michael Weldon.

Send Us Your Feedback

We love to hear from travellers – your comments keep us on our toes and help make our books better. Our well-travelled team reads every word on what you loved or loathed about this book. Although we cannot reply individually to postal submissions, we always guarantee that your feedback goes straight to the appropriate authors, in time for the next edition. Each person who sends us information is thanked in the next edition, the most useful submissions are rewarded with a selection of digital PDF chapters.

Visit lonelyplanet.com/contact to submit your updates and suggestions or to ask for help. Our award-winning website also features inspirational travel stories, news and discussions.

Note: We may edit, reproduce and incorporate your comments in Lonely Planet products such as guidebooks, websites and digital products, so let us know if you don't want your comments reproduced or your name acknowledged. For a copy of our privacy policy visit lonelyplanet.com/privacy.

This Book

This second edition of Lonely Planet's *Best of Vietnam* guidebook was curated by Iain Stewart, who also researched and wrote it along with Brett Atkinson, Austin Bush, David Eimer and Phillip Tang. The previous edition was written by Iain Stewart, Brett Atkinson, Anna Kaminski, Jessica Lee, Phillip Tang and Benedict Walker. This guidebook was produced by the following:

Destination Editor Laura Crawford

Product Editors Ross Taylor, Kate Chapman

Senior Cartographer Diana Von Holdt

Book Designer Mazzy Du Plessis

Assisting Editors Michelle Bennett, Carly Hall, Kate Morgan, Lauren O'Connell, Christopher Pitts, Alison Ridgway

Assisting Cartographer Anita Banh

Assisting Book Designers Michael Weldon, Wendy Wright

Cover Researcher Naomi Parker

Thanks to Michael Huffman, Peter Merrington, Clemens S Ostergaard, Kathryn Rowan

A — Z

Index

Symbols & Map Key

Look for these symbols to quickly identify listings:

- ⊙ Sights
- ⊗ Eating
- ⊕ Activities
- ⊖ Drinking
- ⊛ Courses
- ★ Entertainment
- ⊛ Tours
- 🔒 Shopping
- ⊛ Festivals & Events
- ⓘ Information & Transport

These symbols and abbreviations give vital information for each listing:

🌿 Sustainable or green recommendation

FREE No payment required

- ☎ Telephone number
- ⌚ Opening hours
- Ⓟ Parking
- ⊖ Nonsmoking
- ✳ Air-conditioning
- @ Internet access
- 🛜 Wi-fi access
- ⊠ Swimming pool
- 🚌 Bus
- ⛴ Ferry
- 🚊 Tram
- 🚆 Train
- 📋 English-language menu
- ✏ Vegetarian selection
- ♦ Family-friendly

Find your best experiences with these Great For... icons.

 Art & Culture

 History

 Beaches

 Local Life

 Budget

 Nature & Wildlife

 Cafe/Coffee

 Photo Op

🚴 Cycling

🔭 Scenery

🡥 Detour

🛍 Shopping

🍷 Drinking

🎒 Short Trip

🎫 Entertainment

 Sport

✨ Events

🚶 Walking

👪 Family Travel

🥢 Food & Drink

❄ Winter Travel

Sights

- 🏖 Beach
- 🐦 Bird Sanctuary
- ⊛ Buddhist
- 🏰 Castle/Palace
- ✝ Christian
- ☯ Confucian
- 🕉 Hindu
- ☪ Islamic
- ⊛ Jain
- ✡ Jewish
- 🏛 Monument
- 🏛 Museum/Gallery/ Historic Building
- 🏚 Ruin
- ⛩ Shinto
- 🪯 Sikh
- ☯ Taoist
- 🍷 Winery/Vineyard
- 🐾 Zoo/Wildlife Sanctuary
- ⊙ Other Sight

Points of Interest

- © Bodysurfing
- ⊛ Camping
- ⊛ Cafe
- ⊛ Canoeing/Kayaking
- • Course/Tour
- ⊘ Diving
- ⊛ Drinking & Nightlife
- ⊗ Eating
- ★ Entertainment
- ♨ Sento Hot Baths/ Onsen
- 🔒 Shopping
- ⛷ Skiing
- ⊛ Sleeping
- ⊛ Snorkelling
- ⊛ Surfing
- ⊛ Swimming/Pool
- ⊛ Walking
- ⊛ Windsurfing
- ⊕ Other Activity

Information

- 💲 Bank
- ⊛ Embassy/Consulate
- ⊕ Hospital/Medical
- @ Internet
- ⊛ Police
- ⊛ Post Office
- ☎ Telephone
- 🚻 Toilet
- ⓘ Tourist Information
- • Other Information

Geographic

- 🏖 Beach
- ⊢ Gate
- ⊛ Hut/Shelter
- ⊛ Lighthouse
- ⊛ Lookout
- ▲ Mountain/Volcano
- ⊛ Oasis
- ⊛ Park
-)(Pass
- ⊛ Picnic Area
- ⊛ Waterfall

Transport

- ⊛ Airport
- Ⓑ BART station
- ⊗ Border crossing
- Ⓣ Boston T station
- 🚌 Bus
- 🚡 Cable car/Funicular
- ⊛ Cycling
- ⛴ Ferry
- Ⓜ Metro/MRT station
- ⊛ Monorail
- Ⓟ Parking
- ⊛ Petrol station
- Ⓢ Subway/S-Bahn/ Skytrain station
- ⊛ Taxi
- 🚉 Train station/Railway
- ⊛ Tram
- ⊖ Tube Station
- Ⓤ Underground/ U-Bahn station
- • Other Transport

David Eimer

David Eimer has been a journalist and writer ever since abandoning the idea of a law career in 1990. After spells working in his native London and in Los Angeles, he moved to Beijing in 2005, where he contributed to a variety of newspapers and magazines in the UK. Since then, he has travelled and lived across China and in numerous cities in Southeast Asia, including Bangkok, Phnom Penh and Yangon. He has been covering China, Myanmar and Thailand for Lonely Planet since 2006.

Phillip Tang

Phillip Tang grew up on a typically Australian diet of *pho* and fish'n'chips before moving to Mexico City. A degree in Chinese- and Latin-American cultures launched him into travel and then writing about it for Lonely Planet's *Canada*, *China*, *Japan*, *Korea*, *Mexico*, *Peru* and *Vietnam* guides. See more of his writing at www.hellophillip.com, photos @mrtangtangtang and tweets @philliptang.

Our Story

A beat-up old car, a few dollars in the pocket and a sense of adventure. In 1972 that's all Tony and Maureen Wheeler needed for the trip of a lifetime – across Europe and Asia overland to Australia. It took several months, and at the end – broke but inspired – they sat at their kitchen table writing and stapling together their first travel guide, *Across Asia on the Cheap*. Within a week they'd sold 1500 copies. Lonely Planet was born.

Today, Lonely Planet has offices in Franklin, London, Melbourne, Oakland, Dublin, Beijing, and Delhi, with more than 600 staff and writers. We share Tony's belief that 'a great guidebook should do three things: inform, educate and amuse'.

Our Writers

Iain Stewart

Iain Stewart trained as journalist in the 1990s and then worked as a news reporter and a restaurant critic in London. He started writing travel guides in 1997 and has since penned more than 60 books. Iain's worked on titles including *Mexico, Indonesia, Central America, Croatia, Vietnam, Bali & Lombok* and *Southeast Asia on a Shoestring* for Lonely Planet. He also writes regularly for the *Independent, Observer* and *Daily Telegraph*. He'll consider working anywhere there's a palm tree or two and a beach of a generally sandy persuasion. He lives in Brighton (UK), within firing range of the city's wonderful south-facing horizon. He tweets @iaintravel.

Brett Atkinson

Based in Auckland, New Zealand, Brett is frequently on the road for Lonely Planet. He's a full-time travel and food writer specialising in adventure travel, unusual destinations and surprising angles on more well-known destinations. Craft beer and street food are Brett's favourite reasons to explore places, and he is featured regularly on the Lonely Planet website and in newspapers, magazines and websites across New Zealand and Australia. Since 2005, Brett has covered areas as diverse as Vietnam, Sri Lanka, the Czech Republic, New Zealand, Morocco, California and the South Pacific for Lonely Planet.

Austin Bush

Austin originally came to Thailand in 1999 as part of a language study program hosted by Chiang Mai University. The lure of city life, employment and spicy food eventually led him to Bangkok, and city life, employment and spicy food have managed to keep him there since. These days, Austin works as a writer and photographer. In addition to having contributed to numerous books, magazines and websites, he has contributed text and photos to more than 20 Lonely Planet titles including *Bangkok; The Food Book; Ko Samui Encounter; Laos; Malaysia, Singapore & Brunei*; and *The World's Best Street Food*.

More Writers

STAY IN TOUCH LONELYPLANET.COM/CONTACT

AUSTRALIA The Malt Store, Level 3, 551 Swanston St, Carlton, Victoria 3053
📞03 8379 8000,
fax 03 8379 8111

IRELAND Digital Depot, Roe Lane (off Thomas St), Digital Hub, Dublin 8, D08 TCV4, Ireland

USA 124 Linden Street, Oakland, CA 94607
📞510 250 6400,
toll free 800 275 8555,
fax 510 893 8572

UK 240 Blackfriars Road, London SE1 8NW
📞020 3771 5100,
fax 020 3771 5101

 twitter.com/lonelyplanet
 facebook.com/lonelyplanet
 instagram.com/lonelyplanet
 youtube.com/lonelyplanet
 lonelyplanet.com/newsletter